PRAISE FOR *THE INTERIOR CARMEL*

In this Jubilee Year of Hope, we are encouraged to explore many pilgrimage opportunities, not only in Rome, but across our local dioceses and communities. Scholar and Author John Wu invites readers of *The Interior Carmel* to consider how our time on earth itself is a pilgrimage, and how each soul innately yearns for its true destiny: heaven. Through reflections on the beatitudes and insights drawn from Christian asceticism and Chinese luminaries, Dr. Wu entices readers to experience the joy of discovery and confront the inherent challenges of every spiritual journey.

　　—✠ **ARCHBISHOP SALVATORE J. CORDILEONE**, Archdiocese of San Francisco

Schooled in the Chinese classics, John C. H. Wu embraced Catholicism only after getting to know St. Therese of Lisieux at age 38. He envisaged a future in which the wisdom of the Chinese sages and the Incarnate Wisdom of the Gospel would be together a source of new life to the world. *The Interior Carmel* flows from his conviction that everyone is called to be a saint. In it, he presents the stages of the journey to holiness as the budding of love, the flowering of love, and the ripening of love. He distributes the Beatitudes among the three stages of the journey. It is a long-awaited joy and blessing to see it republished. Wu's quiet and mystical genius will inspire and energize all those interested in the spiritual life and those dedicated to building friendship and mutual understanding between the people of China and the people of the U.S.

　　—**FR. HUGH O'DONNELL**, C.M., the US-China Catholic Association

The Interior Carmel is for Christians who are searching and contemplating the Blessed Trinity in the innermost depth of their being. This book gives peace, joy and clarity to the ones who are steeped in the learnings of the East and West and are living in life of the Spirit.

　　I am deeply moved by the book after reading it carefully. Dr. John C. H. Wu's understanding of the threefold way of love is a path of listening to the Word, understanding the Word, growing in the Word, and putting the Word into practice. Nowadays, when individualism, hedonism, and relativism are threatening human flourishing and social responsibility, the hope for the world lies in understanding as well as practicing of the threefold way of love.

— **CRISTOFORO JOSEMARIA C.S. TOU**, Former Ambassador to the Holy See of Republic of China

The eminent Chinese Catholic John C. H. Wu has bequeathed us a modern masterpiece on the nature and process of the Christian spiritual life. This work is not only a product of great learning but also the fruit of a holy life. The author's intellectual, moral, and spiritual integrity palpitates on every page as he guides the reader on a journey that he himself has known intimately. Perhaps his greatest contribution is his integration of traditional Catholic mystical theology with biblical theology by placing the Beatitudes and the Sermon on the Mount at the center of spiritual progress. Also appealing are his many suggestions and hints about the coinherence between Catholic spirituality and wisdom insights from Confucianism, Daoism, and Buddhism. Truly a timeless work!

— **HUILI (KATHY) STOUT**, Ph.D., University of Dayton

This book is not merely a treatise on Christian spirituality; it is the living witness of an extraordinary man whose soul was transfigured by the boundless love of God, enriched by the profound wisdom of the East. Let us walk with John Wu along this radiant path of love.

— **FR. EMANUELE ANGIOLA**, Ph.D., Fu Jen Catholic University, Taipei

John C. H. Wu, a Chinese layman and a convert to Catholicism, brings his Chinese cultural inheritance to deepen his spiritual growth into the full stature of Christ. Rooted in the Word of God, this book shows the beauty of the lay vocation and invites us to see holiness as the necessary measure of ordinary Christian life.

— **LUCY TONGXIN LU**, Ph.D., Crusaders of Mary

In this one-of-a kind spiritual classic, John C. H. Wu turns our perspective on the seemingly abstract and distant goal of spiritual perfection, or purity of heart, from one that seems bitter and burdensome, and therefore both unattainable and undesirable, to one that perceives the heights of sweetness that come, in stages, from nearness to God, the One who loves us and whom we truly desire. Furthermore, he shows that some ancient Chinese masters and mystics spoke of an analogous journey, such as Confucius's path of aligning one's will to the will of Heaven over the course of a lifetime. In these pages we can see that God has always been stirring the hearts of those in the East as well as the West, and that Christ, the fulfillment of all human love and desire, belongs to all cultures. It is no wonder that one friend, an Asian and a deeply spiritual Catholic, remarked that this is the first book of Catholic spirituality that spoke to her deeply as an Asian person. The reprinting of this book now in our noisy and distracted time is nothing short of glorious. May it be a seed that (to use an idiom Wu himself used seven times in his Chinese translation of the New Testament, 暢茂條達 *chang mao tiao da*) flourishes and bears abundant fruit.

—**JOHN A. LINDBLOM**, Ph.D., Assistant Professor of the Practice at the McGrath Institute for Church Life, University of Notre Dame

SELECTED WORKS BY JOHN C. H. WU

Juridical Essays and Studies. Shanghai: Commercial Press, 1928.

The Legal Systems of Old and New China: A Comparison. Chicago, 1930.

The Art of Law and Other Essays Juridical and Literary. Shanghai: Commercial Press, 1936.

The Science of Love: A Study of the Teachings of Thérèse of Lisieux. Hong Kong: Catholic Truth Society, 1940.

Beyond East and West. New York: Sheed and Ward, 1951. Republished with a foreword by John Wu Jr. Notre Dame, IN: University of Notre Dame Press, 2018.

The Interior Carmel: The Threefold Way of Love. New York: Sheed and Ward, 1953. Republished Taipei: Hwakang Bookstore, 1975. Translated into Portuguese by Redação Minha Biblioteca Católica as *Um chinês e a espiritualidade Carmelita.* Porto Alegre: Minha Biblioteca Católica, 2021.

Fountain of Justice: A Study in the Natural Law. New York: Sheed and Ward, 1955.

Justice Holmes: A New Estimate. Philadelphia: Brandeis Lawyers Society, 1957.

Cases and Materials on Jurisprudence. St. Paul, MN: West Publishing Co., 1958.

Chinese Humanism and Christian Spirituality. New York: St. John's University Press, 1965. Republished Kettering, OH: Angelico Press, 2017. Foreword by Robert M. Gimello.

The Golden Age of Zen. Taipei: National War College, 1967. Republished New York: Image, 1995; and Bloomington, IN: World Wisdom, 2003.

Sun Yat-sen: The Man and His Ideas. Taipei: Commercial Press, 1971.

The Four Seasons of T'ang Poetry. Tokyo: Charles E. Tuttle, 1972.

Jurisprudence: A Treatise, Richly Illustrated with Cases and Readings. Taipei: Hwakang Bookstore, 1976.

The Spiritual Life of Chiang Kai-Shek. Taipei: Hua Hsin Publishing, 1975. Additional editions: 1976, 1983. Republished Taipei: Taipei Central Library, 1987.

The Joyful Spirit of Chinese Philosophy (Joy in Chinese Philosophy). Translated into Chinese by Chu Ping-i. Taipei: Hua Hsin Publishing, 1979. Republished New Taipei: Wisdom Press, 1999.

SELECTED TRANSLATIONS BY JOHN C. H. WU

Lao Tzu's The Tao and Its Virtue. Shanghai: T'ien Hsia Monthly, 1940.

Translation of the Psalms. Shanghai: Commercial Press, 1946.

The Complete New Testament. Hong Kong: Catholic Truth Society, 1949.

Lao Tzu: Tao Teh Ching. Jamaica, NY: St. John University Press, 1961. Republished Boulder, CO: Shambhala Publications, 1989.

SELECTED BOOKS EDITED BY JOHN C. H. WU

An Anthology of Contemporary English Prose. With M. C. Liang (梁森章). 3 vols. Shanghai: Commercial Press, 1935.

Selected Writings on the Constitution. Edited by John C. H. Wu. Compiled by Yu Chung-Chiu. Shanghai: Law Publishing and Translating Co., 1936.

Essays in Jurisprudence and Legal Philosophy. With M. C. Liang (梁森章). Shanghai: Soochow University Law School, 1938.

THE INTERIOR CARMEL

THE INTERIOR CARMEL

The Threefold Way of Love

BY JOHN C.H. WU, OBL. O.S.B., J.D.

Foreword by Vincent L. Wu, Jr.

AROUCA
PRESS

Cover art:
"Lotus and Waterbirds" (modified)
Unidentified artist, active ca. 1300
Yuan dynasty (1271–1368)
Open Access image from The Met

To Mary, Our Lady of Divine Love,
Help of Christians,
Mother most pure,
Singular vessel of devotion,
Mirror of justice,
Virgin most merciful,
Mystical Rose,
Seat of Wisdom,
Cause of our joy.

CONTENTS

The Passing Bear

My grandfather John C. H. Wu, who also bore the given Chinese name "Ching Hsiung," which translates to "passing bear," married his wife Teresa at age 17. This republication of his third book is dedicated to their ninth child, my father, Vincent L. Wu, Sr., who passed away at the age of 90 on April 2nd, 2024. My father was bedridden for over a year, and he passed away shortly after a black bear visited his home in East Hanover, New Jersey. In 60 years of living in a suburban neighborhood, he'd never dream of seeing a bear on his property. Although most people would be alarmed by a visiting black bear, my father was very pleased and comforted and said, "that was my father passing by: Wu Ching Hsiung visited me."

John Ching Hsiung Wu wrote *The Interior Carmel: The Three-fold Way of Love* over a period of 15 years. He began after his conversion to Catholicism at the age of 37 after he was commissioned to translate the New Testament into Chinese upon request of President and Madame Chiang Kai-Shek. This book was first published in 1953 by Sheed and Ward, a Catholic publisher in London. It has been published in many languages since then, and was last republished in Taiwan in 1975. This book was originally granted a "nihil obstat" stamp of approval and imprimatur, the bishop's approval through the efforts of then Right Reverend John L. McNulty, who also recruited John Wu to Seton Hall University, where he pioneered the introduction of Far Eastern studies and established the graduate law program.

Dr. Wu offers a unique perspective by reflecting upon and invoking the wisdom of the Chinese sages including Mencius, Lao Tse and Confucius. He later expands and drills down on this subject in his book, *Chinese Humanism and Christian Spirituality*.[1] *The Interior Carmel* may be regarded as a meditation on how the Eastern philosophies harmonize with Christianity and

---

[1] Republished by Angelico Press in 2017.

as a guide to becoming a better Christian. *The Interior Carmel* is beautifully and clearly written by a Chinese and Catholic scholar, theologian, philosophy professor, statesman, and family man who was educated in China, the U. S., and Europe. The word "carmel" in the first part of the title means "garden" or "vine of God" in Hebrew, reflecting natural beauty and fertility. Mount Carmel is a sacred mountain in Israel and the founding place of the Carmelite order of Sisters, one of the world's most contemplative group of women dedicated to prayer. The second part of the title "The Threefold Way of Love" refers to the three progressive stages for growing closer to God introduced by Saint Thomas Aquinas (the purgative, illuminative, and unitive phases). Dr. Wu refers to these three phases toward sanctity as the "budding, ripening and flowering of love" and explains how the pursuit of mercy and justice outlined by the eight Beatitudes from the Sermon on the Mount fit into the three phases. He also reflects on the principles of three major currents in Chinese philosophy and shows how they fit well with Christianity—Taoism with its doctrine of detachment of material things (purgative phase), Confucianism with its practice of virtues and the search for truth (illuminative phase), and Buddhism with its universal compassion and its leaning toward contemplation (unitive phase)—drawing parallels to Saint Thomas Aquinas' Christian asceticism and mysticism.

In August 1977 I visited my grandfather with my father. During my one month stay in Taiwan, then a curious 16-year-old, I had a taste of my grandfather's accumulated years of wisdom and humor. When talking about possible careers, my grandfather urged me to "follow your interest." Dr. Wu's ambition and interest, as he once wrote to Justice Oliver Wendell Holmes, while he was at The University of Paris on November 23, 1921: "As a Chinese I have a country to save, I have a people to enlighten, I have a race to uplift, I have civilization to modernize". He was successful in his mission, equipping his people with a new constitution and a Chinese translation of the Bible.

Dr. Wu was a man of extraordinary achievement. He served as the head judge of the Shanghai Provisional Court (where he presided over the international settlement court cases), he

1947. Presentation of John C. H. Wu's translation of the New Testament to Chiang Kai-Shek, Ningbo, China. John C. H. Wu was Madame Chiang's and CKS's spiritual advisor and he published a biography of CKS's spiritual life in 1975. (Photo from Wu Family personal collection.)

Rome, 1947. Wu Family with Pope Pius XII (*Life Magazine*, April 14, 1947, page 92-93). Original caption: "BIG FAMILY was honored by Pope Pius XII when he posed in the Vatican with Dr. John C. H. Wu (wearing horned-rimmed glasses), Chinese Minister to the Holy See. Also present were the members of Dr. Wu's immediate family, which includes Mme. Wu (at the Pope's right), nine sons, four daughters, and one son-in law. Besides his family, Dr. Wu brought with him to Rome his own Chinese translations of the New Testament and the Book of Psalms. A leading Chinese Catholic layman and government career man, Dr. Wu helped draft China's constitution."

John Wu wrote on page 325 in *Beyond East and West*, Chapter 20, "The Diplomacy of Love": "It was the 16th of February, 1947—Quinquagesima Sunday. The weather was fine; the skies were smiling; my heart was singing for joy. I was to present my credentials to The Holy Father, Pius XII. It was the first time in the diplomatic history of The Holy See that a Catholic ever represented a non-Catholic nation."

San Francisco, 1952, on the way from Hawaii to NJ. United Airlines Advertisement. (Photo from Wu Family personal collection.)

John Wu (kneeling) with his family while being blessed by his newly ordained son, Fr. Peter A. Wu, on June 6, 1961 at Maryknoll, Ossining, NY.

Yangmingshan, Taipei, Taiwan, August 1977. Grandson Vincent L. Wu, Jr. with Dr. John C. H. Wu. (Photo from Wu Family personal collection.)

drafted a new constitution for the Republic of China (the basis of Taiwan's current constitution), he represented China at the signing of the United Nations Charter in 1945, and he was China's Minister Plenipotentiary to the Vatican from 1947 to 1949, under Pope Pius XII. After the fall of mainland China to the Communists, he moved to the United States, where he taught Chinese philosophy at the University of Hawaii and he later served as a professor of Law and Philosophy at Seton Hall University in South Orange, New Jersey.

During my visit to Taiwan I asked my grandfather who do you admire most? He said, "Abraham Lincoln, because he was a self-made man, but of course without assassination!" No one laughed, so he said, "Did you hear me, I'm going to say it again: but of course without assassination", and this time everyone laughed. John Wu had a great sense of humor. He compared and contrasted the sense of humor of people from his east-west travels. As one of the writers and editors of *The T'ien Hsia Monthly*, an English language magazine published in Shanghai, he remarked: "Westerners are seriously humorous, and Easterners are humorously serious."

One afternoon, in Yangmingshan, my grandfather was enjoying watching Chinese opera on television while lying down on a canopy bed. He asked me to improve the television reception. The TV antenna was accessible and was mounted on a fence post in the backyard. I ran back and forth to the backyard 5 times adjusting the position of the antenna with no improvement in the television picture. John Wu then said, "Vinnie, you fixed it too good, it's getting worse! Please lie down next to me and I will show you how I read a book." He then proceeded to use a double-ended blue and red pencil and marked his thoughts and questions in the margins of the book. He noted that a pencil, unlike a pen, works even when you are lying down.

The Interior Carmel follows Dr. Wu's spiritual autobiography *Beyond East and West*, originally published in 1951,[2] which introduced his journey from his Chinese heritage to Catholicism. He was so eager to publish *The Interior Carmel* that he hoped

---

[2] Republished in 2018 by University of Notre Dame Press.

to release it before *Beyond East and West*, but the publisher Sheed and Ward believed it would be best to introduce John Wu to the world through his autobiography first. Earlier, in 1940, Dr. Wu had published *The Science of Love*, which recounts his spiritual transformation after reading the autobiography of Saint Thérèse of Lisieux and thereafter was so moved that he embraced Catholicism at the age of 37.

This book will resonate with anyone seeking to understand the spiritual life as a dynamic process. Written from a unique perspective of a completely Chinese and completely Catholic scholar, *The Interior Carmel* offers both a roadmap for personal growth and an intellectual framework for understanding the inner workings of love and sanctity. Dr. Wu's intellectual and spiritual journey exemplifies the harmony between his Chinese heritage, his Catholic faith, and his profound dedication to service.

I invite you to explore this work with an open heart and mind. Dr. Wu's words will guide you along your own spiritual ascent, inspiring you to walk the path of love, wisdom, and grace. May you spend some time with John Wu, China's "Passing Bear," as I did during the summer of 1977, and may this book serve as a handbook for your own journey toward becoming the saint you were born to be.

VINCENT L. WU, JR.
Grandson and Co-founder of
The Dr. John C. H. Wu Institute

This is an impersonal book because it contains the basic potentialities of all persons. It has been written by a man of extraordinary learning and wisdom, but it is the story of love.

Dr. John C. H. Wu is one of the world's most brilliant minds, a scholar and author of many well-known legal and literary books. He has sat in the councils of the wise, listened in hallowed halls of learning, and gained international fame in his trysts with men. But Dr. Wu is a convert to Christianity, one who has tasted the sweetness of the Savior and the world has lost its savor.

Those who are interested in love of science alone and ignorant of the science of love will read these pages with difficulty. Dr. Wu lives the theme of Christ since he became a convert, the theme of love. As Archbishop Yupin once remarked:

> For most Chinese an act of genuine love often means far more than a set of brilliant, but cold, arguments. Of course, there are times when logic must be used, but in everyday life, according to Chinese reasoning, the human necessities should be equally taken into consideration. Western philosophers like Kant and Hegel may be admired by some Chinese at times, but their rigid systems of thinking prove to be too extreme, too mechanical and, therefore, not sufficiently human, so far as the Chinese are concerned. In this respect, the Chinese are truly Confucius' disciples. Confucius put his emphasis on *Jen* (love, brotherhood) and *Chung Yung* (golden mean). As a matter of fact, both his moral code and his political philosophy were based on these two concepts. *Jen* and *Chung Yung* are the two cardinal virtues by which all human actions are to be measured.

Dr. Wu shows that man can live in the world with the spirit of the cloister. These pages reveal a simple, solid thought; viz., we did not come into the world to become lawyers, judges, scholars, craftsmen. We were born to become saints, and in every human being the seed of sanctity lies ready for the planting, the nurturing, and the ripening. Dr. Wu does not despise learning or any other accomplishments of man, but he holds that all things should feed the fire of love. He believes in putting first things first. As one sees him each morning kneeling before the altar, one feels that the wisdom of the law is lost in the humanity of a suppliant, and the knowledge of a man is sublimated in the prayers of a child.

Dr. Wu follows the concept of St. John of the Cross, who believed that sanctity was an evolution, a growing, a nurturing. He called it a voyage to Heaven and described the journey in three ways: (1) the Way of Purgation—of cleansing, of mortification, and of meditation; (2) the Illuminative Way—when the gifts of the Holy Ghost inspire us to pure acts of charity and justice; (3) the Unitive Way—the moment of perfect contemplation with God.

Timid souls look upon the three ways as difficult, almost impossible roads. They leave the heights of sanctity to the courageous and the foolhardy, and they are satisfied with the mediocrity of the easy journey. Dr. Wu remembers that Our Lord described the road to sanctity in very simple terms when he invited men saying, "Come, follow Me." And later, opening His mouth, He taught men saying:

> Blessed are the poor in spirit: for theirs is the kingdom of heaven;
> Blessed are the meek: for they shall possess the land;
> Blessed are they that mourn: for they shall be comforted;
> Blessed are they that hunger and thirst after justice: for they shall have their fill;
> Blessed are the merciful: for they shall obtain mercy;
> Blessed are the clean of heart: for they shall see God;
> Blessed are the peacemakers: for they shall be called the children of God;
> Blessed are they that suffer persecution for justice' sake: for theirs is the kingdom of heaven.

Do you agree that poverty in spirit, meekness, and sorrow cleanse the soul? *Purgative Way*

Do you agree that justice and charity are the inspiration of a God-like man? *Illuminative Way*

Do you agree that it is the clean of heart who shall see God, the peacemakers who shall be called the children of God, and those who suffer persecution for justice' sake who shall inherit the kingdom of heaven? *Unitive Way*

If you do, then you agree with Dr. Wu. If you agree with Dr. Wu, you can live in the world with the spirit of the cloister. You can lead an active life and live in contemplation. You can become a Saint.

RIGHT REVEREND JOHN L. MCNULTY, PH.D.
Seton Hall University, South Orange, N. J.
Office of the President
Oct. 11, 1952
Feast of the Maternity of Our Blessed Mother

The Growth of Love

The moral life of man may be likened to travelling to a distant place: one must start from the nearest stage. It may also be likened to ascending a height: one must begin from the lowest step (Tse Sze in *The Golden Mean*).

I do not want suddenly to attain the loftiest heights of sanctity. I desire to progress gradually (St. Bernard in *Sermons on the Canticle of Canticles*).

1. THE IDEA OF PROGRESS

The idea that our interior life must grow, and that in its growth it usually passes through certain stages or phases, is not peculiar to Christianity. We find the same idea, for instance, in Buddhism, which asserts that one begins with abstention from evil, passes through the period of confirmation in the virtues, and finally arrives at the state of wisdom. In Confucianism, one speaks of "entering the door," "ascending to the hall," and "being admitted into the secret chamber." There is no question that Confucius conceived of the way of wisdom and goodness as a growing process consisting of three progressive phases. "To know about it," he said, "is not so good as to take interest in it; to take interest in it is not so good as to rejoice in it." Using a homely analogy drawn from his agricultural environment, he said, "There are cases in which the blade springs, but the plant does not go on to flower! There are cases where it flowers but produces no fruit." These words recall one of the parables of Christ: "Thus is the kingdom of God, as when a man casteth seed upon the earth—night and day he sleepeth and riseth, and the seed is shooting up and growing, he knoweth not how. Of itself the earth beareth the crop—first the blade, then the ear, then the full-formed grain in the ear" (Mark 4:26–28).[1]

---

[1] Rev. Cuthbert Lattey, S. J., trans., *The New Testament in The Westminster Version of the Sacred Scriptures* (London: Longmans, Green and Co., 1936).

It should, of course, be noted that neither Confucius nor Buddha moved in the same sphere as Christ. Theirs is the sphere of nature, while His is the sphere of grace. He comes from heaven and bears witness of what He has seen and heard, while they are of earth, and from the earth they speak. But the point is that even grace is sown upon the earth, that is, human nature; and, therefore, the life of grace has to grow according to the gradual steps followed in the normal development of human nature, and is subject to the rhythms of life as symbolized by "night and day."

In the life of grace, as in the life of natural morality and wisdom, ripeness is all. In one as in the other, one must continuously grow toward ripeness; for not to advance is to fall back. The reason why so many Christians are frustrated and stunted is that they do not realize the vital importance of continual progress in the spiritual life, and pay but scant attention to the laws of interior growth. They are so fascinated by the progress of the physical sciences and material civilization that they seem to have no time for, nor attraction to, the things of the spirit. In thinking of modern times, one is often reminded of what Christ said to the Pharisees and Sadducees: "You know then how to discern the face of the sky: and can you not know the signs of the times?" (Matt. 16:3).

One of the reasons why the spiritual life has become such an unattractive subject to most people is that it is too often treated statically rather than as a dynamic process. Man has a natural desire for change and growth; for, as St. Thomas Aquinas says, "It is natural to human reason to advance gradually from the imperfect to the perfect" (*Summa Theologica*, I-II, Q.98, Art. 1).[2] When, therefore, the idea of progress in the spiritual life is not sufficiently emphasized, the natural desire for progress will seek its outlets somewhere else. But progress presupposes a right orientation; if, therefore, it is pursued apart from the spiritual life, which alone can give it the right direction, then it is apt to be an aberration. As St. Augustine would say, "You ran well, but you were off the track."

---

[2] Translation by the Fathers of the English Dominican Province (Benziger).

In fact, nothing can be more progressive than Christianity. As Belamy says, "If there is any doctrine that favors the true development of human activity and impresses on liberty a continuous ascent to the supreme good, it is certainly the Catholic dogma of variable justification and progressive sanctity with no limit but the infinite. Grace, then, truly merits the name of supernatural life and has, therefore, the phases of growth and virility. It is comparable to an edifice in which each good work is a stone and the stories are always ascending until the roof reaches the heavens."[3] Progress is the law of life, and this law is rooted in the will of God. For, as Terrien has pointed out, "It is part of the order of divine Providence that no being receives from the very first instant the final perfection which it ought to achieve. In all things there must be growth, with the concomitant tendency to a better state. Everything here below is subject to this law. All things must pass from a less perfect to a more perfect state, from incipient goodness to consummate goodness. This is true in the works of nature, the production of art, and the wonderful works of grace itself."[4] Even the Word Incarnate *"advanced in wisdom, and age, and grace with God and men"* (Luke 2:52). That is to say, He grew in human wisdom and experience as He grew in age. If that is true of Christ, True Man and True God, how much truer it should be of us who are mere men! How hard must we strive to improve ourselves constantly, by the help of grace, so as to fulfill our high destiny!

The Christian ideal of perfection is absolute. "Be you therefore perfect, as also your Heavenly Father is perfect" (Matt. 5:48). But our attainment of perfection admits of degrees. In his exposition of the spiritual doctrine of St. Augustine, Pierre Pourrat has said, "In fact, as long as we are on earth there is always room in us for an increase in charity.... The perfection, therefore, to which a Christian can attain is only relative. It consists in tending unceasingly and without flagging or desistance toward absolute perfection. This, however, remains an

---

[3] *La vie surnaturelle*, 284. Quoted in John G. Arintero, *The Mystical Evolution in the Development and Vitality of the Church*, trans. Jordan Aumann, O. P. (St. Louis: B. Herder Book Co., 1949), vol. 1, 98, note 48.

[4] *La grace et la gloire*, I, 154. Quoted in Arintero, vol. 1, 197.

ideal which must be the more indefatigably pursued inasmuch as it is not altogether to be fully attained."[5] In other words, relative perfection is "a constant endeavor towards that which is best, towards that fullness of charity when sin is no longer committed; it is a voyage, so to speak, in which we sail onwards towards our fatherland, which is heaven: it is a forward march without a halt; a race towards the most perfect, a mounting upwards to God."[6]

Even in heaven there can be no monotony of perfection. In the words of Father J. P. Arendzen: "God remains unfathomable even to the greatest of His saints. They see Him, but none can see to the very depths of His divine being. God is a world, a wide universe, which none of the Blessed has ever totally explored. Even after millions of cycles of ages, neither Mary, the Queen of heaven, nor Michael, the Prince of the heavenly host, shall exhaust the greatness of the divine majesty. It is an ocean on which the little craft of created intelligence can forever press forward in all directions, for it is a sea without a shore. As a pretty, many-colored insect on swift wings floats on the summer breeze and allows itself to be driven along in the seemingly boundless air; as a lark rises in the apparently boundless sky, so do the Blessed roam about in the limitless wideness of God."[7]

2. THE THREE STAGES

We can learn a great deal about the working of the law of growth from the life of Confucius. He lived to be seventy-two. Shortly before his death, he summed up the progress of his life in the following words:

> At fifteen I set my heart upon the pursuit of wisdom.
> At thirty I stood firm.
> At forty I was free from illusions.
> At fifty I understood the will of Heaven.

---

[5] Pierre Pourrat, *Christian Spirituality*, trans. W. H. Mitchell (New York: P. J. Kenedy & Sons, 1927), vol. 1, 186–87.

[6] Ibid., 187.

[7] J. P. Arendzen, *What Becomes of the Dead?* (New York: Sheed & Ward, 1951), 37.

> At sixty my interior ear was docile.
> At seventy I could follow the desires of my heart without
>   overstepping the boundaries of right.

It will be seen that he had completed the first stage of his life by thirty. From that time up to around fifty, he gave himself a strict discipline in the exercise of moral virtues and in purification from delusions and erroneous ways of thinking, and that led him to the understanding of the will of Heaven. From fifty, he grew more and more docile and responsive to the subtle ways of Divine Providence, so that by the end of his life he could follow the dictates of his heart without fear of transgression. Guided by the light of natural reason, occasionally helped, perhaps, by special illuminations from above, he spent his whole life in the pursuit of wisdom, and attained a moral greatness unrivaled in the history of China.

Confucius was not only a great man, but a great teacher. He put his program of education in a nutshell when he said, "Let the pupil be first stimulated by the study of poetry, then given a firm footing by the exercises of the laws of right conduct, and finally perfected by the cultivation of music." Like all his pithy sayings, this is not to be taken in too literal a sense; but the idea it suggests is clear enough. The making of a perfect man follows three stages. First, the desire for goodness and wisdom must be aroused and nourished by means of poetry, or whatever may correspond to it. Then comes the second stage, when one is to be subjected to a thorough moral discipline in order to be confirmed in the virtues. Finally, one reaches the state of harmony, where what was accomplished formerly by effort becomes spontaneous, and the virtues which were assiduously acquired and practiced are harmonized and organically fused, to produce, as it were, a second nature.

How fundamentally sound Confucius's program of education is, can be judged by the striking similarity it bears to the method of the Divine Teacher Himself as embodied in the Psalm of the Good Shepherd (Ps. 23). This psalm is so simple that he who runs can read it and feel its charms; but at the same time it is so profound that even the greatest saints and

sages, I dare say, would not be able to fathom its meaning. It
is like a shell from the ocean-beach, murmuring, to the atten-
tive ear, "mysterious union with its native sea." The language
is the language of a poet, but the music is the music of the
spheres. Let me quote the psalm in full that we may study it
more closely:

(1)

The Lord is my shepherd, I shall not want.
He maketh me to lie down in green pastures;
He leadeth me beside the waters of rest.
He restoreth my soul.

(2)

He guideth me in the paths of righteousness for his
   name's sake.
Yea, though I walk through the valley of the shadow of
   death,
I will fear no evil, for thou art with me.
Thy rod and thy staff, they comfort me.

(3)

Thou spreadest before me a table in the presence of
   mine enemies.
Thou anointest my head with oil;
My cup runneth over.
Surely goodness and mercy shall follow me all the days
   of my life.
And I shall dwell in the house of the Lord unto length
   of days.[8]

As will be seen, the psalm falls, quite naturally, into three
parts, which symbolize the three consecutive phases in the
progress of the life of grace. There runs through them all the
love of God, in whom "we live and move and have our being"
(Acts 17:28). There is really only one Way, the Way of Love,
which is the bond of perfection; but it is equally clear that the
Way has three stages, as pictured in the three stanzas. The first

---

[8] *The New Psalter of Pius XII in Latin and English*, translated by Rev. Charles
J. Callan, O. P. (New York: Wagner, 1949).

corresponds to what is traditionally known as the Purgative Way, or the Way of beginners; the second, to the Illuminative Way, or the Way of proficients; and the third, to the Unitive Way, or the Way of the perfect. They also recall to mind the three successive biddings Christ gave to St. Peter before His Ascension: *Feed my lambs, Shepherd my sheep,* and *Feed my sheep* (John 21:15–17).

It is to be noted that, while the Psalm of the Good Shepherd presents the growth of spiritual life from the angle of divine grace, Psalm 1 presents the same thing from the angle of human effort. Let me reproduce the opening verses of Psalm 1:

(1)

Blessed is the man who follows not the counsel of the
    ungodly,
Nor walks in the ways of sinners,
Nor sits in the company of the scornful.

(2)

But his heart is in the law of the Lord,
And on His law he meditates day and night.

(3)

And he shall be like a tree which is planted near the
    running waters, which shall bring forth its fruit, in
    due season,
And his leaf shall not fall off: and all whatsoever he
    shall do shall prosper.

The Holy Scriptures form a seamless tunic, whose folds fit into one another perfectly. As the Holy Spirit is their Author, we must invoke Him in order to get at their hidden meanings. For, as St. Paul says, "The Spirit searches all things, yea the deep things of God" (1 Cor. 2:10). It is only by "combining spiritual with spiritual" that we can arrive at the Truth; and it is only with "the mind of Christ" that we understand the mind of God (1 Cor. 2, 13 and 16).

Many psalms chart out the course of our spiritual progress under the figures of pilgrimage. To give just one example, Psalm 83:

(1)

Blessed is the man whose help is from Thee,
When he has pilgrimages in his heart.

(2)

Passing across a parched valley, they shall make it a
    source of wells,
And the first rain shall clothe it with blessings.

(3)

They shall go from strength to strength:
They shall see the God of gods in Sion.[9]

Does this not present beautifully the budding, the flowering,
and the ripening of love?

Christ has summed up the three stages of our spiritual life in
words at once simple and profound: *Ask and it shall be given you;
seek and you shall find; knock and it shall be opened to you.* You ask for
graces and gifts and even for your daily bread, so that you may
be provided for in your journey of life, and they will be given
to you inasmuch as they are necessary means to enable you to
reach your destination. But in this you are thinking primarily
of your own needs. So your love is more or less self-centered
and possessive. You look upon God chiefly as your benefac-
tor. When you advance a stage higher, you begin to seek Him
because of His attractions; and this plainly is a higher form
of love than merely to expect gifts from Him. The higher you
rise, the more beautiful he appears to your eyes. Then comes a
point where you are so enamored of Him that you cannot help
knocking at the door of His inner chamber in order that you
may be united with Him forever. When it will be opened to
you depends upon His good pleasure; but knock you must. If
you are so lucky as to be admitted into His intimate company,
you will enjoy the liberty of the children of God, as free as a
butterfly. But it must be remembered that before one becomes
a butterfly, one must pass through the larval stage and that of
the chrysalis. There is no Easter without Good Friday.

---

[9] *The Psalms: A Prayer Book*, trans. Professors of the Biblical Institute (New
York: Benziger Brothers, 1947).

3. THE BUDDING OF LOVE

Christ has sketched for us not only the three stages, but also the eight degrees of Love in the form of Beatitudes. Let us try to see how well these stages and degrees dovetail with one another.

The three stages are traditionally known as the Purgative Way, the Illuminative Way, and the Unitive Way. I prefer to call them the budding, the flowering and the ripening of love, because there are not three ways, but only one Way, the Way of Love, although the Way may roughly be divided into three successive stages. The eight Beatitudes as Christ announced them from the Mount are as follows:

(1) Blessed are the poor in spirit, for theirs is the kingdom of heaven.

(2) Blessed are they that mourn, for they shall be comforted.

(3) Blessed are the meek, for they shall inherit the land.

(4) Blessed are they that hunger and thirst after justice, for they shall have their fill.

(5) Blessed are the merciful, for they shall find mercy.

(6) Blessed are pure of heart, for they shall see God.

(7) Blessed are the peacemakers, for they shall be called the children of God.

(8) Blessed are they that suffer persecution for justice's sake, for theirs is the kingdom of heaven. Blessed are ye when they shall revile you and persecute you and speak all that is evil against you, untruly, for my sake: be glad and rejoice, for your reward is very great in heaven. For so they persecuted the prophets that were before you (Matt. 5.3–12).

It is to be noted that with reference to the second and third Beatitudes, I follow here the order of the Greek text rather than that of the Vulgate, as is done in the Westminster version by the Reverend Cuthbert Lattey.

Now, there are two ways of considering the Beatitudes. One way is to regard any one of them as a ladder to heaven, with ascending steps within itself. Just as there are many mansions in Our Father's house, so there are many ladders to them. The

other way is to regard all the Beatitudes in the order that Christ
has presented them as so many ascending steps of one single
ladder. So far as I know, St. Augustine was the first to treat
them in this way. St. Thomas Aquinas, following St. Augustine, has classified them into three groups. The first three Beatitudes — of the poor in spirit, those who mourn, the meek —
have to do with "the withdrawal of man from those things in
which sensual happiness consists" (*S. T.*, Ia, IIae, Q.69, Art.
4). The Beatitudes of justice and mercy "belong to the works
of active happiness." The Beatitudes of the pure in heart and
the peaceful "belong to contemplative happiness." As to the
eighth Beatitude, St. Thomas regards it as the confirmation and
consummation of all the preceding ones.

It is clear that St. Thomas's threefold division of the Beatitudes corresponds to the three stages on the Way of Love. St.
Augustine had said, "As soon as charity is born it takes food;
after taking food, it waxes strong; and when it has become
strong, it is perfected" (*In prim. canon. Joan., Tract.* v). Commenting on these words, St. Thomas writes: "For at first it is
incumbent on man to occupy himself chiefly with avoiding sin
and resisting his concupiscences, which move him in opposition to charity: this concerns beginners, in whom charity has
to be fed or fostered lest it be destroyed: in the second place
man's chief pursuit is to aim at progress in good, and this is the
pursuit of the proficient, whose chief aim is to strengthen their
charity by adding to it: while man's third pursuit is to aim
chiefly at union with and enjoyment of God: this belongs to
the perfect who *desire to be dissolved and to be with Christ*" (*S. T.*,
IIa, IIae, Q. 24. Art. 9).

Now, in the budding of love, the soul is awakened to the
utter worthlessness of earthly riches and worldly honors, on
the one hand, and to the infinite riches and ineffable glories
of the kingdom of heaven on the other. "Vanity of vanities,"
sighed the splendid Solomon, "vanity of vanities, and all is
vanity" (Eccles. 1:2). "I am poor and needy, and my heart is
wounded within me" (Ps. 108:22), said another king, David.
To realize that "a man's life does not consist in having more
possessions that he needs" (Luke 12:15) is to be "poor in spirit."

St. Angela of Foligno said that "To know God's allness and man's nothingness: that is perfection." I do not know whether it is perfection; at least, it is the beginning of wisdom. We cannot too often remind ourselves that "man is insufficient without God because without God he would not even be," and that "there is an abyss of nothingness at the very heart of our being."[10] It was no accident that the prodigal son came to himself before he returned to his father. This thought is in line with the idea of St. Catherine of Siena that there is an interior cell with twin chambers within us, one of which is the chamber of self-knowledge and the other the chamber of the knowledge of God. "It is in the chamber of self-knowledge that one learns his wretchedness, because he sees with his spiritual eye his defects and his nothingness, and he sees in truth. And when the man knows himself, he knows also the goodness of God towards him."[11] Cardinal Bérulle also said, "Abnegation is founded on the greatness of God, and on the state of the creature drawn from nothing and tending to nothingness by his own condition and owing to sin, and also on another kind of nothingness of self through grace."[12] This may be called the doctrine of triple nothingness, corresponding, perhaps, to the triple fullness of Being. Likewise, St. Teresa of Ávila has said, "It is absurd to think that we can enter Heaven without first entering our own souls — without getting to know ourselves, and reflecting upon the wretchedness of our nature and what we owe to God, and continually imploring His mercy."[13] To acknowledge our nothingness, then, is a sign of sanity, which is the foundation of sanctity. Not only are we nothing, but the whole universe apart from God is nothing. Certainly, St. John of the Cross was not exaggerating when he declared, "All the wealth and glory of all the creatures, in comparison with the wealth which is God, is supreme poverty and wretchedness."[14]

---

[10] F. J. Sheed, *Theology and Sanity* (New York: Sheed & Ward, 1946), 330.

[11] Père S. Bézine, O. P., ed., *Mystique de Sainte Catherine de Sienne: Extraits de ses lettres* (Paris: Éditions du Cerf, 1947).

[12] Pourrat, *Christian Spirituality*, vol. 3, 347.

[13] Teresa of Avila, *The Complete Works of St. Teresa of Jesus*, trans. E. Allison Peers (New York: Sheed & Ward, 1946), vol. 2, 218.

[14] John of the Cross, *The Complete Works of St. John of the Cross*, trans. E.

This insight is the first step in what Father Gerald Vann calls "the quest for self-loss in God."[15] Without this initial insight, there can be no talk of the spiritual life; for the spiritual life is nothing but a self-realization through self-immolation in Christ.

But insight alone does not make a saint. For, although the spirit may be willing, the flesh is weak. Like Lazarus, we may already have been raised from the dead by the voice of Christ, but we are still "bound feet and hands with winding bands," which symbolize our evil habits and the propensities of our fallen nature. The old Adam in us dies extremely hard. As St. Paul says, "For the flesh lusteth against the spirit: and the spirit against the flesh: for these are contrary one to another: so that you do not the things that you would" (Gal. 5:17). He has elsewhere presented our pathetic condition in even more graphic terms: "For I am delighted with the law of God according to the inward man, but I see another law in my members, fighting against the law of my mind and captivating me in the law of sin that is in my members. Unhappy man that I am! Who shall deliver me from the body of this death? The grace of God, by Jesus Christ our Lord" (Rom. 7:22–24).

This struggle of the inner man against the concupiscence of our body costs tears of anguish and contrition, but it leads to the salutary knowledge that we can do nothing of ourselves, that it is by the grace of God that we can conquer ourselves, and that the grace of God comes only through our abiding in Christ. Our relation with Christ is infinitely closer than any human relation can possibly be. It can best be symbolized by the Vine and its branches, for we are members of the Mystical Body of which Christ is the Head.

In short, by ourselves we can never bring our body to subjection; it is only by virtue of our being branches of the true Vine that we can receive the sap which is the grace of God.

One of the most charming psalms of David is on the wonderful medicinal power of confession. He says:

Allison Peers (Westminster, MD: Newman Press, 1953), vol. 1, 28.
[15] Gerald Vann, O. P., *St. Thomas Aquinas* (New York: Benziger Brothers, 1947).

> Because I was silent my bones grew old; whilst I cried
> out all the day long.
> For day and night thy hand was heavy upon me: I am
> turned in my anguish, whilst the thorn is fastened.
> I have acknowledged my sin to thee: and my injustice I
> have not concealed.
> I said: I will confess against myself my injustice to the
> Lord. And thou hast forgiven the wickedness of my
> sin....
> Thou art my refuge from the trouble which hath
> encompassed me: my joy, deliver me from them that
> surround me (Ps. 31).

Every time one goes to the confessional with a sincere heart, God welcomes him and feasts him with a fattened calf. My good friend Dr. Paul Sih has described beautifully how he felt after his first general confession: "My heart was filled with happiness and I came out a changed being. I was free, as free as a bird in the air. I was pure, as pure as white snow. My wife wondered what had happened to me when she observed that I was so joyful that I could have jumped over the sky and gladly joined the 'Dragon Lanterns Parade' in the moon!" This bears out the words of our Lord: *Blessed are they that mourn, for they shall be comforted.* Indeed, heaven and earth shall pass away, but the words of Our Lord shall not pass away.

This leads us to the Beatitude of meekness. Now, according to St. Thomas, while the Beatitude of those who mourn has to do with the conquering of concupiscible passions, the Beatitude of the meek has to do with the overcoming of the irascible passions. With the help of divine grace and the gift of piety, one grows in patience, calmness, serenity, and self-possession. The French word for meekness is *douceur*, which means sweetness. I imagine St. Francis of Sales was thinking of meekness when he said, "You can catch more flies with a spoonful of honey than with a hundred barrels of vinegar."

To be meek is to be contented with one's lot, to lie low; and to lie low is, according to the Chinese Philosopher Lao Tse, to be a king. "Why is the ocean the king of all rivers and streams?" he asks; and his answer is: "Because it lies lower than all of them." This figure finds a parallel in the words of Our Lord: *Blessed are the meek, for they shall possess the earth."*

David was singing of the joy of meekness when he said:

> The Lord is the portion of my inheritance and my cup:
> It is thou that wilt restore my inheritance to me.
> The lines are fallen unto me in goodly places: for my
>   inheritance is goodly to me (Ps. 15).

This is, perhaps, one of the pleasantest periods one can experience in one's spiritual journey. There is something idyllic about it. The Divine Physician has restored your soul, and you feel like one who has just recovered from a grave and prolonged illness. Your passions have been duly subordinated to reason. In the calm of convalescence you feel contented, and want to enjoy your rest for some time. You even think that you can advance no further. You say to Christ, as Peter did on Mount Tabor, "Lord, it is good for us to be here." But He tells you, "It is expedient that I go."

4. THE FLOWERING OF LOVE

As a matter of fact, so far you have only known the consolations of God, not the God of consolations. So far, you have been acting like the young silkworm that feeds greedily on the tender mulberry leaves. Now it is time for the larva to molt, to fast, to mount, to spin its silk, and to be prepared to become a chrysalis. In plain words, you are still extremely imperfect. Your ideas of God are sensual and narrow. Your love of God is possessive. You think of Him as belonging to yourself. Your heart is attached to the consolations He has showered upon you. In order to lead you to a higher plane, your Divine Lover withdraws His consolations, and you, who have in your ignorance identified His consolations with Himself, feel keenly His absence. You say to yourself, "He no longer loves me. I am no longer what I used to be." You will moan with David:

> O God, my God, to thee do I watch at break of day.
> For thee my soul hath thirsted; for thee my flesh, O
>   how many ways!
> In a desert land, and where there is no way, and no
>   water (Ps. 62).

> As the hart panteth after the fountains of water; so my
>   soul panteth after thee, O God.
> My soul hath thirsted after the strong living God; when
>   shall I come and appear before the face of God?
> My tears have been my bread day and night, whilst it is
>   said to me daily: Where is thy God? (Ps. 41).

The Psalmist felt an unspeakable nostalgia when he remembered how he had "walked in the throng and gone before them to the house of God in the midst of the sounds of joy and praise in a festive gathering." So he was really more homesick for those festive days in the temple of God than for God Himself.

The truth is that God has never left us. In fact, He is nearer to us now than before. It is His stirring within us that produces this hunger and yearning. He deals with us as a mother with her child, "who warms it in her bosom, nourishes it with her milk, feeds it with tender and delicate food, carries it in her arms and fondles it. But as the child grows up the mother withholds her caresses, hides her breasts, and anoints them with the juice of bitter aloes; she carries the infant in her arms no longer, but makes it walk on the ground, so that losing the habits of an infant, it may apply itself to greater and more substantial pursuits" (St. John of the Cross, *The Dark Night of the Soul*).

With this we clearly enter upon a new phase in our spiritual life, which consists in the Beatitude of hunger and thirst for justice and that of mercifulness. This is the central part of our life. Our own house being more or less at rest, we begin actively to practice the love of God and the love of our neighbor. These two Beatitudes form an inseparable pair; for justice to God requires mercifulness to our neighbor. In the words of Father Gerald Vann, "If you learn to treat God as your Father you will automatically come to think of men as your brothers, and to love them as your brothers precisely in the unity of God's family, so that your love for them and for Him is one single love."[16]

---

[16] Gerald Vann, O. P., *The Divine Pity* (New York: Sheed & Ward, 1946), 53.

Nothing can be so intriguing as the study of man's spiritual metamorphosis, but the present phase is the most dramatic of all. In the former phase Christ had drawn us to our Father's house; but now the Father has drawn us to the Son, telling us, "If you want to be My true children, follow the example of My Son, so that you may be by grace what He is by nature." In this stage your favorite prayer is apt to be the *Anima Christi*, or something to the same effect. From the bottom of your heart you cry:

> Soul of Christ, sanctify me.
> Body of Christ, save me.
> Blood of Christ, inebriate me.
> Water from the side of Christ, wash me.
> Passion of Christ, strengthen me.
> O good Jesu, hear me.
> Within Thy wounds hide me.
> Suffer me not to be separated from Thee.
> From the malignant enemy defend me,
> In the hour of my death call me,
> And bid me come unto Thee,
> That with Thy saints I may praise Thee
> For ever and ever. Amen.

You are more and more assimilated to the mind and heart of Christ, and with that grows your devotion to the Blessed Virgin, for no human being knows His mind and heart as well as the Mother. In the meantime, your love of the Holy Eucharist becomes an ever-increasing passion, since you know that this is the best preparation for your spiritual union with Him. Some time or other, the Holy Spirit moves you to whisper to Christ, "Lord, what shall I render to You for Your wonderful love of me?" He answers you in a whisper, "Do not always say 'me, me, me, me....' Remember there is a big Me in you. Love Me, love My brothers!" This is inevitable, for, as St. Thomas says, "Whoever loves another, must in consequence also love those whom that other loves and who are united with him. But men are loved by God, seeing that for them He has prepared the enjoyment of Himself as their last end. Therefore as one is a lover of God, so must he be a lover of his neighbor."[17] In a note to this passage, Father Rickaby quotes the proverb: *Love me, love my dog.* In this light you come to appreciate St. Francis's *Canticle of Brother Sun.* It is a marvelous privilege to be a Christian. A Christian can enjoy all the lyrical ecstasies of a pantheist at their very Source, and without the danger of being drowned in the ocean of creatures. The truth is that, as God contains all things in Himself, so His lovers carry in their hearts all other creatures. In the words of St. Leo the Great, "Christian poverty possesses all things, for it possesses the master of all things."

"God is love," says St. John, the Beloved Disciple, "and he who abides in love abides in God, and God in him." Perhaps the highest form of fraternal love is to share our Beloved with others. The more we share, the more we have. The less we share, the less we have, until even the little that we have is taken away from us. As Father Frederick W. Faber says in his *All for Jesus;* "Indeed, we shall never prosper with the work in our souls, if we do not strive to advance the interests of Jesus in the souls of others."

No work is nobler than that of the apostolate. "How beautiful are the feet of them that preach the gospel of peace, of them that bring glad tidings of good things!" (St. Paul quoting from Isaias; see Rom. 10:15) "For we are the good odour of Christ unto God, in them that are saved and in them that perish. To one indeed the odour of death unto death: but to the others the odour of life unto life" (2 Cor. 2:15–16). This is the supreme office that a man can aspire to; there goes with it the power over life and death of men.

5. THE RIPENING OF LOVE

However, like all powers, it is not free from pitfalls. I think it was Lord Acton who said, with reference to political power: "All power corrupts, and absolute power corrupts absolutely." This also applies to spiritual power, because our fallen nature is so deep-rooted in us that it would take a whole lifetime

---

[17] Thomas Aquinas, *Of God and His Creatures*, trans. Rev. Joseph Rickaby, S. J. (London: Longmans, Green, and Co., 1905), 277.

to uproot it entirely. You remember in what high spirits the seventy-two disciples returned from their first missionary trip, reporting to Christ, "Lord, even the devils are made subject to us in thy name" (Luke 10:17). Christ, who knew what is in man, discerned at once their inborn tendency to attach their hearts to the fruits of their labors, and bade them to raise their minds to heaven and fix their eyes on their ultimate destiny, saying, "You, instead of rejoicing that the devils are made subject to you, should be rejoicing that your names are enrolled in heaven" (Luke 10:20).

How many zealous missionaries and lay apostles are stunted in their spiritual development because they set too much store by what they have accomplished and are unconsciously infected by a kind of partisan spirit, a group egoism! So long as you are not completely detached from the fruit of your hands, your love for God is not pure. This leads us to the Beatitude of the clean of heart, which corresponds to the passive purification of the spirit. This purification is necessary because, in the words of Fr. Garrigou-Lagrange, "The stains of the old man still remain like rust that will disappear only under the action of a purifying fire.... The root of the higher faculties of intellect and will is still deeply tainted with pride, personal judgment, and self will."[18]

This is the most painful period of one's spiritual life, but it is also the most crucial. John Tauler was probably speaking of this period when he said, "When the Heavenly Father resolves to adorn a soul with sublime gifts and to change it in special wise, it is not His custom to cleanse it gently, rather is He wont to bathe it in an ocean of bitterness, to plunge and sink it as He did the prophet Jonah."

One of the causes of this bitterness is that, the more illumined one's soul is by the divine light, the more one becomes conscious of sin. It is, in effect, like sunlight shining through some vent into a dark room, revealing countless specks of hitherto unsuspected dust dancing in its ray. David was in that state when he cried:

---

[18] Réginald Garrigou-Lagrange, O. P., *The Three Ages of the Interior Life*, vol. 2 (St. Louis, MO: B. Herder Book Co., 1948), 358–59.

> Withhold not thou, O Lord, thy tender mercies from me:
>   thy mercy and thy truth have always upheld me.
> For evils without number have surrounded me: my iniq-
>   uities have overtaken me and I was not able to see.
> They are multiplied above the hairs of my head: and my
>   heart hath forsaken me (Ps. 39).

David was not alone in experiencing this terrible night; for another Psalmist wrote the *De Profundis*:

Indent as per format

> If thou, O Lord, wilt mark iniquities: Lord, who shall
>   stand it?
> For with thee there is merciful forgiveness: and by rea-
>   son of thy law, I have waited for thee, O Lord.
> My soul hath relied on his word: my soul hath hoped
>   in the Lord.
> `From the morning watch until night, let Israel hope in
>   the Lord (Ps. 129).

"It is a question here of fruitful spiritual suffering and of a spiritual winter that prepares the germination of a new spring,"[19] writes Garrigou-Lagrange. Before your soul can take wing, it must be buried in its cocoon, completely dead to the world and to self.

The best way for a soul in this state to conduct itself is in complete abandonment to the good pleasure of the Lord, and in absolute confidence in His power to cure even the cancer of self-will and the leprosy of evil desires. Let Him operate in you, and trust in His power to Cure you. Say to Him with David: "Create a clean heart in me, O God, and renew a right spirit in me" (Ps. 50:12). Approach Him as the wise leper did: "Lord, if thou wilt, thou canst make me clean." And He will certainly stretch forth His hand and touch you, saying, "I will: be thou cleansed" (Luke 5:12–14). The more hopeless you are in yourself, the more hopeful you are in the Lord. Only keep your heart open and let Christ, the Eternal Sun, shine into it, and He will purify it and cause it to open out in His light, until it overflows with the joy and sweetness it has received.

---

[19] Garrigou-Lagrange, *Three Ages*, 2:360.

This introduces you into the unitive stage, where what the mystics call "spiritual betrothal" and "spiritual marriage" take place. I should prefer to speak of it in terms of the consummation, so far as is possible in this life, of our birthright as children of God. We have seen that in the first stage the Son led you to the Father, and in the second, the Father led you to the Son. In this third stage, Father and Son together pour Their Spirit of Love into your heart; and "because you are sons, God hath sent the Spirit of his son into your hearts, crying: Abba, Father" (Gal. 4:6). Only then have we begun to live on the deeper levels of reality. "Most of us," as Mother St. Austin says, "live on the surface of ourselves; underneath is a fathomless sanctuary where 'Spirit and spirit can meet.' That is the secret place where the Holy Ghost, the Love of the Father and of the Son, makes love to us."[20] When you have the spirit of the Son, then you have *His* freedom, *His* peace, and *His* joy, which the world cannot take away from you.

Perhaps as good a description as can be found of the unitive state has been given by John Tauler in his sermon in preparation for Whitsuntide:

> St. Augustine says that there is a mysterious place deep in the soul that is beyond time and this world, a part higher than that which gives life and movement to the body; true prayer so raises the heart that God can come into this innermost place, the most disinterested, intimate, and noble part of our being, the seat of our unity. It is His eternal dwelling-place. And into this grand and mysterious kingdom He pours the sweet delight of which I have spoken. Then is man no longer troubled by anything: he is recollected, quiet, and really himself, and becomes daily more detached, spiritualized, and contemplative, for God is within him, reigning and working in the depths of his soul.[21]

---

[20] John A. Nageleisen, *The Divine Crucible of Purgatory*, trans. from the German (New York: P. J. Kenedy & Sons, 1893), 101.

[21] Paul de Jaegher, S. J., ed., *An Anthology of Mysticism*, trans. Donald Attwater (Westminster, MD: Newman Press, 1950), 84.

In this state, you attain, on the supernatural plane, the stage that Confucius attained on the natural plane, when he could follow the dictates of his heart without transgressing the boundaries of right. The season of songs has come, and the music, says St. Bernard, "is not a noise of the mouth, but a shout of the heart; not a sound of the lips, but a tumult of internal delights; a harmony of wills, not of voices." You would be like a musician who is so full of his art that, without any effort, all that he does therein is perfection, and whose apparent improvisations, when closely examined, would be found in perfect conformity with prescribed rules. "Without rule, yet exactness itself; without measure, yet nothing better proportioned; without reflection, yet nothing better managed; without effort, yet nothing more efficacious; without forethought, yet nothing better fitted to unforeseen events."[22]

Being united with their God, such happy souls are truly beyond the categories of active or contemplative life. They are actively contemplative, and contemplatively active. God is their Love and their All. "If He wishes them to be passive, passive they will be; if active, then active; or if contemplative, then will they rejoice in contemplation. They know interiorly that it is God who has made ready the inner room of their soul, and He wishes to dwell therein to the exclusion of all His creatures."[23] They are "all things to all men" without being attached to anything.

Happy the soul who can say: "I am become in his presence as one finding peace" (Cant. 8:10). Night or day, in season or out of season, for better or for worse, for richer or for poorer, such a soul is wedded to the tremendous Lover, and finds Him more and more lovable as the years go by. In these circumstances life is a veritable prelude to heaven.

It may not be unfitting to conclude this section with an old Chinese love-song which, spiritually interpreted, will perhaps give an inkling of the joy of the saints:

---

[22] Jean-Pierre de Caussade, *Abandonment to Divine Providence* (New York: Benziger Brothers, 1887), 127.
[23] Attwater, *An Anthology of Mysticism*, 82.

Cold is the wind, chill the rain.
The cock crows *kikeriki*.
Now that I have seen my Love,
Peace has come to me.

The wind whistles, the rain drizzles.
The cock crows *kukeriku*.
Now that I have seen my Love,
My sickness is healed too.

The wind and the rain darken the day.
The cock ceases not to crow.
Now that I have seen my Love,
My joy ceases not to grow.

6. RECAPITULATION

It must not be imagined that after one has arrived at the unitive stage, all the virtues acquired during the preceding stages are thrown overboard. On the contrary, they are deepened and perfected and vitally integrated in a harmony of Love. Faith merges into actual experience of the ways of Providence. It is turned into boundless confidence in His wisdom and goodness, reinforced by the knowledge that "To them that love God, all things work together unto good" (Rom. 8:28) Hope becomes a longing for the ultimate union with God. In the earlier stages, you love because you hope. In this stage, you hope because you love. What you desire is not so much His blessings as Himself. You would pray with St. Gertrude: "I hold Thee fast as mine own with all the love of my heart; and even though Thou bless me a thousand times ere Thou go, yet never will I let Thee go" (*The Exercises of St. Gertrude*). All moral virtues and intellectual knowledge pass into love and become its attributes. Love is just, temperate, prudent and courageous. Love "believes all things" and "hopes all things." Even the seven gifts of the Holy Spirit are absorbed into love and become its qualities. Love vibrates with the spirit of holy fear, piety, knowledge, fortitude, good counsel, understanding and wisdom. For, as the Maritains have written, "In us, as well as in God, love must proceed from the Word, that is from the spiritual possession of the truth, in Faith. And just as everything which is in the Word is found once more in the Holy Spirit, so must all that we know pass into our power of affection by love, there only finding its resting-place."[24]

When one is in the unitive state, all the virtues take on heroic proportions, heroic not in one's own eyes, but in the eyes of others. Poverty in spirit becomes complete denudation and perfect adaptability to all kinds of circumstances. In the words of Régamey, "What does poverty in spirit mean, then, but living in such a way as to play the parts forced on us by circumstances without becoming attached to any of them. If we are professors—not becoming pedants; priests—not hardened into ways of clericalism; if we attain some success—not pontificating; if we never reach any special position—not being vulgar. Every element in life must serve to increase our human qualities rather than bury them."[25] Tears are shed over the miseries of the whole creation, including oneself. "Who is weak and I am not weak? Who is scandalized and I am not on fire?" (2 Cor. 11:29). As to humility and meekness, they become, as it were, *ontological*, springing from the transparent knowledge of one's nothingness; so that when one hears praises of oneself, one feels actually "like an impostor whose tricks have been discovered."[26] The thirst for God is turned into "a fountain of water, springing up into life everlasting" (John 4:14). Mercifulness takes the form of a fruition of Love. One can understand the great vow of St. Thérèse *to spend her heaven in doing good on earth*. One becomes a mother of souls, the Father being the Holy Spirit. On this point, Father Arintero has made an interesting comment: "Procreation of fructification does not kill or weaken that mutual affection, or cause it to

---

[24] Jacques Maritain and Raïssa Maritain, *Prayer and Intelligence*, trans. Algar Thorold (London: Sheed & Ward, 1928), 3.

[25] Pie Raymond Régamey, *Poverty: An Essential Element in the Christian Life*, trans. Rosemary Sheed (New York: Sheed and Ward, 1949), 117.

[26] Louis Lallemant, *Spiritual Doctrine of Father Louis Lallemant of the Society of Jesus*, originally compiled in 1694 by the Jesuit Pierre Champion under the title *Doctrine spirituelle*, with a Life of Lallemant also written by Champion, ed. Alan G. McDougall (Westminster, MD: Newman Press, 1955), 289.

be lost. Rather it augments and strengthens it in such a way that she ever retains her youth and gains even greater fertility. The more fruitful the soul in good works and the more it fructifies for God, the more vigorous and beautiful and radiant in glory does it become and the more pleasing it is to the divine Spouse."[27] Even imperfections and weaknesses become an occasion of joy and strength; as St. Paul says, "When I am weak, then I am strong." In the meantime, the gift of understanding makes you realize God's absolute transcendence, and that there is no understanding Him, after all. And you are glad of your ignorance, because that assures you that the beauties of your God are inexhaustible, so that the freshness of His glory will never pass, even in heaven. With this blissful ignorance, you enter upon a second childhood, without which no one can enter heaven. But, although the being of God is unfathomable, and although in this life we can only see Him indirectly in the effects of His power and goodness, yet His light shines upon us so that we can reflect it in our lives. Contemplation, in this life, is nothing but an awareness of being shone upon by God and reflecting His glory as in a mirror. His shining upon us transforms us "into the same image from glory to glory" (2 Cor 3:18). This is the work of the Spirit of Love.

Finally, the gift of wisdom harmonizes all things from one end to the other, beginning with the Alpha and resting in the Omega. For wisdom "reaches from end to end mightily, and orders all things sweetly" (Wisd. 8:1). Wisdom infuses into you the wonderful insight that Love is all, and that the same Love that moves the sun and the other stars is throbbing in the heart of your heart and in the soul of your soul. The Way of Love starts from Love and ends in Love. All the eight Beatitudes are in reality only one: Blessed are you who love, for you shall be loved by God. Christ has summed up the whole process of our spiritual life in a magnificent promise: "If anyone love me, he will keep my word, and my Father will love him, and we will come to him, and will make our abode with

---

[27] Arintero, *The Mystical Evolution in the Development and Vitality of the Church*, 1:166.

him" (John 14.23). Note how marvelously He has portrayed the active and passive phases of the Supreme Romance of Love between God and man. From the standpoint of fruition, the active phase is negative, while the passive is positive. Only the words of the Holy Spirit can illustrate this wonderful teaching of Our Lord:

> Mercy and truth have met each other: justice and peace have kissed.
> Truth is sprung out of the earth: and justice hath looked down from heaven.
> For the Lord will give goodness: and our earth shall yield her fruit.
> Justice shall walk before him: and shall set his steps in the way (Ps. 84).

PART ONE

THE BUDDING OF LOVE

"There is but one sorrow," wrote Léon Bloy, "and that is to have lost the Garden of Delights, and there is but one hope and one desire, to recover it. The poet seeks it in his own way, and the filthiest profligate seeks it in his. It is the only goal."

These words have a special bearing on the first stage of our spiritual life. At the start of our journey, we must have the right orientation. While all people are seeking to recover the lost Garden of Delights, only the saints have found it, because they did not follow their own ways, but the Way of God as revealed in the Person and teachings of Christ. For us wayfarers, the all-important thing is to know the Way. As Alice Meynell has it:

> Thou art the Way.
> Hadst Thou been nothing but the goal,
> I cannot say
> If Thou hadst met my soul. (*From* "I Am the Way")

The budding of love begins with a radical revaluation of values. Christ teaches us where to look for the object of our love and where not to look for it. "Lay not up to yourselves treasures on earth, where the rust and moth consume, and where thieves break through and steal; but lay up to yourselves treasures in heaven, where neither the rust nor the moth consume, and where thieves do not break through, nor steal. For where thy treasure is, there is thy heart also" (Matt. 6:19–20). By talking in terms of "treasures," He condescends to our level, for He who created human nature knows how possessively inclined we all are. In order to lift our hearts from earthly riches, He promises us the reward of heavenly riches. St. Thomas Aquinas who sees the Beatitudes as being arranged in the ascending order, has this to say about the first three Beatitudes:

> For the first three Beatitudes concerned the withdrawal of man from those things in which sensual happiness consists: which happiness man desires by seeking the object of his natural desire, not where he should seek it, viz.

in God, but in temporal and perishable things. Wherefore the rewards of the first three Beatitudes correspond
to these things which some men seek to find in earthly
happiness. For men seek in external things, viz. riches
and honours, a certain excellence and abundance, both
of which are implied in the kingdom of heaven, whereby
man attains to excellence and abundance of good things
in God. Hence Our Lord promised the kingdom of
heaven to the poor in spirit. Again, cruel and pitiless men
seek by wrangling and fighting to destroy their enemies
so as to gain security for themselves. Hence Our Lord
promised the meek a secure and peaceful possession of
the land of the living, whereby the solid reality of eternal
goods is denoted. Again, men seek consolation for the
toils of the present life, in the lusts and pleasures of the
world. Hence Our Lord promises comfort to those who
mourn (*S. T.*, Ia IIae, Q. 69. A.4).

It is clear that in the first stage of the spiritual life, grace
makes use of the psychological process of sublimation — sublimation, not in the sense that the Freudian school uses it,
but as understood by Dom Thomas Verner Moore. As Moore
has pointed out, the term "sublimation" comes from the science of chemistry. "In chemistry, sublimation is one of the
processes by which a salt may be purified. If a volatile salt is
heated beneath a bell jar, it vaporizes and the vapor rises to the
cool dome of the jar and there crystallizes in its pure state."[1]
Thus, sublimation means a restoration to its rightful object of
the fundamental craving of human nature for happiness. It
means an adjustment of our mind to what Frank Sheed calls
"the landscape of reality." As he says, "We see our life as a road
with a beginning and a goal, for we know the realities from
which, through which, and to which it proceeds."[2]

Sublimation means putting first things first. It means love
returning to its First Principle. It does not require us to inhibit
all human desires and cravings. What it demands is that we

---

[1] Paul D. MacLean, *The Driving Forces of Human Nature and Their Adjustment* (New York: Grune & Stratton, 1953), 314.
[2] Ibid., 365.

should subordinate everything to our supreme end, for our hearts are made for God. As Christ Himself has told us, our Father knows that we have physical and social needs, but we must first seek the Kingdom of God and His justice, and all the other things will be given to us besides. We have to eat and drink, but this does not mean that we should make a god of our belly. Whatever we do, so long as it is not a sin, we can do it for the glory and pleasure of God.

The task of the first phase of our spiritual life is the reintegration of our nature. But as Matthias Scheeben says:

> In Christian justification, the whole of original justice, including its lower, material factors, is not given back to us. The full order and harmony of all the faculties of the soul are not restored. Inordinate concupiscence, particularly, is not completely suppressed and tamed. Thus there is lacking in us some of the order and harmony that pertained to Adam's justice; there is lacking the integrity of nature by which grace had originally been made so close an ally of nature, and had exercised such power in nature.[3]

On the other hand, we must realize the fact that "as living members of Christ we have a higher dignity, a greater sanctity, and a more glorious power of pleasing God, than we should possess in virtue of grace alone, or than Adam possessed before his sin."[4] *O felix culpa, quae talem ac tantum meruit habere Redemptorem!* (Preface of the Blessing of the Paschal Candle, Holy Saturday). It is, then, by virtue of our incorporation in Christ that grace is the seed of glory. That is why St. Leo said, *"Agnosce, Christiane, dignitatem tuam"*—Learn, O Christian, thy dignity. To quote Scheeben again:

> Christian justice, notwithstanding the lack of an external complement, is in many respects more sublime, more bountiful, and more mysterious than original justice. The man who is restored to grace in Christ is, for all the

---

[3] Matthias Joseph Scheeben, *The Mysteries of Christianity*, trans. Cyril Vollert (St. Louis: B. Herder Book Co., 1946), 628.

[4] Ibid., 625.

frailty of his nature, more intimately and wonderfully
united to God than was Adam in the complete integrity
of his nature. His state of justice is a greater supernatural
mystery than Adam's state, and is all the more a mystery inasmuch as his state is not accompanied, as Adam's
was, by a transfiguration of the whole nature, but is hidden under the infirmity, the misery, and the poverty of
nature, like a pearl buried in mud, and is visible only to
the eyes of strong faith. Externally and in the lower faculties of his soul the justified Christian, unlike Adam, is
still under the law of the sin, death, and corruption that
came into existence with original sin. But the God-man,
with His Holy Spirit, dwells in the profoundest depths of
his soul, in the most hidden part of his being; and amid
the wreckage of sin builds Himself a temple that is the
more sacred and precious the less it can be desecrated
and damaged by the surrounding debris.[5]

From the standpoint of the temporal order, at least, we
cannot help saying the Redemption is more wonderful than
the Creation, and Sanctification is the most wonderful of all.
At the marriage of Cana the steward said to the bridegroom,
"Every man at first setteth forth good wine, and when men
have well drunk, then that which is worse. But thou hast kept
the good wine until now" (John 2:10). These words seem to
have a deep symbolic meaning not only for the growth of the
Church throughout the ages, but also for our spiritual life.

In the first stage, our principal duty is to cooperate with
grace in purifying ourselves. The purification cannot be perfect,
but it is the indispensable condition for rising to the higher
stages, in which the purification will be continued, though not
as the principal *leitmotif*, as is the case in the first stage.

---

[5] Scheeben, *The Mysteries of Christianity*, 630.

I

The Reversal of Values

Blessed are the poor in spirit, for theirs is the kingdom of heaven.

1. WE ARE ALL PASSING SHADOWS

"We are all passing shadows," says a holy priest. In fact, these words form the constant refrain of all his speeches and conversations. Every time I hear it, I feel a thrill in my heart. Thank God that our life here on earth is but a temporary exile! The fact that we have a true Home to look forward to gives us the necessary courage to face all the vagaries and vicissitudes of life without blinking, and to undergo all the trials and tribulations without flagging.

One either succumbs to the pathos of life or rises above it. The children of the world, however successful and however brilliant they may be, will inevitably succumb to it. Only the children of Light can triumph over it, and say: "*O grave where is thy victory? O death, where is thy sting?*"

Walter Pater wrote: "We have an interval, and then our place knows us no more. Some spend this interval in listlessness, some in high passions, the wisest, at least among 'the children of this world,' in art and song. For our one chance lies in expanding that interval, in getting as many pulsations as possible into the given time." This would indeed be a sensible way of spending our life, if there were no God, no future life, no Home awaiting us at the end of our journey. If that were the case, then "*Let us eat and drink, for tomorrow we shall die.*" But the irony of it is that with such a pathetic philosophy of life, even eating and drinking would bring no real joy. How much more healthy and cheerful the outlook of St. Paul, who says, "Whether you eat or drink, or whatsoever else you do, do all to the glory of God!" (1 Cor. 10:31).

Only the saints are happy. They have peace in Christ, and their faith in the Holy Trinity is confirmed by a lifelong experience and intimate intercourse with Them. To take just one instance out of a million, Blessed John Almond, immediately before his execution, said: "One hour overtaketh another, and though never so long, at last cometh death. And yet not death; for death is the gate of life unto us whereby we enter into everlasting blessedness. And life is death to those who do not provide for death, for they are ever tossed and troubled with vexations, miseries, and wickedness. To use this life well is the pathway through death to eternal life."

Every little happening and anecdote of our pilgrimage acquires an eternal significance if we refer it to God, our Origin, our Home, and our Way. The saints, who realize this in their very bones, are the true realists; the rest of us are mere daydreamers. How wise the prayer of St. Gertrude: "O Almighty God, I sanctify, dedicate and consecrate to Thee every beating of my heart, and every pulsation of my blood; and I desire to make this compact with Thee, that their every movement shall say to Thee, Holy, holy holy, Lord God of Sabaoth: and I beseech Thee to impart this meaning to them, so that they may be before Thy Divine Majesty as the unceasing echo of that heavenly canticle which seraphim sing without ceasing unto Thee. Amen, amen."

Now, here is the paradox: If we regard our earthly existence as our abiding home, we become homeless waifs; if, on the other hand, we regard ourselves as birds of passage, we feel at home even in our exile. Similarly, if we regard ourselves as somebody, we are nobody; if we regard ourselves as nobody, we are somebody. The Lord empties the full, but fills the empty. The more we are emptied of ourselves, the more we are filled with God. This presents in its essence the whole process of the spiritual life, with its polarity of negative and positive phases, or, as the Chinese would express it, the *Yin* and *Yang* aspects.

This polarity between nature and grace, man and God, is patent in all the Beatitudes, of which the first is: *Blessed are the poor in spirit, for theirs is the kingdom of heaven.* This constitutes the starting-point of the way of love, and gives, as it were, a bird's-eye view of the whole way.

The phrase "poor in spirit" has been variously interpreted by a host of commentators. Some have identified it with humility. To St. Augustine, for instance, to be poor in spirit is "not to have an inflated spirit." Others have identified it with the spirit of detachment. In order to attach oneself to God, one must be detached in interior disposition from all things that are not God. One cannot serve both God and mammon. Still others have taken "poor in spirit" to indicate a voluntary embracing of poverty, the actual relinquishment of all possessions.

To my mind, humility and detachment are the effects of the spirit of poverty, but not to be identified with it. As to the voluntary embracing of a life of poverty, it is an expression of the spirit of poverty, but not its only possible expression. As to the voluntary embracing of a life of poverty, it is an expression of the spirit of poverty, but not its only possible expression. The spirit of poverty is essentially an outlook on life, a philosophy of happiness, an insight into the true value of things. In one word, the spirit of poverty consists, metaphysically, in seeing "the universe and everything in it (ourselves included) as held in existence from moment to moment by nothing save God's continuing will to hold it (including ourselves) there";[1] and, ethically, in setting our hearts upon God and loving Him above all things. It recalls the image of the abyss of misery calling for the abyss of mercy to fill it with its plenitude.

2. THE IMPORTANCE OF BEING EMPTY

Among the Oriental sages, no one seems to have a better understanding of the importance of being empty than Lao Tse, who was an elder contemporary of Confucius. Here is what he says:

> Bend and you will be whole.
> Curl and you will be straight.
> Be empty and you will be filled.
> Wither and you will be renewed.
> Have little and you will gain.
> Have much and you will be lost.

These are some of the "seeds of the Logos" that God had

---

[1] Sheed, *Theology and Sanity*, 104.

sown in the Far East before the Incarnation of His Son. If John the Baptist was "the Voice crying in the wilderness," Lao Tse was at least a fore-echoing of that Voice. Let us listen to the Voice itself:

> Prepare ye the way of the Lord, make straight his paths.
> Every valley shall be filled: and every mountain and hill
>   shall be brought low: and the crooked shall be made
>   straight, and the rough ways plain.
> And all flesh shall see the salvation of God
> (Luke 3:4–6).

The Magnificat sung by the Blessed Virgin when she was pregnant with the Word made flesh reveals the same lesson of the importance of emptiness:

> My soul doth magnify the Lord.
> And my spirit hath rejoiced in God my Saviour.
> Because he hath regarded the humility of his hand-
>   maid; for behold from henceforth all generations
>   shall call me blessed.
> Because he that is mighty, hath done great things to
>   me; and holy is his name.
> And his mercy is from generation unto generations, to
>   them that fear him.
> He hath shewed might in his arm: he hath scattered
>   the proud in the conceit of their heart.
> He hath put down the mighty from their seat, and hath
>   exalted the humble.
> He hath filled the hungry with good things; and the
>   rich he hath sent empty away (Luke 1:46–53).

Just as Jesus is the fruit of her womb, so the Beatitudes are contained in an embryonic form in her song of joy.

All spiritual life begins with an initial insight as to our poverty and helplessness, and the absolute necessity of the grace of God. It is only because the Lord is our shepherd that we shall want for nothing. It is only because Christ has given us the kingdom of heaven that our very poverty is turned into a blessing. All that we need to do is to see eye to eye with Christ and be willing, heart and soul, to accept His blessing; but we must acknowledge that even that insight and that good will come from His grace.

I want to borrow a passage from Blessed John Ruysbroeck's *The Adornment of the Spiritual Marriage,* to illustrate in a symbolic manner the meaning of the spirit of poverty:

> Now understand this: when the sun sends its beams and its radiance into a deep valley between two high mountains, and, standing in the zenith, can yet shine upon the bottom and ground of the valley, then three things happen: the valley becomes full of light by reflection from the mountains, and it receives more heat, and becomes more fruitful, than the plain and level country. And so likewise, when a good man takes his stand upon his own littleness, in the most lowly part of himself, and confesses and knows that he has nothing, and is nothing, and can do nothing of himself, neither stand still nor go on, and when he sees how often he fails in virtues and good works: then he confesses his poverty and his helplessness, then he makes a valley of humility. And when he is thus humble, and needy, and knows his own need; he lays his distress, and complains of it, before the bounty and the mercy of God. And so he marks the sublimity of God and his own lowliness; and thus he becomes a deep valley. And Christ is a Sun of justice and also of mercy, Who stands in the highest part of the firmament, that is, on the right hand of the Father, and from thence He shines into the bottom of the humble heart; for Christ is always moved by helplessness, whenever a man complains of it and lays it before Him with humility. Then there arise two mountains, that is, two desires; one to serve God and praise Him with reverence, the other to attain noble virtues. Those two mountains are higher than the heavens, for these longings touch God without intermediary, and crave His ungrudging generosity. And then that generosity cannot withhold itself, it must flow forth; for then the soul is made to receive, and to hold, more gifts.

It is to be noted that Ruysbroeck was not writing a commentary on the first Beatitude; but I have found no commentary which presents more clearly the very spirit of it. The careful reader will not fail to see that Christian poverty is not to be cultivated as an end in itself, but rather as a necessary condition for being filled with the infinite riches of the kingdom of heaven. It takes two to make a romance; and it is well known that in the Supreme Romance between God and the soul, the soul must always play the role of the feminine. It is for God to give, it is for us to receive. For what have we got that we have not received from Him? True, it is more blessed to give than to receive; but this is said of our relations with our neighbor; *vis*-à-*vis* God, we have absolutely nothing to give, for our humble offerings to Him are really His gifts to us. If we make a complete dedication of our lives to Him, He is so generous as to accept it as though it were our gift, just as a fond father gratefully accepts from the hands of his children a birthday gift which they have bought with his own money. Such is the tenderness of a father's heart, that the poorer and more helpless his child is, the more dearly he loves him, and the more solicitous he is for his welfare. So long as the child remains docile, his very helplessness touches the heart of the father. If this is true of the human father, it must be eminently true of our Father in heaven. It is no wonder that St. Paul, who knows the heart of God so well, should have said, "For when I am weak, I am strong." He knows the heart of the Father, because he has the mind of the Son, from whom all true wisdom flows as from its living fountain.

3. THE MIND OF CHRIST

It was St. John Chrysostom who said, "The mind of Paul is the mind of Jesus." In his Epistle to the Philippians, St. Paul writes:

> Have this mind in you which was also in Christ Jesus, who, though he was by nature God, did not consider being equal to God a thing to be clung to, but emptied himself, taking the nature of a slave and being made like unto men. And appearing in the form of man, he humbled himself, becoming obedient to death, even to death on the cross. Therefore God also has exalted him and bestowed upon him the Name that is above every name, so that at the name of Jesus every knee should bend of

those in heaven, on earth and under the earth, and every tongue should confess that the Lord Jesus Christ is in the glory of God the Father (2:5–11).[2]

Now here is the living embodiment of the spirit of poverty in its plenitude. Christ, *in whom dwells all the fullness of the Godhead bodily* (Col. 2:9), emptied Himself to such an extent that He could say of Himself, "I am a worm and no man, the reproach of men and the outcast of the people" (Ps. 21:7). This infinite condescension is hard for us finite beings to comprehend in its full purport. Even to think of it makes the mind reel. But its lesson for us is clear enough. He had to empty Himself in order to fill us. All that we need to do is to take our stand upon our emptiness in order to be filled. He detached Himself from His true riches and glory as God, so that He might share them with us. The only price that we have to pay for all this is a wholehearted and grateful acceptance of His ineffable gifts; and we only need to detach ourselves from false riches and vain glories, to which we foolishly cling. God became a "worm" that we worms may become gods. Our salvation and our deification is thus a gift from God. That is why Our Lord said to the disciples, "Freely you have received, freely give." Again, in the Apocalypse, the idea of grace as a free gift of God is emphasized: "And he that sat on the throne said: Behold, I make all things new. . . . I am Alpha and Omega: the beginning and the end. To him that thirsteth, I will give of the fountain of the water of life, freely" (21:5–6).

The recognition that our spiritual life is a free gift from God does not preclude the necessity of our effort and cooperation. God has given us talents to be used to the best of our judgment and ability. But we must understand that even these talents are not owned by us; they are only held by us as trustees, with God as the true owner and with our neighbor as the beneficiary. So we have no right to waste or abuse our talents; for we are accountable to God for the use we have made of them. And

---

[2] *The New Testament of Our Lord and Savior Jesus Christ: Translated from the Latin Vulgate.* Confraternity of Christian Doctrine Edition (Paterson, NJ: St. Anthony Guild Press), 1941.

even if we have done everything that we are commanded to do, we must still feel, "We are unprofitable servants; we have done what it was our duty to do" (Luke 17.10). This is not a mere Oriental politeness, but a candid statement of the truth. If we do not see the truth, we are simply under a delusion. As Piers Plowman has it:

> For we are all Christ's creatures.
> And of His coffers rich.
> And Brethren of one blood.
> Alike beggars and earls.

Perhaps no man has worked than St. Paul, and yet he was ever aware of the paramount importance of grace, of the fact that without Christ he could do nothing. As he said, "I am the least of the' apostles, who am not worthy to be called an apostle, because I persecuted the Church of God. But by the grace of God, I am what I am: and his grace in me hath not been void, but I have laboured more abundantly than all they; yet not I, but the grace of God with me" (1 Cor. 15:9–10). With St. Paul, the knowledge of self and the knowledge of God worked together like double currents of electricity to produce a magnificent light and warmth. "For God, who commanded the light to shine out of darkness, has shined in our hearts, to give the light of the knowledge of the glory of God, in the face of Christ Jesus. But we have this treasure in earthen vessels that the excellency may be of the power of God, and not for us." In our spiritual life, nature constitutes the negative current, while grace functions as the positive current; and neither is dispensable in the Divine scheme of things. It is thanks to nature that "In all things we suffer tribulation"; it is thanks to grace that "we are not distressed." It is thanks to nature that "we are straitened"; it is thanks to grace that we "are not destitute." It is thanks to nature that "we are cast down"; it is thanks to grace that "we perish not." It is thanks to nature that we always bear about in our body the dying of Jesus; it is thanks to grace that "the life also of Jesus may be made manifest in our mortal flesh" (2 Cor. 4:6–12). The result of this marvelous cooperation is that we are "as deceivers and yet true, as unknown, and yet known, as dying, and behold we live; as chastised, and not killed; as sorrowful, yet always rejoicing; as needy, yet enriching many; as having nothing, and possessing all things" (2 Cor. 6:8–10). The long and short of it is that, as Jacopone da Todi puts it, "This spirit of poverty possesses so ample a bosom that Deity Itself takes up its dwelling there." And is it not a pity to have the kingdom of God in our bosom and yet to depart from it in order to seek after creatures? But man is a funny animal. "That which is of little or no profit takes up our thoughts; and that which is above all things necessary is negligently passed over; for the whole man sinks down into outward things, and unless he quickly recover himself, he willingly continues immersed in them" (*Imitation of Christ*, III, 44). How many Christians take to heart the words of Christ that "a man's life does not consist in having more possessions than he needs," and that "what is exalted in the sight of men is an abomination before God"?

4. THE BEGGAR WHO WAS A KING

In the fourteenth century, so the story goes, there was a great theologian who prayed for the space of eight years that God would vouchsafe to direct him to a man who might show him the way of truth. On a certain day, after having prayed more fervently than usual, he heard a voice from heaven, which said to him, "Go out to the porch of the church, and there you will meet with a man who will teach you the way of truth." On going thither he found a poor beggar, whose feet were covered with sores, dirt and mire, and all the clothes on his back not worth three farthings. "Good morning!" he saluted him. To which the beggar replied, "I never remember having had a bad morning." "God prosper you," said the doctor. "What do you mean?" asked the beggar, "I never was otherwise than prosperous." "I wish you all happiness," replied the doctor. "Why," said the poor man, "I never was unhappy." "God bless you," said the doctor; "but explain yourself, for I cannot well understand your meaning."

"That I shall do very willingly," answered the beggar. "I said that I never had a bad morning, because if I am hungry,

I praise God; if I suffer cold, I praise God; if it hail, snow, or
rain, if the weather be fair or foul, I give praise to God; if I am
miserable and despised by all the world, I still give praise to
God; and therefore I have never had a bad morning. I said that
I never was otherwise than prosperous, because, having learned
to live with God, I know for certain that all He does must
necessarily be for the best; and therefore whatever happens
to me by His will, or His permission, whether it be pleasant
or disagreeable, sweet or bitter, I always receive with joy, as
coming from His merciful hand, for the best; and therefore I
have never been otherwise than prosperous. Again, I said that
I had never been unhappy, because I have resolved to adhere
to the divine will alone, and have so absolutely relinquished
my self-will as to will always whatever God wills, and therefore
have never been unhappy."

Then the doctor asked him, "Where do you come from?"
"From God," he answered. "But tell me who or what are you,"
said the doctor. "I am a king," replied he. "But where is your
kingdom?" asked the doctor. "My kingdom," he replied, "is in
my soul; for I can govern my senses, exteriorly and interiorly,
so absolutely that all the affections and powers of my soul are
in perfect subjection to me; which kingdom is doubtless more
excellent than all the kingdoms of this world." The doctor then
asked him how he had attained to this perfection. He answered,
"By silence, by meditation, and by always tending to a union
with God, for I could never rest in anything less than God;
and now, having found God, I enjoy peace and everlasting rest."

The fact is that the saints are at once the poorest and the
richest of people. Not all the saints are beggars in actual fact,
but they are beggars at heart. If they are rich, they do works
of corporal charity, knowing as they do that their wealth is
not their own, but must be used according to the will of God.
While they live in the world, they are not of it. They have taken
the words of St. Paul to heart: "This therefore I say, brethren:
the time is short; it remaineth that they also who have wives,
be as if they had none: and they that weep, as though they
wept not; and they that rejoice, as if they rejoiced not; and
they that buy, as though they possessed not; and they that use

this world, as if they used it not; for the fashion of this world passeth away" (1 Cor. 7:29–31). All depends on a right valuation of things. "If we value things rightly," Fray Francisco de Osuna says, "we ought to reckon corruptible gold and silver as sand in comparison with what is divine and incorruptible. We should lay up treasures in heaven, sending our heart after them to make it recollected, for according to St. Augustine, the rich man who makes his possessions serve God and his soul as best he can, finds no difficulty in drawing near to God; for though he may own riches in abundance, his heart is attached not to them but to God."[3]

Because of this right valuation of things, the saints do not mind being actually poor. This is even true of philosophers and scholars whose central interest is in the pursuit of wisdom rather than in the acquisition of material wealth. Confucius, for instance, once said to his pupils, "With coarse food to eat, plain water to drink, and a bent arm for a pillow—there is joy even in such a state. As for wealth and honor obtained by improper means, they are to me as a floating cloud" (*Analects*, 7.15). Among his pupils, he had the greatest admiration and love for Yen Huei, who died before him. "What a good man was Huei!" he said, "A single bowl of rice; a single ladle of water; living in a mean alley! Others could not have borne such misery; but Huei was always joyful!" (Ibid., 6.9). Confucian scholars of all ages have admired Yen Huei's indifference to poverty. A great philosopher of the Sung Dynasty, Chou Tun-yi (1017–1073), commenting on the joy of Yen Huei, said, "Now, riches and honor are loved by all men; yet Yen Huei did not love them nor seek after them, but remained happy in poverty. Was his heart different from others? The fact is, there is something infinitely more honorable and lovable than those things; and Yen Huei, seeing as he did what was of greater value, forgot what was of lesser value. When one sees what is of greater value, one's heart is at peace and one is wanting in nothing. When one is wanting in nothing, one is indifferent to

---

[3] Francisco de Osuna, *The Third Spiritual Alphabet*, trans. A Benedictine of Stanbrook (Westminster, MD: The Newman Bookshop, 1931), 297.

external circumstances. And it is only when one is indifferent to external circumstances that one can adapt oneself equally well to any of them. This is why Yen Huei was a sage second only to Confucius."

Mencius, whose position in Confucianism is similar to that of St. Paul in Christianity, worked out a philosophy of values by distinguishing two kinds of nobility. There is a nobility of man; there is a nobility of Heaven. To be an earl, a cabinet minister, or a great officer—this belongs to the nobility of man. Love, justice, loyalty, good faith, and unwearied joy in goodness—all these are of the nobility of Heaven. "In the good old days," Mencius observed, "men cultivated the nobility of Heaven, and the nobility of man came to them in its train. The men of the present day, on the other hand, cultivate the nobility of Heaven as a means of courting the nobility of man; and when they have obtained the latter, they throw away the former." This reminds us of modern politicians, who, while running for election, go to church in order to impress the people with their piety and trustworthiness, but after they have got what they want cease to be churchgoers. It is hard to imagine how human nature can sink so low as that. But God is not mocked. For whatever position they may have got by their hypocrisy is temporary, while the price they have to pay is something permanent. Extreme is their delusion, as Mencius would say, for in the end they lose both the nobility of Heaven and the nobility of man. And Mencius further observes: "To desire to be honored is the common mind of men. But all men have in themselves that which is truly honorable. Only they do not think of it" (*The Works of Mencius*, XI, Chapters 16 and 17).

All these Chinese moral philosophers, in seeking after love, justice, loyalty, good faith, and unwearied joy in goodness, were really seeking after the "unknown God." They were faithful to their natural lights, and it is not to be doubted that God smiled on their sincere efforts to perfect themselves, for all good proceeds from God.

The Christian philosophers, enlightened by the light of revelation, have an unerring measure for judging all things, and penetrate into the very secrets of the Divine Mind. They know the value of things with a greater certitude than even the greatest of Oriental sages. "Is it not a shame," asks Blessed Henry Suso in all simplicity, "to have the kingdom of God in one's soul and depart from it in order to think of creatures?" This question brings to a focus all the groanings of the spirit of man. All of us feel an abysmal void within us which can be filled only by God. We have tried to fill it with rubbish; and our unhappiness mounts with the heap. This rubbish must be turned out before God can dwell in us.

Perhaps no one has swept his soul cleaner than St. John of the Cross. "All the being of creation," he declares, "compared with the infinite being of God is nothing. And therefore the soul that sets its affections upon the being of creation is likewise nothing in the eyes of God, and less than nothing." He says further: "All the grace and beauty of the creatures, compared with the grace of God, is the height of ungracefulness and unattractiveness." "All the wisdom of the world and human ability, compared with the infinite wisdom of God, are pure and supreme ignorance, even as Saint Paul writes *ad Corinthios*, saying: *Sapientia hujus mundi stultitia est apud Deum.* The wisdom of this world is foolishness in the eyes of God." Again he says: "All the dominion and liberty of the world, compared with the liberty and dominion of the spirit of God, is the most abject slavery, affliction and captivity." And finally: "All the delights and pleasures of the will in all the things of the world, in comparison with all those delights which are God, are supreme affliction, torment and bitterness." "All the wealth and glory of all the creatures, in comparison with the wealth which is God, is supreme poverty and wretchedness."[4]

There you have a terrific manifesto of Christian valuation. It is not easy for modern man, torn as he is from his deepest roots, to accept this scale of values. And yet, unless we are perfectly convinced that every word in this manifesto is nothing but the truth, there can be no talk of the spiritual life. The Holy Father, Pius XII, raised a thought-provoking query in his first encyclical, *Summi Pontificatus*: "What age has been, for all

---

[4] *Works*, 1:28.

its technical and purely civic progress, more tormented than ours by spiritual emptiness, and deep-felt interior poverty?" The awareness of this bottomless "spiritual emptiness" and "interior poverty" in our age of unprecedented material civilization—this awareness is the prerequisite to a genuine Christian awakening. It seems to me that no words are so appropriate to our age as those that Our Lord addressed through St. John to the church of Laodicea: "These things saith the Amen, the faithful and true witness, who is the beginning of the creation of God: I know thy works, that thou art lukewarm, and neither cold nor hot. I would that thou wert cold or hot. But because thou art lukewarm, and neither cold nor hot, I will begin to vomit thee out of my mouth. Because thou sayest, I am rich, and made wealthy, and have need of nothing: and knowest not that thou art wretched, and miserable, and poor, and blind, and naked. I counsel thee to buy of me gold fire tried, that thou mayst become rich; and mayest be clothed in white garments, and that the shame of thy nakedness may not appear; and to anoint thy eyes with eyesalve, that thou mayst see" (Apoc. 3:14–18). These words depict exactly the present state of the world. And yet, if only we have ears to hear what the Spirit is saying to us, our age is the most hopeful of all ages. The re-Christianization of the world does not necessarily entail the actual destruction of material civilization. No, Christ comes only to fulfill, not to destroy. All that is required of us is a sincere change of heart, and this utterly naked and wretched age of ours can yet be a king. Mark the encouraging words of Our Lord, immediately following that terrible rebuke: "Such as I love," He says, "I rebuke and chastise. Be zealous therefore, and do penance. Behold, I stand at the gate, and knock. If any man shall hear my voice, and open the door, I will come in to him, and will sup with him, and he with me. To him that shall overcome, I will give him to sit with me in my throne; as I also have overcome, and am set down with my Father in his throne" (Apoc. 3:19–21). Can there be a more earnest call than this? Let us answer Him, "Come in, O Lord, and open the door for us; for the lock of our door is so hopelessly out of order that our own key can no longer open it. O Beloved

Jesus, come in to sup with us. Do not look at our preparations, look at our dispositions! Open the door with Thy own key; or else we shall be stifled to death!"

Christian theologians have never taught that material things are intrinsically bad. What they do teach is that they must be subordinated to the ultimate end of man. They are not unreal, but they belong to an infinitely lower level of reality than God, the Supreme Reality. In his *Fulgens Radiator,* Pope Pius XII gives us a most salutary counsel that

> ...while engaged in manual or intellectual pursuits, all should strive continually to lift their hearts to Christ, having that as their chief concern, and to burn with perfect love of Him. For the things of the earth, of the whole world cannot satisfy the mind of man which God created for Himself; rather their function given them by their Creator is to move and lift us by gradual steps to the possession of God.... Above all, let this not be forgotten, that looking beyond the fleeting things of earth we must daily and increasingly strive after heavenly and lasting goods, whether we be engaged in intellectual work or study or in a laborious trade; when we shall have gained that goal, then and then only will it be given to us to enjoy true peace, undisturbed repose and everlasting happiness.

This may serve as a fitting commentary on the words of Christ that we should seek first the kingdom of God and His justice, and all the other things that we need shall be given us besides (Matt. 6:31–33).

In fact, only the saints are truly rich. They began by renouncing everything less than God; but after they have found God, who is all and possesses all, they are rich with the richness of God. Certainly St. John of the Cross was not boasting when he declared:

> The heavens are mine, the earth is mine, and the nations are mine: mine are the just, and the sinners are mine: mine are the angels and the Mother of God; all things are mine, God Himself is mine and for me because Christ is mine and all for me. What dost thou then ask for, what

dost thou seek for, O my soul? All is thine, all is for thee; do not take less, nor rest with the crumbs that fall from the table of thy Father. Go forth and exult in thy glory, hide thyself in it, and rejoice, and thou shalt obtain all the desires of thy heart.

When one is rich with the richness of God, one can have a taste of the joy of God when He looked at the heavens and the earth which He had created and saw that they were good. The English poet and mystic Thomas Traherne showed a profound insight when he wrote: "You never enjoy the world aright till the sea itself floweth in your veins, till you are clothed with the heavens and crowned with the stars; and perceive yourself to be the sole heir of the whole world, and more than so, because men are in it who are ever one sole heirs as well as you. Till you can sing and rejoice and delight in God, as misers do in gold, and kings in sceptres, you can never enjoy the world."[5]

---

[5] Thomas Traherne, *Centuries of Meditations*, ed. Bertram Dobell (London: The Editor, 1908).

II

Mortification

Blessed are they that mourn, for they shall be comforted.

The way of penance and of My commandments seems at first hard and painful, but as one advances, it becomes sweet and easy. In the way of evil, on the contrary, the beginnings are delightful, but later come pain and danger (Our Lord to St. Catherine of Siena).

1. MORTIFICATION AND ABUNDANT LIFE

Christ came that we might have life, and have it more abundantly (John 10:10). But there is no other way to that abundant life than mortification. This sounds like a paradox, but the truth is that to be a Christian is to put on the New Man, and in order that the New Man may live, the old man in us must die. The unfortunate thing is that the old man dies hard; and this is the reason why the life of a Christian is a continual warfare against the evil tendencies and habits of his old self.

This very struggle, painful as it is, is a sure sign of our vitality and a perennial source of our joy. As St. Paul would put it, we appear "as dying and behold we live: as chastised and not killed: as sorrowful, yet always rejoicing." Alphonsus Rodriguez has likewise said: "The fish that is alive swims against the stream, but a dead one is carried down with it; so, to know whether the Spirit of God lives within us or not, we need only see whether we go against the current of our passions, or whether we permit ourselves to be carried along by their impetuosity."

There is nothing morbid about mortification, which is but another name for self-denial. I do not know of any religion or moral philosophy worthy of the name that preaches self-indulgence rather than self-denial. Here is a good passage from *Bhagavad-Gita:*

Who knows the Atman[1]
Knows that happiness
Born of pure knowledge:
The joy of sattwa.[2]
Deep his delight
After strict self-schooling:
Sour toil at first
But at last what sweetness,
The end of sorrow.

Senses also
Have joy in their marriage
With things of the senses,
Sweet at first
But at last how bitter:
Steeped in rajas,
That pleasure is poison.
Bred of tamas
Is brutish contentment

In stupor and sloth
And obstinate error:
Its end, its beginning
Alike are delusion.[3]

These two stanzas illustrate the point brought out so graphically by Bishop Fulton Sheen: "There are only two philosophies of life: one begins with the fast and ends with the feast; the other begins with the feast and ends with the headache."[4]

Confucius lamented that he had not seen a man whose love of virtue equaled his love of woman (*Analects*, 9.17). By that he meant that if only a man could love virtue as intensely as he would love the beauty of women, he would be a perfect man. Mencius, the greatest exponent of Confucianism, said that the

---

[1] soul
[2] wisdom
[3] Swami Prabhavananda and Christopher Isherwood, trans., *The Song of God: Bhagavad-Gita*, with an introduction by Aldous Huxley (London: Phoenix House, 1947), 166.
[4] St. John Eudes, *The Life and the Kingdom of Jesus in Christian Souls*, trans. A Trappist Father of The Abbey of Our Lady of Gethsemani, with an introduction by Fulton J. Sheen (New York: P. J. Kenedy & Sons, 1946), xix.

distinction between a great man and a small man is that the former follows the superior part of his nature, whereas the latter follows the inferior part. In this he anticipated what St. Vincent de Paul said: "He who permits himself to be led and governed by the inferior or animal part of his nature deserves the name of beast rather than that of man."

Among Chinese philosophers, Lao Tse, the Founder of Taoism, was even more emphatic than the Confucians on self-conquest and the curbing of desires. He went to the extent of saying:

> The five colors blind the eye.
> The five tones deafen the ear.
> The five flavors cloy the palate.
> Racing and hunting madden the mind.
> Rare goods tempt men to do wrong.
>
> Therefore, the Sage attends to the heart not the eye.
> He prefers what is within to what is without.

To Lao Tse, no one who is addicted to self-indulgent living can ever attain to Tao.

I suppose no one would call William Shakespeare an ascetic; yet one of his sonnets is an excellent presentation of the philosophy of mortification:

Body and Soul

> Poor Soul, the centre of my sinful earth,
> Fooled by those rebel powers that thee array,
> Why dost thou pine within, and suffer dearth,
> Painting thy outward walls so costly gay?
> Why so large cost, having so short a lease,
> Dost thou upon thy fading mansion spend?
> Shall worms, inheritors of this excess,
> Eat up thy charge? is this thy body's end?
>
> Then, Soul, live thou upon thy servant's loss
> And let that pine to aggravate thy store;
> Buy terms divine in selling hours of dross;
> Within be fed, without be rich no more:—
> So shalt thou feed on Death, that feeds on men,
> And Death once dead, there's no more dying then.

2. MORTIFICATION AND LOVE

When I was a mere boy, I heard an interesting story from my elder brother, who was a great reader of popular novels. A chivalrous scholar of a noble family fell in love with a girl of another noble family. As there was no way of seeing her, he hit upon an ingenious idea. He sold himself as a slave into the girl's family in order that he might see her every day. I do not remember how the story ended, but I still remember two lines of a poem in his praise:

> For the sake of Miss Pearl Phoenix,
> The nobleman was willing to be a slave.

Where there is genuine love, there is generosity and all sacrifices or mortifications seem light and sweet. "Jacob served seven years for Rachel; and they seemed but a few days, because of the greatness of his love" (Gen. 29:20). If this is true of natural love, how much more so it should be of the love of that Beauty, ever ancient and ever new! As St. Teresa of Ávila said: "Since I have had the happiness to know Jesus Christ, of beholding faint glimpses of that ravishing beauty, nothing created can find a place in my heart, all things earthly are distasteful to me." *Gustato spiritu, desipit omnis caro*—once you have tasted the spiritual, the carnal is wholly insipid. But how is it that most of us do not seem to have any glimpse of that ravishing beauty, nor any taste of the ineffable sweetness of Christ? Because, as Lao Tse said, "the five colors blind the eye, and the five flavors cloy the palate." The soul turns to the Light as naturally as the sunflower turns to the sun, but the body drags it down. St. Catherine of Genoa is extremely enlightening on this point: "By a natural instinct a soul aspires to delight. Blinded by the body, it seeks delight only through the body, which leads it from one thing to another that they may feed together. But the soul, having a capacity for infinite things, cannot through the body find aught to quiet it: like a senseless thing it lets itself be led by the body, yet is never satisfied."[5]

---

[5] St. Catherine of Genoa, *Treatise on Purgatory; The Dialogue*, trans. Charlotte Balfour and Helen Douglas Irvine (London: Sheed & Ward, 1946), 48.

In other words, the soul is frustrated on account of the inordinate desires of the flesh. Herein lies the necessity of mortification, which is not an end in itself but a means to an end. The end is union with God through transformation in Christ. As à Kempis says, "Free me from evil passions and heal my mind of all disorderly affections; that, being healed and well purified within, I may become fit to love, courageous to suffer and constant to persevere" (*Imitation*, III, 5). In the words of Evelyn Underhill, mortification "is a process, an education directed towards the production of a definite kind of efficiency, the adjustment of human nature to the demands of its new life. Severe, and to the outsider apparently unmeaning—like their physical parallels the exercises of the gymnasium—its disciplines, faithfully accepted, do release the self from the pull of the lower nature, establish it on new levels of freedom and power."[6] To use the language of Spiritual Alchemy, one must tame the Green Lion before one can give him wings.

Love is the motivating power behind the mortification of all earnest seekers of God. In his treatise, *The Praise of Love*, Hugh of St. Victor has written: "Love alone, since the beginning ever persuadeth the servants of God to fly the seductions of this world, to tread pleasure under foot, to restrain fleshly concupiscence, to subdue desire, to despise honor—in one word, to spurn all the allurements of this present existence, and to brave death for the sake of the eternal life."

Christ Himself set the supreme example of mortification by His forty days' fast in the desert. When He was tempted by the devil to change the stones into bread, what was His answer? He said: "It is written, 'Not in bread alone doth man live, but by every word that proceedeth from the mouth of God'" (Matt. 4:4). It is to be noted, He does not say that man does not need bread at all. No, He knows too well that we have need of it. What He does say is that we must never make the belly our God. For we don't live to eat, but eat to live.

---

[6] Evelyn Underhill, *Mysticism: A Study in the Nature and Development of Man's Spiritual Consciousness*, 12th ed. (New York: E. P. Dutton, 1930), 218.

St. Paul, in his First Epistle to the Corinthians, compares
our spiritual life to racing. "Know you not that they that run
in the race, all run indeed, but one receiveth the prize. So run
that you may obtain. And every one that striveth for the mastery refraineth himself from all things. And they indeed that
they may receive a corruptible crown: but we an incorruptible
one. I therefore so run, not as at an uncertainty: I so fight,
not as one beating the air. But I chastise my body and bring it
into subjection: lest perhaps, when I have preached to others,
I myself should become a castaway" (9:24–27).

In St. John Fisher's *A Spiritual Consolation*, there is comparison between the life of hunters and the life of religious persons.
I quote a passage:

> What life is more painful and laborious of itself than
> is the life of hunters, which most early in the morning
> break their sleep and rise when others do take their rest
> and ease? And in his labor he may use no plain highways
> and the soft grass, but he must tread upon the fallows,
> run over the hedges and creep through the thick bushes,
> and cry all the long day upon his dogs, and so continue
> without meat or drink until the very night drive him
> home. These labours be unto him pleasant and joyous,
> for the desire and love that he hath to see the poor hare
> chased with dogs.
>
> Verily, verily, if he were compelled to take upon him
> such labors, and not for this cause, he would soon be
> weary of them, thinking them full tedious unto him;
> neither would he rise out of his bed so soon, nor fast so
> long, nor endure these others labors, unless he had a very
> love therein. For the earnest desire of his mind is so fixed
> upon his game that all these pains be thought to him but
> very pleasures. And therefore I may well say that love is
> the principal thing that maketh any work easy, though
> the work be right painful of itself, and that without love
> no labor can be comfortable to the doer. The love of
> his game delighteth him so much that he careth for no
> worldly honor, but is content with full simple and homely
> array. Also the goods of the world he seeketh not for, nor
> studieth how to attain them; for the love and desire of

his game so greatly occupieth his mind and heart. The pleasures also of his flesh he forgetteth by weariness and wasting of his body in earnest labor. All his mind, all his soul, is busied to know where the poor hare may be found. Of that is his thought, and of that is his communication, and all his delight is to hear and speak of that matter, every other matter but this is tedious for him to give ear unto; in all other things he is dull and unlusty, in this only quick and stirring; for this also to be done, there is no office so humble, nor so vile, that he refuseth not to serve his own dogs himself, to bathe their feet and to anoint them where they be sore, yea, and to cleanse their stinking kennel, where they shall lie and rest them. Surely if religious persons had so earnest a mind and desire to the service of Christ as have these hunters to see a course at a hare, their life should be unto them a very joy and pleasure.[7]

3. THE PRACTICE OF MORTIFICATION

In the practice of mortification, some self-knowledge is of great help. Each of us has his own particular psychical make-up. If you happen to belong to the choleric type, it is well to remember that your chief enemy to be mortified is anger. If you are of the phlegmatic type, your chief enemy is sloth, or what the Middle Ages called acedia. If you are sanguine, you must beware particularly of lust, pride and self-complacency, and you should try to temper your zeal with moderation and regulate it with prudence. If you are melancholic, you must try to be cheerful by cultivating the virtue of hope.

In mortifying the old man in us, we must first attack its worst habits, just as in taking prisoners we should first capture the captain. Let me quote to you a Chinese poem which has some bearing on this point:

Bows should be drawn with a firm hand and strong,
And the arrows you use should be sharp and long.
In shooting men, shoot first the horses they ride;

---

[7] St. John Fisher, *A Spiritual Consolation and Other Treatises*, ed. D. O'Connor (London: Burns & Oates, 1935), 16–18.

In taking prisoners, first capture the *Wang*.[8]
In killing, be sure to keep within the limits of necessity.
In defending a kingdom, to go beyond the borders
    would be wrong.
For the object is to ward off aggression and invasion,
And not to indulge in massacres and devastation.

It is well to remember that mortification is a medicine which must be applied with discretion, to suit the case of the particular individual, for what is medicine to one may be poison to another. Take just one instance. St. Ignatius Loyola was in his youthful days a highly bred Spanish gentleman of refined personal habits. "As he was somewhat nice about the arrangement of his hair, as was the fashion of those days and became him not ill, he allowed it to grow naturally, and neither combed it nor trimmed it nor wore any head covering by day or night. For the same reason he did not pare his finger or toe nails; for on those points he had been fastidious to an extreme" (*Testament*, Cap. ii).

In him it was nothing but good sense; for he knew his own weakness and he was trying to straighten the bent stick, as it were, by bending it the other way. On the other hand, for us to imitate him in a concrete way would be like the case of an ugly woman in ancient China imitating the knit brows of Hsi Sze, the Chinese Venus, and becoming more ugly than ever. In imitating the saints, we must take care to follow their spirit, rather than their particular ways. In fact, the function of all the saints is to remind us of Jesus. As Clare Boothe Luce has observed, "The portrait of a saint is only a fragment of a great and yet incomplete mosaic — the portrait of Jesus." In practicing mortification, we must strive to choose what is the most hidden, not what is the most manifest. As Christ Himself has told us, "And when you fast, be not as the hypocrites, sad. For they disfigure their faces, that they may appear unto men to fast. Amen, I say to you, they have received their reward. But thou, when thou fastest, anoint thy head and wash thy face: that thou appear not to fast, but to thy Father who is

---

[8] The King.

in secret. And thy Father who seeth in secret will repay thee" (Matt. 6:16–18).

One of the best things that have been said on this subject is to be found in St. Thérèse's comment: "Far from being like to those great souls who, from their childhood, practice all sorts or macerations, I made my mortification consist solely of *breaking my will, keeping back a word of retort, rendering little services without making much of them, and a thousand other things of this kind.*"[9] Thus, mortification becomes a great bundle of little sacrifices.

These words can be displeasing to none but those spirits of whom Bossuet speaks, "to whom the simple and common life is repugnant because, beguiled solely by the senses and far from a sincere conversion, they will admire only what they regard as inimitable."

4. TRIALS AND AFFLICTIONS

So far, I have only touched upon mortification in its *active* phase. Now I want to say something about *passive* mortification, which consists in the grateful acceptance of trials and afflictions sent or permitted by the all-wise and all-merciful Father for our good.

The Book of Proverbs says: "My son, reject not the correction of the Lord: and do not faint when thou art chastised by him. For whom the Lord loveth, he chastiseth: and as a father in the son he pleaseth himself" (Prov. 3:11). Commenting on these words, St. Paul writes: "Persevere under discipline. God dealeth with you as with his sons. For what son is there, whom the father doth not correct? But if you be without chastisement, whereof all are made partakers, then are you bastards and not sons" (Heb. 12:7–8).

Recently, I have read a book by C. S. Lewis: *The Problem of Pain*. Speaking of an erroneous conception of Divine Love, he said with a find irony, "We want, in fact, not so much a Father in Heaven as a grandfather in heaven—a senile benevolence

---

[9] Thérèse of Lisieux, *The Spirit of Saint Thérèse de l'Enfant Jésus: As Shown Forth by Her Writings and the Testimony of Eyewitnesses*, trans. Carmel of Kilmacud, Stillorgan (London: Burns Oates & Washbourne, 1925), 150.

who, as they say 'liked to see young people enjoying themselves' and whose plan for the universe was simply that it might be truly said at the end of the day 'a good time was had by all.'"[10] And then he follows it up by a remarkable statement: "If God is Love, He is, by definition, something more than mere kindness."[11]

Now, this reminds me of a very touching scene recorded in a Confucian classic. Tseng-Sheng, one of the greatest disciples of Confucius, was dying. A boy attendant, in his innocence, made the remark, "Oh, what a beautiful mat the Master is lying on! It is the mat of the Great Officers!" Tseng-Sheng's sons were annoyed and tried to hush him. But Tseng-Sheng had heard those words. So he said to his sons that the mat was a present from a friend, but as he himself was no Great Officer, it would be against the laws of propriety to die on it. His sons pointed out that he was already worn out and was in no condition to be moved. The father became indignant and said, "As a wise adage has it, a gentleman loves others with virtue and rectitude; whereas a small man loves others with indulgence! Your love for me is not as great as that of the boy!" They were compelled to yield, and changed the mat for him. A few minutes later, the old man died.

There is, of course, no comparison between God's love and a gentleman's love. But relatively speaking, the gentleman's love is nearer to God's love than a small man's love is. God loves us too much to be over-indulgent with us. He wants us to be perfect. Like Father, like son. "You shall be holy, because I am holy."

No modern writer has given a better account of the relationship between Divine Providence and our sufferings than Dom Pierre-Celestine Lou Tseng-Tsiang. In his paper on Madame Leseur, he said:

> God has guided me by ways which I did not comprehend before, to lead me to the point where I am now. These ways have for me, as for Elizabeth Leseur, entailed great

---

[10] C. S. Lewis, *The Problem of Pain* (New York: Macmillan, 1943), 28.
[11] Ibid., 29.

trials. But trials are nothing else than the divergences from the thoughts of God of our own desires. The trials are sent us in order to make us pass from the narrowness of our poor hearts to the magnanimity of the Heart of God. We experience then, as Elizabeth Leseur has pointed out, an enlargement of our being, a dilation of heart, of which we had no idea before; we lose nothing of life and we see opening before us a new landscape as beautiful as it is immense. But this is not obtained without efforts, nor without failures and sufferings.

This reminds me of some lines in Francis Thompson's *The Hound of Heaven*:

> All which I took from thee I did but take
> Not for thy harms
> But just that thou might'st seek it in My arms.

There is a species of plum-tree in China, which blossoms in the depth of winter. Its flowers are yellow. Its fragrance is ethereal. There is a Chinese saying about it which contains a great deal of wisdom: "Were it not for the biting cold of the winter, how could there be such lovely flowers and such unearthly fragrance?" This is but a flowery way of presenting the second Beatitude: *Blessed are they that mourn, for they shall be comforted.*

In order to attain this Beatitude, both self-discipline with the aid of grace, and discipline given us by God and gratefully accepted by us, are necessary. The former is called *active* mortification; the latter, *passive*. The Western mentality is more inclined to the active; the Eastern mentality understands better the passive. In this connection, let me quote to you some penetrating words of Bishop Fulton Sheen: "It is apt to be an error of the Eastern World to think that God does everything and man does nothing; it is apt to be the error of the Western World to believe that man does everything and God does nothing. The Oriental thus ends in Fatalism and the Occidental in Pride."[12]

---

[12] Fulton J. Sheen, *Philosophy of Religion: The Impact of Modern Knowledge on Religion* (New York: Appleton-Century-Crofts, 1948), 253.

The one is as bad as the other. Let us, therefore, each beware of his own inclination and guard against it. Let us try to achieve a living synthesis of Predestination and Free Will, so that the one does not become Fatalism and the other does not become Pride.

III

Meekness

Blessed are the meek, for they shall inherit the land.

1. HUMOR AS AN INGREDIENT OF MEEKNESS

I have often reflected that humor is an essential ingredient of Christian perfection. A humorous man laughs at himself, while a wit laughs at others. In this definition, wit is pagan, but humor is Christian. The devil may be witty, but he cannot be humorous. For there is something sharp and venomous about wit, and something mellow and kind about humor.

Recently, in reading *The Divine Pity*, by Gerald Vann, O. P., in a good chapter on "Meekness" I came across this striking passage:

> It is important to remind ourselves often that the cultivation of a right sense of humor can be one of the forms of piety. Cultivate a sense of humor in yourself about other people and in other people about yourself: learn to laugh rather than be vexed by other people's foibles, but learn the ability also to laugh at your own. It is not a virtue to be uncritical; on the contrary; but you have to be sure that your judgments are not hasty or spiteful, and that the growth of the power of criticism is accompanied by a growth in gentleness. Acquire the sort of personality that people will instinctively take their troubles to: and you will acquire it by learning to be pious and to love. (52)

Meekness is a tree rooted in humility and watered by humor; it flowers in the form of a serene mellowness, and bears the fruit of docility to the Holy Ghost.

Someone has said that good humor is nine-tenths of Christianity. Anyways, it is nine-tenths of meekness, and meekness is the foundation of a full Christian life. In a saint, humor serves to relieve the tension between grace and nature, thus making it possible to conquer nature in a graceful way. For instance, no one could like the idea of leprosy, but when Father Damien discovered the symptoms of leprosy on his own person, he said, "Well, at any rate, in future when I preach, instead of saying 'My dear brethren,' I shall be able to say 'My fellow lepers.'" No one likes to see one's precious plans frustrated, but when St. Philip Neri was in great adversity he said, "I thank Thee, Lord God, with all my heart that things are not going as I wish, but as Thou dost." This act of thanksgiving makes us smile, but it is so genuine that by comparison our own acts of thanksgiving are pale and colorless. Oftener than not our prayer takes the form of "Our will be done in heaven as it is on earth," rather than "Thy will be done on earth as it is in heaven." The saints have a way of laughing us into sanctity. It is well known that when climbing the scaffold, St. Thomas More said to the Lieutenant of the Tower, "Assist me up, coming down I will look after myself." Similarly, Blessed John Kemble, on the day of his execution, asked for time first to finish his prayers and then to smoke a pipe of tobacco. One does not have to smoke a pipe in order to become a saint, but such a spirit of composure in the face of death and in the heat of suffering is typical of the meek. Only the meek can be truly strong. One of the recent victims to fall into the hands of Communists in China was young Chiao, an ex-seminarian and a gentle boy. He was brought before the students' assembly to be accused publicly. Chiao was calm and self-possessed. When he was told to kneel, he refused, saying "I can kneel only to God." He was then beaten to the ground and forced to his knees. After the usual procedure, he was told to rise. This time he refused to get up. When asked why, he replied: "I haven't finished my prayer to God yet."

It is needless to multiply instances. Suffice it to say that humor flows from meekness, which, in turn, is replenished by it. It helps grace to score a victory over nature, not violently, but in a subtle and unobtrusive way.

Good humor mellows you and keeps you cheerful even in the face of unpleasant events. As St. Francis de Sales has said, *"Un saint triste est un triste saint"*—a sad saint is a sorry sort of a saint. Besides being an implement of your own sanctification, good humor has an educative and apostolic value. I remember reading somewhere an anecdote about this same St. Francis. A Sister rushed into his room, and abruptly asked him, "What shall I do in order to become a saint?" Francis answered, "I think God wants you to shut the door more gently." I am sure the Sister had a good laugh and never repeated her fault. Recently, I was delighted to read in Dorothy Day's *The Long Loneliness* an account of the humor of St. Teresa of Ávila and how it affected the author:

> Once when she was travelling from one part of Spain to another with some other nuns and a priest to start a convent, and their way took them over a stream, she was thrown from her donkey. The story goes that our Lord said to her, "That is how I treat my friends." And she replied, "And that is why You have so few of them." She called life a "night spent in an uncomfortable inn." Once when she was trying to avoid that recreation hour which is set aside in convents for nuns to be together, the others insisted on her joining them, and she took castanets and danced. When some older nuns professed themselves shocked, she retorted, "One must do things sometimes to make life more bearable." After she was a superior she gave directions when the nuns became melancholy, "to feed them steak," and there were other delightful little touches to the story of her life which made me love her and feel close to her. I have since heard a priest friend of ours remark gloomily that one could go to hell imitating the imperfections of the saints, but these little incidents brought out in her biography made her delightfully near to me. So I decided to name my daughter after her.[1]

For all we know, were it not for the delightful humor of Teresa, Dorothy Day might never have known the light.

And who knows how many have been induced to study the Faith by the humor of G. K. Chesterton? The devil has painted

---

[1] Dorothy Day, *The Long Loneliness: The Autobiography of Dorothy Day* (New York: Harper & Brothers, 1952), 140–141.

the Catholic Church as frightfully solemn and severe, in order to keep souls away from her. The devil is clever, but certainly he has no sense of humor.

But the masterpiece of Christian humor is to be found in what St. Luke wrote about the trial of St. Paul before the governor Festus and King Agrippa. Paul's defense was growing into a sermon, when Festus interrupted him by saying in a loud voice, "Paul, thou art mad; they are driving thee to madness, these long studies of thine." Instead of being angry, Paul answered affably, "No, most noble Festus, I am not mad; the message which I utter is sober truth. The king knows about all this well enough; that is why I speak with confidence in his presence. None of this, I am sure, is news to him; it was not in some secret corner that all this happened." Then addressing himself to Agrippa, he said, "Dost thou believe the prophets, King Agrippa? I am well assured thou dost believe them." At this, Agrippa, trying to evade answering, said to Paul, "Thou wouldst have me turn Christian with very little ado." "Why," said Paul, "it would be my prayer to God that, whether it were with much ado or little, both thou and all those who are listening to me today should become just as I am, but for these chains" (Acts 26:24–29).

If no one was converted on this occasion, it can be attributed to no fault in Paul. As for me, I must admit that this incident played no small part in my conversion. It was a thrill to perceive that the real king was the man in the chains, while the one who sat on the throne was but a slave. It dawned suddenly upon my mind that there was another scale of values different from that of the world, and that it was Festus, not Paul, who was mad; and it was Agrippa, not Paul, who was in chains.

2. MEEKNESS AND STRENGTH OF CHARACTER

Meekness is not to be confused with weakness of character, or a spineless conformity to the ways and conventions of the world. On the contrary, it presupposes a high degree of self-possession, which enables a man to adapt himself to his environment without losing his central harmony. As St. Thomas Aquinas has put it, "Meekness is a virtue which supposes a noble soul; that is, those who possess this virtue are superior to all one may say or do to them. Though they receive indignities from others in word or action, they preserve their tranquility and lose not their peace of soul."

There is therefore nothing abject or slavish about meekness. *Tout au contraire*, the meek man is the free man. For, if one's tranquility and peace of soul can be disturbed by the actions or words of others, then one is truly a slave to others. If, on the other hand, one can maintain one's equipoise in the face of insults, then one enjoys true independence and freedom. In fact, nothing is so dignified as self-mastery in the spirit of piety. Let one illustration suffice. In the life of St. John Eudes, one finds a remarkable episode: "One of his companions having given him a blow on the face, John, while keenly alive to the insult, at once fell on his knees and offered the other cheek in accordance with the Gospel precept." Now, who is the more dignified, the one who gave the blow, or the one who received it?

A great Buddhist monk wrote a song on calumny:

> Let them slander, let them abuse!
> Who tries to burn the sky only wearies himself out.
> When I hear their words, I feel like drinking the sweet
>   dew.
> They purge me! I suddenly enter into the Ineffable!
>
> If you are able to regard gossip as charity,
> The slanderer becomes your spiritual guide.
> Let no bad words provoke anger in you.
> Else can one reveal the supernatural power of loving
>   patience?

If a Buddhist could have attained such a high state of spiritual life, what a shame on us if we could not do the same with the living example of Christ before us and with His grace working in us! It is, indeed, not easy to take in other people's criticisms of us as if we were drinking the sweet dew. But a rational consideration will, perhaps, help us in this matter. Other people's criticisms of us may be either just or unjust. If they are just, of course, they hurt you to the quick, for truth hurts. But what is there to prevent you from reforming yourself in accordance with the criticisms, thus making the critic your spiritual guide? You should be happy to learn a lesson without being charged for it. What difference does it make to you whether the criticism was made in good faith or with malice? Even if it was made maliciously, it does not hurt your soul, so long as you do not resent it. If the criticism is unjust, then you are in a still better position, for you can offer it cheerfully as a little cross to be united with the Cross of Christ. Of course, in the matter of self-mastery as in all spiritual exercises, it is easier said than done. The saints are not insensitive people; but by trusting themselves in the hands of Providence they achieved self-mastery in the midst of the most provoking and trying of circumstances.

Christian meekness means primarily filial obedience to the will of God. The Apostles were truly meek when they said to the Sanhedrin: "Judge for yourselves whether it would be right for us, in the sight of God, to listen to your voice instead of God's. . . . We ought to obey God rather than men" (Acts 4:19 and 5:29). According to St. Augustine, meekness is nothing but obedience to the truth. Secondarily it involves the gentle manner in which this obedience to God expresses itself. As St. Jerome says, "Meekness is a mild virtue, it is kindly, serene, gentle in speech, gracious in manner, it is a delicate blending of all the virtues. Kindness is akin to it, for, like meekness, it seeks to please; still it differs from the latter in that it is not as winsome and seems more rigid, for though equally prompt to accomplish good and render service, it lacks that charm, that gentleness that wins all hearts" (*Commentary on Galatians* 5:20). It is well known that St. Jerome was, by nature, anything but meek. But if he was swift to anger, he was just as swift to remorse; if he was severe on the shortcomings of others, he was even more so on his own. As the story goes, when Pope Sixtus V looked at a picture of the saint representing him in the act of striking his breast with a stone, he said, "You do well to carry that stone, for without it the Church would never have canonized you." I suppose it was the very fact that he was high-tempered that made him extol the virtue of meekness. Only

God knows how much energy is needed to master oneself when one happens to be fiery in nature, as most Christian saints are. In their case, therefore, meekness means intense energy under intense control; it has nothing in common with the idea of a milk-and-watery character, a nice person who simply lets himself be shoved around. A meek person is not a goody-goody any more than a roughneck is a strong character. As Confucius said, "The goody-goodies are thieves of goodness." They are thieves because they only appear good, but are not really good.

Confucius conceived a hierarchy of personalities. The highest order consists of persons who follow the Golden Mean; the second consists of those who are fiery and expansive; the third, of those who are anxious to seem correct; and the lowest order consists of worldly mediocrities, or the goody-goodies. The fiery and expansive, though they may err by over-enthusiasm, are at least earnest seekers of the way. The scrupulous are at least diligent in avoiding evil. Both of these classes can be educated to follow the Mean—the former, by the inculcation of patience and prudence, the latter by encouragement. Confucius welcomed them both. The only class of people for whom he had the greatest contempt were the "nice people of the village." The trouble with these "nice people of the village" is, according to Mencius, that "if you want to criticize them, they seem so unimpeachable; if you want to lampoon them, they seem so perfect; they conform entirely to the current conventions and identify themselves thoroughly with the decadent ways of the times. Their principles have a semblance of honesty and decency, their conduct has a semblance of purity and uprightness. Everybody likes them and they are pleased with themselves. But it is impossible to lead them into the ways of Emperors Yao and Shun" (*Works*, VII, II, 36). In other words, these nice people are rational in everything except first principles. They would mock at the enthusiasts by saying, "Why should they be so idealistic? Look at them: their words do not correspond to their conduct, and their conduct does not measure up to their words. They only say, 'The Ancient Sages! The Ancient Sages!'" They cavil at the scrupulous by saying, "Why are they so supercilious toward the world, and so cold and aloof in their conduct?" Their own philosophy is: "Since we are living in the present world, we must conform ourselves to the present world; and if we are successful, we should be contented." Such respectable people are affable, sociable, self-complacent, and wise in the eyes of their fellows. But spiritually they are more hopeless than harlots.

The meek, or the true gentlemen, are so far from the goody-goodies that they belong to the first order of persons, those who follow the Golden Mean. They are as careful in avoiding evil as the scrupulous, but they know that the avoidance of evil is only the beginning of goodness. They are as eager for goodness as the idealists; but they know that goodness must be cultivated with patience and perseverance, and they are careful to check words against conduct. How matter-of-fact Confucius was can be seen in these words: "A gentleman observes four principal laws; I have not been able to observe a single one of them. I have not yet been able to perform those duties toward my father which I ask of my son, nor those duties toward my superiors which I ask of my inferiors, nor those duties toward my elder brother which I ask of my younger brother; I have not been able to do first to my friends what I wish them to do for me. Is not he truly a gentleman, who in the practice of the ordinary virtues and in his daily conversations attempts to avoid even the least faults, who is always afraid to promise more than he can do, and lives so that his actions correspond with his words and his words with his actions?" The meekness of Confucius was rooted in his humility, which, in turn, sprang from self-knowledge. His character represents a balance of strength and tenderness. As his disciples observed, "The Master is affable yet dignified, severe without being harsh, respectful without formality." This is meekness in the true sense of the word.

Christian meekness is even higher, because, besides possessing the natural qualities of Confucian meekness, it is ordered to the supernatural love of God, and perfected by grace. Speaking of the first Christians, Bossuet said: "They are strong in the face of peril; but they are tender in their love of their brethren; the almighty Spirit who guides them well knows the secret of reconciling the most opposite tensions.... He strengthens and He softens, but in a manner all His own. For these are the same hearts of the disciples, which seem as diamonds in their invincible firmness, and which yet become human hearts and hearts of flesh by brotherly love."

Somehow, meekness always recalls to my mind the image of jade. Confucius made a comparison between the virtues of the gentleman and the qualities of jade. What he says can be applied, even with more appropriateness, to Christian meekness:

Tse Kung said to Confucius, "Allow me to ask the reason why the superior man sets a high value on jade, and but little on soapstone. Is it because jade is rare and soapstone plentiful?"

Confucius replied,

> It is not because the soapstone is plentiful that he thinks but little of it, nor because jade is rare that he sets high value on it. The superior man of ancient times found in jade the symbol of virtue. Soft, smooth, and glossy, it symbolizes lovingkindness; fine, compact and solid, it symbolizes intelligence; angular, but not sharp and cutting, it symbolizes justice; when suspended on a thread, it looks as though it would fall to the ground — in this it is akin to humility; when struck, it yields a note, clear and prolonged, yet sharply defined in its termination — in this it is like music; its flaws do not cover its beauty, nor its beauty its flaws — in this it represents loyalty; with its interior light radiating on all sides, it recalls sincerity; bright as a brilliant rainbow, it is like heaven; its mysterious essence being formed in the hills and streams, it is akin to the earth; standing out conspicuous in the symbols of rank, it can be likened to virtue; esteemed by all under the sky, it can be likened to the Tao (Li Ki, Bk. 48).

3. THE EXAMPLE OF ST. THÉRÈSE

St. Thérèse of Lisieux was by nature extremely sensitive. Until the Christmas Eve of 1886, when she received the priceless gift of her complete conversion she had been very childish in some of her ways and feelings. As she tells us, "My extreme sensitivity made me almost unbearable, and all arguments against it were simply useless; I could not correct myself of this miserable failing."[2] She gives us an interesting account of how she used to weep for the most trivial cause:

> I was most anxious, for instance, to advance in virtue, yet I went about it in a strange way. I had never been accustomed to wait on myself, or do any house work, and Céline always arranged our room. Now, however, with the intention of pleasing Our Lord, I would sometimes make my bed, or, if Céline happened to be out, I would bring in her plants and cuttings. Since it was for Our Lord's sake that I did these little things I ought not to have looked for any return. But, alas! I did look for thanks, and if, unfortunately, Céline did not seem surprised and grateful for my small services, I was disappointed, as my tears soon showed. Again, if I unintentionally offended anyone, far from making the best of it, I fretted until I became quite ill, thus increasing my fault instead of repairing it. Then when I began to be reconciled to the blunder, I would cry for having cried.[3]

The turning point of Thérèse's spiritual life occurred after the midnight Mass in 1886. We shall let her tell her own story:

> I must tell you here, dear Mother, the circumstances under which I received the priceless grace of my complete conversion. On reaching home, after midnight Mass, I knew I should find my shoes in the chimney-corner, filled with presents, just as when I was a little child, a fact which proves that I was still treated as a baby. Papa loved to watch my enjoyment, and to hear my cries of delight as I drew each fresh surprise from the magic shoes, and his pleasure added considerably to mine.
>
> But the hour had come when Our Lord desired to free me from the failings of my childhood, and take from me even its innocent pleasures. He permitted that Papa, instead of indulging me in his usual way, should feel annoyed, and as I went upstairs I overheard him say:

---

[2] St. Thérèse of Lisieux, *The Little Flower of Jesus: A New and Complete Translation of "L'Histoire d'une Âme,"* trans. T. N. Taylor (New York: P. J. Kenedy & Sons, 1927), 86.
[3] *The Little Flower of Jesus*, 83–4.

"All this is far too babyish for a big girl like Thérèse, and I hope this is the last time it will happen." These words cut me to the very heart, and Céline, knowing how sensitive I was, whispered: "Don't go down just yet, you would only cry if you looked at your presents before Papa." But Thérèse was no longer the same — Jesus had transformed her. Choking back my tears, I ran down to the dining room, and making every effort to still the throbbing of my heart, I picked up my shoes and gaily drew out the presents one by one, looking all the time as happy as a queen. Papa joined in the laughter and there no longer appeared on his face the least sign of vexation. Céline thought she must be dreaming, but happily it was a sweet reality, and Thérèse had once for all regained the strength of mind which had left her when she was four and a half.[4]

One cannot help marveling at the way the Divine Artist deals with souls. He made use of the extreme sensitivity of Thérèse and transmuted it into an extreme responsiveness to the whisperings of the Holy Spirit! He does not destroy our nature, but raises us at precisely our weakest point. In the case of Thérèse, He opened her eyes to the supernatural value of suffering, and Thérèse, the docile disciple, used her native sensitivity in the exploration of the opportunities for suffering and sacrifices in her daily life. Thereafter, she was no longer egocentric; she became Christocentric. As she says, "Love and a spirit of self-forgetfulness took possession of my heart, and thenceforward I was perfectly happy."[5] She realized that Our Lord redeemed the world by suffering, not by enjoying life, that His way is not a way of roses, but the way of the Cross. If, therefore, we wish to resemble Jesus, we have to take up our daily cross, and learn of Him in His meekness and humility of heart. Our meekness consists in our willingness to suffer for Him and with Him. No one is more sensitive to suffering than Thérèse, but no one has a profounder insight into its value. In her Letters, she never wearies of expounding her philosophy of suffering. An example is the following letter to Céline:

---

[4] *The Little Flower of Jesus*, 86–7.
[5] Ibid., 87.

Let us not fancy we can love without suffering, without
suffering deeply. Our *poor nature* is there, and it is not there
for nothing! It is our wealth, our livelihood! It is so precious that Jesus came on earth on purpose to make it His
own. Let us suffer bitterly, that is without courage!. . . . "Jesus suffered with *sorrow*: could the soul be suffering if
there were no sorrow?" And here are we wanting to suffer generously, greatly. . . . Céline!. . . . What folly!. . . . We
want never to fall?—What does it matter, my Jesus, if
I fall at every instant, for thereby I *see* my weakness and
that for me is a great gain. Thereby *You see* what I can do,
and so You will be moved to carry me in Your arms. . . . If
You do not, it is because it pleases You to see me *on the
ground* . . . so I am not going to be disquieted, but shall go
on stretching out to You arms of supplication and full of
love! I cannot believe You would abandon me!. . . . "When
the saints were at Our Lord's feet, that is when they found
their cross." Dearest Céline, sweet echo of my soul!. . . . If
you knew my misery . . . oh! If you knew! Sanctity lies not
in saying beautiful things, or even in thinking them, or
feeling them: it lies in truly willing to suffer.[6]

The best way to acquire meekness is to meditate constantly
on the Passion of Our Lord, and to gaze at Him on the Cross.
Then probably you will be able not only to put up with all the
little pin-pricks in your daily intercourse with the world, but
even to prize them as so many diamonds given to you by God
Himself for your adornment. You will still feel pain, of course,
but you will accept it with gratitude as a token of His love. For,
as Père Pichon put it, "God would turn the world upside down
to find suffering to give to a soul upon which His divine gaze is
fixed with ineffable love."[7] Thérèse saw this truth so clearly that
she could write in all simplicity, "To those who love *more*, He
gives more suffering, to those who love less, less."[8] That this is
no exaggeration, but a sober statement of the Christian teaching,
will be borne out by a quotation from the Prince of Apostles:

---

[6] St. Thérèse of Lisieux, *Collected Letters of St. Thérèse of Lisieux*, edited by
Abbé Combes, translated by F. J. Sheed (London: Burns, Oates, 1949), 101.
[7] Ibid., 90.
[8] Ibid., 89.

This doing is thankworthy before God. For unto this are you called: because Christ also suffered for us, leaving you an example that you should follow his steps. *Who did no sin, neither was guile found in his mouth.* Who, when he was reviled, did not revile: when he suffered he threatened not, but delivered himself to him that judged him unjustly. Who in his own self bore our sins in his body upon the tree: that we, being dead to sins, should live to justice: by whose stripes you were healed (1 Peter 2:19–24).

Thus Christian meekness is nourished by the filial affection for God, strengthened by the example of Christ, and deepened by the Mystery of Redemption.

4. SOME MORE EXAMPLES

Let me give you some examples of meekness, from Father Lasausse's *Short Meditations*:

Philip II of Spain once spent several hours of the night in writing a long letter to the Pope. He gave it to his secretary to fold and seal. The secretary had been sleeping, and, half awake, he took a bottle of ink instead of sand to pour over the writing. Perceiving his mistake, he was inconsolable. The king very quietly said: "The fault is not very great, there is still more paper," and sat down the rest of the night to write a second letter, without showing the least displeasure with his secretary.

St. Jane Frances having been grossly insulted by a young gentleman, who was inconsolable because she had received into her community a young lady whom he wished to marry, this worthy daughter of St. Francis of Sales said to her companions: "I never heard a panegyric which pleased me more."

St. Francis of Sales was charged with having shown too much mildness to a young man who was incorrigible in his faults, incapable of listening to reason. "What would you have me do?" replied the saint. "I did my best to arm myself with an anger that was no sin; but to tell the truth, I was afraid to squander in a quarter of an hour the spoonful of sweetness which I have labored during twenty years to collect in the vase of my heart. In trying to save this young man from shipwreck by rigor and severity, I might myself have been drowned with him."

"You are astonished because I suffer with tranquillity what you have just heard," said St. Francis of Sales to a religious who had witnessed injurious language addressed to him. "Do you not see that God has ordained, from all eternity, the grace He has given me to support voluntarily this opprobrium? Should I not drink the chalice which has been prepared by the hands of so good a Father?"[9]

Meekness is based on humility and humility is based on truth, and the truth is that we have nothing good in ourselves, for whatever good we may have is received from and sustained by God. That is why when a truly humble man is praised for his good qualities, he feels like a thief, or, in the expressive words of Father Lallemant "like an impostor whose tricks have been discovered."[10] Only a certain courtesy prevents him from retorting to his well-meaning friends, "I am afraid you are paying compliments to the wrong person"; for the right Person is always God. Christ was speaking in His capacity as Man when He said to the young man who called Him "Good Teacher": "Why call me good? There is none good but God."

5. MEEKNESS AND HUMILITY

The relation between meekness and humility may be summed up in a few words: meekness is the full unfolding of humility. In the Rule of St. Benedict, twelve degrees of humility are enumerated. You will note that humility grows from the interior to the exterior. On this point it is well to remember the maxim of Blessed Henry Suso: "The interiority that reaches the exterior is an interiority more interior than the interiority that remains in the interior only." At any rate, the higher degrees of humility reach and permeate the exterior and blend into meekness. In his commentary on the twelfth degree of humility, Dom Delatte remarks: "If humility be really in the heart it will appear in the body also, and will regulate all its movements; it will

---

[9] Abbé Lasausse, *Short Meditations for Every Day of the Year*, trans. Mrs. James O'Brien (New York: Benziger Brothers, 1890), 100, 101, 111, 118.
[10] Ibid., 280.

be like a new temperament, a nature made in humility replacing the old. This external manifestation is a thing natural and necessary: it is the very consequence of our oneness of being."

Logically, humility is more fundamental than meekness; but in the process of time and in spiritual growth, meekness is the ripening of humility.

This reminds me of what Confucius said about filial piety: "When the true son has deep love, he will necessarily possess the spirit of harmony; when he has the spirit of harmony, he will necessarily radiate an atmosphere of gladness; when he has the atmosphere of gladness, he will necessarily have gentle and sweet manners" (Li Ki).

These words come near to the Christian idea of meekness, if we would lift them to the spiritual plane. A deep filial love for God will spontaneously beget in us the spirit of harmony and mildness, and make us radiate an atmosphere of joy and gladness, and behave sweetly and cordially towards others. Thus, we see that love is at the bottom of it all; but it takes time and practice for Love to acquire some mellowness so as to attain the state of meekness.

In the first two periods which we discussed in the previous chapters, Love was already there, but it was not as mellow and sweet as in this period of the spiritual life. Love is like wine: the older the better. St. John of the Cross has given us a very beautiful comparison between new wine and old wine:

> In the new wine the lees have not yet been thrown off, and not settled, wherefore the wine ferments, and its goodness and worth cannot be known until it has well settled on the lees and the fermentation has ceased. Until that time there is great likelihood of its going bad; it has a rough and sharp taste, and to drink much of it is bad for the drinker; its strength is chiefly in the lees. In old wine the lees are digested and settled, so that there is no longer any fermentation going on in it as there is in new wine; it can be well seen that it is good, and it is quite safe from going bad, for that fermentation and bubbling which might cause it to do harm is all over; and thus it is a marvel if wine that is well prepared goes bad and spoiled. It has a pleasant flavor, and

the strength is in the substance of the wine and no longer in the taste, wherefore a draught of it gives the drinker
good health and makes him strong.[11]

6. A CHINESE PHILOSOPHER OF MEEKNESS

Outside of Christendom, the greatest philosopher of humility
and meekness is, perhaps, Lao Tse, the founder of Taoism and
the author of Tao Teh Ching, which John Cowper Powys has
called "the noblest classic of quiet wisdom." Lao Tse is against
all violence. For, as he says:

> A whirlwind does not last a whole morning,
> Nor does a summer shower last a whole day.

He is against all forms of pride and self-complacency:

> One who displays himself does not shine.
> One who justifies himself has no glory.
> One who boasts of his own ability has no merit.
> One who parades his own success will not endure.
> In Tao these things are called "unwanted food and
>   extraneous growths,"
> Which are loathed by all things.
> Hence, a man of Tao does not set his heart upon them
>   (24).

Thus, to Lao Tse all external things are unessentials, the only
thing essential is the Tao.

> Therefore, the Sage embraces the One,
> And becomes the pattern of the world.
> He does not make show of himself,
> Hence he shines;
> He does not justify himself,
> Hence he is glorified.
> He does not boast of his ability,
> Hence he gets his credit;
> He does not brandish his success,
> Hence he endures;
> He does not compete with anyone,
> Hence no one can compete with him.

---

[11] *Works*, 2:325–26.

> Indeed, the ancient saying: "Bend and you will be
> whole" is no idle word.
> Nay, if you really attain wholeness, the world will flock
> to you (22).

Lao Tse is for the soft and tender as against the rigid and hard.

> When a man is alive, he is soft and supple;
> When he is dead, he becomes hard and stiff.
>
> Therefore, hardness and stiffness are companions of death;
> While tenderness and softness are companions of life (76).

I think he would have given a hearty approval to what Dietrich von Hildebrand has written about meekness: "The aspect of which meekness embodies a specific expression is that of a *serene mellowness* inherent in the perfect attitude of love: the softening quality of love by virtue of which it becomes, as it were, a tangible substance, which might be described as 'fluid goodness.'"[12] I like especially the term "fluid goodness," and I am tempted to borrow it to give a hint at the spirit of the Taoistic philosophy of life. For Lao Tse harps upon the virtues of water:

> The highest form of goodness is like water.
> Water benefits all things without striving with them,
> And rests in places loathed by all.
> Therefore, it comes near to the Tao (8).
>
> Nothing is softer and weaker than water;
> Yet, for overcoming the hard and strong, there is noth-
> ing like it,
> For nothing can take its place.
> That the weak overcomes the strong, and the soft over-
> comes the hard,
> This is known by all but practised by none.
>
> Therefore, the Sage says:
> To receive all the dirt of a country is to be the lord of
> its soil-shrines.
> To bear the calamities of a country is to be the king
> of the world.
> Indeed, Truth sounds like a paradox (78).

---

[12] Dietrich von Hildebrand, *Transformation in Christ: On the Christian Attitude of Mind* (New York: Longmans, Green, 1948), 329.

I would not call this a prophecy about the Messias; but I as a Christian cannot help considering it as a prelude of Christianity. As the Psalmist says, "In Thy light shall we see light." Since all lights, whether natural or supernatural, come from God, a scribe steeped in the Kingdom of God should be able to bring forth from his storeroom "things new and old" without too much incongruity between them; because whether old or new they flow from the one living Source, which is neither old nor new. To my mind, things new and old must meet beyond old and new, just as the East and the West must meet beyond the East and the West.

In this connection, I am reminded of some profound words of Meister Eckhart on nature and grace: "Let God work within you and ascribe it to Him, and do not trouble yourself whether He works through His grace or through your nature, for both are His: nature and grace." Pope Pius IX has also said, "Although faith is above reason, there can never be found any real dissension or real disagreement between them, since they both have their origin from the same source of unchanging and eternal truth, God" (*Qui pluribus*). The same may be said of God's works of Creation, Redemption and Sanctification. Although we attribute in a special way the work of Creation to the Father, that of Redemption to the Son, and that of Sanctification to the Holy Spirit, it is well to remind ourselves that the Three Divine Persons are One. It is true that the work of Creation has been spoiled by man's disobedience, but it is not wholly spoiled, and therefore grains of truth are to be found in the philosophies and religions of all peoples. So long as they are grains of truth, they belong to God, because according to the saying of Saint Ambrose, which Saint Thomas Aquinas delighted to quote, "every truth, whoever said it, comes from the Holy Spirit." In fact, it is the Light of Revelation that enables a Christian to judge all things, while he himself is judged by no man. (See 1 Cor. 2:15.) As Father Otto Karrer has put it: "Christianity is 'the fulfilment of all religions,' not only because it possesses in the pure state all religious values, but because it comprehends in their utmost extent and fullness values elsewhere scattered and fragmentary."[13] To use an analogy, Christ is the Sun who gives light to the whole world, while the Church is like the biconvex lens through which His luminous rays are brought together and focused in order to cast fire on earth. We must put our soul under this focus so that it may be inflamed with divine love.

To conclude this chapter, I would like to introduce some beautiful images of meekness, which have impressed me profoundly. The first is found in Psalm 130:

> Lord, my heart is not proud, nor are mine eyes haughty,
> Neither do I aspire after great things or matters above me.
> Indeed I have behaved and calmed myself,
> As a little child on the lap of its mother,
> As a little child, so is my soul within me.

This leads us to the words of St. Francis of Sales, who may be called the Saint of Meekness *par excellence*: "I admire the Little Infant of Bethlehem. He Who knew all things, Who had so great power, suffered them to do as they pleased with Him, without ever saying a word." To borrow the words of Lao Tse, we can say of Christ, True God and True Man: "He knows the masculine, but keeps to the feminine. He knows the white, but keeps to the black. He knows the glorious, but keeps to the humiliations" (28). Who but the Word Incarnate can be said to have fulfilled perfectly these words? All dark sayings become clear when they are seen in the Light of Revelation.

It was Lao Tse also who said:

> How does the sea become the king of all streams?
> Because it lies lower than they.
> Hence it is the king of all streams (66).

Is this not a good commentary on the third Beatitude? *Blessed are the meek, for they shall inherit the land.*

---

[13] Otto Karrer, *Religions of Mankind*, trans. E. I. Watkin (London: Sheed & Ward, 1936), 210.

PART TWO

THE FLOWERING OF LOVE

SPECIAL INTRODUCTION

It is not always easy to distinguish one stage of the spiritual life from another. In general outline, however, the distinguishing marks of each stage are clear enough. Perhaps the commonest experience of beginners on the way is the abundance of sensible consolations that God gives to them, or allows them to enjoy, in order to sustain their efforts in reforming their habits and to confirm their faith. As St. John of the Cross says in *The Ascent of Mount Carmel*:

> It is lawful, and even expedient, for beginners to feel a sensible pleasure in Images, Oratories, and other visible objects of devotion, because they are not yet entirely weaned from the world, so as to be able to leave the latter wholly for the former. They are like children to whom, when we want to take anything from them which they hold in one hand, we give something to hold in the other, that they may not cry, having both hands empty (Bk. III, Ch. xxxix).

Aside from the assistance gained from visible objects of devotion, sometimes God stoops to our level by giving us some exterior sign of his presence — causing us, for instance, to smell the mysterious fragrance of incense, or to receive the gift of tears. I supposed that every new convert must receive some such favor. In this connection, Hilda Graef has written an illuminating passage:

> It is true that we must not attach ourselves to pleasant devotional feelings and must not seek them for their sake. But in the beginning of the spiritual life God will always give them. For we are creatures of sense, and fallen creatures at that; and as long as we are still powerfully attracted by the pleasures of sense, God in His mercy provides for us spiritual pleasures to wean us gradually from the coarser ones which we have so far indulged. We should gratefully accept them. Hence we should not despise the consolations God sends us. We should gratefully accept them; but we should at the same time be

very conscious that it is only because we are so weak, not because we are in any way advanced in the spiritual life, that God sends us these delights. . . . They have nothing to do with mystic union. They are passing attractions, "sensible consolations," as spiritual writers call them, given to us to be counter-attractions to the sensuous attractions of the world.[1]

In order to make us advance in the way of love, God will sooner or later withdraw these exterior supports from us, and we shall experience a period of aridity. This is a critical period, in which we either rise higher or fall into laxity, allowing our spiritual growth to be arrested. Let us listen again to what St. John of the Cross has to say:

> The reason why some spiritual persons never enter perfectly into the true joys of the spirit is that they never succeed in raising their desire for rejoicing above these things that are outward and visible. Let such take note that, although the visible oratory and temple is a decent place set apart for prayer, and an image is a motive to prayer, the sweetness and delight of the soul must not be set upon the motive and visible temple, lest the soul should forget to pray in the living temple, which is the interior recollection of the soul.[2]

It is time to remember the words of St. Paul, that our bodies are living temples of the Holy Spirit, who dwells in us. The time has come for us to worship God "in spirit and truth."

From the standpoint of prayer, the second stage upon which we are entering now is marked by an increasing inwardness and fervency in our love of God. From the standpoint of the active life, it is marked by an intensive exercise and cultivation of all the virtues, moral as well as theological, especially the virtue of fraternal charity. From the standpoint of grace, it is marked by the incipient infusion of supernatural light; and you have begun to savor the things of heaven, and to see eye-to-eye with Our Lord.

---

[1] Hilda C. Graef, *God in Our Daily Life* (Westminster, MD: Newman Press, 1951), 125.
[2] *Works*, 1:322–23.

When St. Peter asked Our Lord, "What of us, who have forsaken all, and followed thee?" (Mark 10:28), he was still a beginner; it is obvious that his love for Him was far from pure. He was serving Him from self-interest. His love was mercenary and calculating. It was not ardent enough to overwhelm reason. Of course, God is just, and no good action on our part, however little it may be, will go unrewarded. But to think principally of the reward in serving Him is to show how weak our love is. What a different man Peter became after his second conversion, which took place after he had wept bitterly over his denials. He became head-over-heels in love with Christ. When He manifested Himself on the beach of the sea of Tiberius, Simon Peter, hearing John say that it was the Lord, "girt up the fisherman's cloak, which was all he wore, and sprang into the sea" (John 21:7). There was no human reason why he should have acted with such impetuosity, for the boat, St. John tells us, was only two hundred cubits from the land. Evidently his love had overwhelmed his reason. This impetuosity is characteristic of the Flowering of Love.

To take another instance: When Thérèse of Lisieux was eleven she received her First Communion, and she was able to offer her little Jesus a splendid sheaf of sacrifices and 2,773 ejaculatory prayers, all duly counted. In a beginner, this is as it ought to be. But as she grew in wisdom and in grace, she no longer counted the sacrifices and ejaculations. Everything was reduced to love. She said to a Sister, "There is only one way of compelling God not to judge us: we must take care to appear before Him empty-handed. Lay nothing by, spend your treasures as fast as you gain them. Were I to live to be eighty, I should always be poor, because I cannot economise. All my earnings are immediately spent on the ransom of souls."[3]

When your prayer grows in simplicity, it is a sure sign that you are making progress along the way. The important task of this stage of the spiritual life is to dispose yourself for union with God. To that end, there is no other way than by cultivating a love for the cross. Perhaps you will find the following

---

[3] St. *Thérèse of Lisieux, The Little Flower of Jesus*, 310.

simple prayer to Christ by Blessed Thérèse Couderc of help
to you:

> I unite myself to Thy perpetual, unceasing, universal Sac-
> rifice. To Thee I offer myself for all the days of my life
> and every instant of the day, according to Thy most holy
> and adorable will. Thou wert the Victim of my salvation.
> I desire to be the victim of Thy love. Accept my desire,
> receive my offering, hear my prayer. May I live by love,
> may I die of love, and may the last beat of my heart be
> an act of the most perfect love.[4]

I do not mean that you have to recite the exact words. But
some such prayer said from the bottom of your heart during
the Mass, especially at the Offertory, will greatly help you
to assimilate the interior dispositions of the Sacred Heart of
Christ, and thus prepare yourself for the unitive stage.

According to St. Thomas, the Beatitudes of justice and mercy
belong to the active life (*S. T.*, Ia, Iae, Q. 69, Art. 3 and 4).
Commenting on this, Fr. Garrigou-Lagrange writes:

> "Blessed are they that hunger and thirst after justice: for
> they shall have their fill." To desire justice, perfect order,
> is the effect of the virtues; but to hunger and thirst after
> it, to be tormented by this hunger, is the fruit of a loftier
> inspiration.
>
> This thirst for justice should not become a bitter zeal
> with regard to the guilty; consequently Our Lord says:
> "Blessed are the merciful: for they shall receive mercy."
> Attentive to the sufferings of others, the merciful are
> able to give that counsel which reanimates and encour-
> ages. Accordingly the spirit of counsel corresponds to this
> beatitude.
>
> This union of justice and mercy is one of the most
> striking signs of the presence of God in the soul; for He
> alone can intimately harmonize virtues that are appar-
> ently so contradictory.[5]

---

[4] Eileen Surles, *Surrender to the Spirit: The Life of Mother Thérèse Couderc*,
R. C. (New York: P. J. Kenedy, 1951), xiii.
[5] Réginald Garrigou-Lagrange, O. P., *Christian Perfection and Contemplation: According to St. Thomas Aquinas and St. John of the Cross*, trans. Sister
M. Timothea Doyle, O. P. (St. Louis: B. Herder Book Co., 1937), 133.

It would seem that they are using the words "justice" and "mercy" in the sense that Shakespeare used them when he wrote in *The Merchant of Venice*:

> The quality of mercy is not strained,
> It droppeth as the gentle rain from heaven
> Upon the place beneath: it is twice blest;
> It blesses him that gives and him that takes;....
> And earthly power doth then show likest God's
> When mercy seasons justice.

In the present book, I am using the word "justice" in a wider sense, so as to include our desperate desire to render to God his due. (See *S. T.*, IIa, IIae, Q. 80.) As St. Thomas says, "Whatever man renders is His due, yet it cannot be equal." The fact that it cannot be equal is the very cause of our hunger and thirst. St. Thomas quotes a verse from Psalm 115: *What shall I render to the Lord for all the things that he hath rendered to me?* Commenting on this, he says, "In this respect *religion* is annexed to justice since, according to Tully, it consists in offering service and ceremonial rites of worship *to some superior nature that men call divine.*" In short, "*They who hunger and thirst for justice* are they who ardently long for spiritual perfection."[6]

One may add that spiritual perfection consists in the love of God and the love of our neighbor as ourselves.

The Beatitudes of justice and mercy, therefore, belong to the center of our spiritual life. They correspond to the middle part of the Mass, embracing the Offertory and the Canon, where the priest says, "Let us give thanks to the Lord our God," and you respond, "it is right and just," and he rejoins you by saying, "It is truly right and just...." We can also pray in the words of Dom Guéranger: "All that we have, O Lord, comes from Thee, and belongs to Thee; it is just, therefore, that we return it to Thee. But, how wonderful art Thou in the inventions of Thy immense love! This bread which we are offering

---

[6] Catholic Biblical Association, *A Commentary on the New Testament* (New York: Catholic Book Publishing Co., 1942), 48. See also Amleto Giovanni Cicognani, *Canon Law: Its Nature, Sources, and History.* Translated by J. O. Horgan. Westminster, MD: Newman Press, 1949.

to Thee, is to give place, in a few moments, to the Sacred Body of Jesus. We beseech Thee, receive, together with this oblation, our hearts, which long to live by Thee, and to cease to live their own life of self."[7] In this middle part of the Mass, we also practice mercy and fraternal charity by praying for others, whether living or dead.

In attending the Mass, we must not do it as a matter of formality; we must try to assimilate its spirit, so that we may live the Mass. Not the least important of the lessons it gives us is the progress of love.[8] You will realize that the Mass is the perfect embodiment of the threefold way of love. The first part, called "the Mass of the Catechumens," corresponds to the budding of love. There the keynote is the *Confiteor*, and the principal interior disposition is the willingness and eagerness to learn the truth. The middle part, called "the Mass of the Faithful," corresponds to the flowering of love, whose keynote is the spirit of sacrifice. The third part, called "the Banquet of the Faithful," corresponds to the ripening of love, whose keynote is peace and joy. It is not for nothing that the word "peace" is so often repeated in the Communion. "Mercifully grant peace in our days." "The peace of the Lord be always with you." "O Lord Jesus Christ, who saidst to Thy Apostles, Peace I leave with you, My peace I give unto you; look not upon my sins, but upon the faith of Thy Church; and vouch-safe to grant her peace and unity according to Thy will." It is also significant that before we receive the Holy Eucharist, we pray to be delivered "from all evils, past, present and to come," and we say the *Confiteor* once more. To my mind, this signifies that before we can enjoy the beatitude of peace, we must undergo a thorough and radical purification, which corresponds to the beatitude of the pure of heart.

Thus, the whole Liturgy of the Church forms a seamless tunic with her spiritual doctrine. "This is the will of God, your sanctification." Every prayer, every ceremony, and every

---

[7] Dom Prosper Guéranger, *The Liturgical Year*, trans. Laurence Shepherd. vol. II (New York: Benziger Brothers, 1910), 39.

[8] It was my former confessor, Father Nicholas Maestrini, who first pointed out this lesson to me.

Sacrament that Christ has instituted is for your sanctification, so that God may be glorified in you. They are all ordained to the practice and actualization of the Sermon on the Mount, which may be called the Constitution of the Kingdom of Heaven, of which the Beatitudes form the worthy preamble.

In the stage of the spiritual life with which we are dealing now, a Christian must particularly beware of the danger of exteriorization and of, in the words of John Morley, "letting his religion spoil his morality."[9] As Dom Marmion says, this thought may be compared with certain words of Bossuet: "One is uneasy if he has not said his rosary or other fixed prayers, or if he has omitted some *Ave Maria* in a decade; I do not blame him; God forbid! I have only praise for religious exactitude in exercises of piety. But who can endure to have this same person easily breaking four or five precepts of the Decalogue daily without troubling, and treading under foot the holiest duties of Christianity without scruple?.... Undeceive your-selves, Christians.... In doing works of supererogation, take care not to forget those that are of necessity."[10] The spirit of Phariseeism never dies. Let us never forget the words of Christ: "Woe to you, scribes and Pharisees, hypocrites; because ye tithe mint and dill and cummin, and ye have neglected the weightier things of the Law — justice and mercy and faith. These things it behoved you to do, nor yet to neglect those others. Blind guides, who strain out the gnat but swallow the camel" (Matt. 23:23 in the Westminster version).

It may be asked by some reader: Since St. Thomas calls the Beatitudes of justice and mercy the Beatitudes of the active life, are they equally applicable to those living in the cloister? I answer that we must not confuse the contemplative state with the contemplative life, nor the active state with the active life. Those who are living in the cloister are in the contemplative state — that is, in the environment most conducive to the con-templative life. But this does not mean that they have no active

---

[9] John Morley, *The Life of William Ewart Gladstone*, vol. 2 (London: Mac-millan and Co., 1903), 158.
[10] Dom Columba Marmion, *Christ, the Life of the Soul*, trans. Mother Mary St. Thomas (St. Louis, MO: B. Herder Book Co., 1922), 216n.

life, nor that those who live in the world are precluded from the contemplative life. In fact, the active life of the cloistered can be just as intense as that of anyone outside. In the first place, as St. Teresa of Ávila says, "To pray for those who are in mortal sin is the best kind of almsgiving."[11] Furthermore, there are many opportunities for practicing justice and mercy among the members of the same religious community, who see one another day in and day out. Anyone who wishes to learn the ways of fraternal charity will do well to read Chapter X of the autobiography of the Little Flower. Here a few quotations will do: "Now I know that true charity consists in bearing all my neighbor's defects, in not being surprised at mistakes, but in being edified by the smallest virtues." "When I show charity towards others I know that it is Jesus who is acting within me, and the more closely I am united to Him, the more dearly I love my Sisters. Should I wish to increase this love, and should the devil bring before me the defects of a Sister, I hasten to look for her virtues and good motives." "There are, of course, no enemies in Carmel; but, after all, we have our natural likes and dislikes. We may feel drawn towards one Sister and may be tempted to go a long way round to avoid meeting another. Well, Our Lord tells me that this last is the Sister I must love and pray for, even though her manner might lead me to believe that she does not care for me." What a keen psychologist she was can be gathered from her comment on the words of Christ: *"Give to every man that asks, and if a man takes what is thine, do not ask him to restore it"* (Luke 6:32). "To give to everyone that asks," she says, "is less pleasant than to give to everyone that asks," she says, "is less pleasant than to give spontaneously and of one's own accord. Again, if a thing be asked in a courteous way consent is easy, but if, unhappily, tactless words have been used, there is an inward rebellion unless we are perfect in charity. We discover no end of excuses for refusing, and it is only after having made clear to the guilty Sister how rude was her behavior, that we grant *as a favor* what she requires, or render a slight service which takes, perhaps, one-half of the time we

---

[11] *Works*, 2:330.

have lost in setting forth the difficulties and our own imaginary rights."[12] This is an instance of how psychology, or whatever science can help us to know ourselves, may be turned into an instrument of charity. In fact, all our knowledge and learning should minister to love.

As to the question whether those of us who are living in the world can aspire to the contemplative life, I will answer by the words of St. Teresa of Ávila:

> I believe that, through His goodness, there are many such souls in the world: they are most desirous not to offend His Majesty: they avoid committing even venial sins; they love doing penance; they spend hours in recollection; they use their time well; . . . . they are very careful in their speech and dress and in the government of their household if they have one. This is certainly a desirable state and there seems no reason why they should be denied entrance to the very last of the Mansions; nor will the Lord deny them this if they desire it, for their disposition is such that He will grant them any favour.[13]

St. Gregory the Great has likewise said: "Holy men who are obliged by the necessity of their employments to engage in outward ministrations, are ever studiously betaking themselves to the secrets of their hearts; and there do they ascend the height of most inward thought, while they put aside the tumults of temporal activities and at the summit of their contemplation search out the sentence of the divine will" (*Mor.*, xxiii. 38).[14]

---

[12] *The Little Flower of Jesus,*, 162–165.

[13] *Works*, 2:221.

[14] Dom Cuthbert Butler, *Western Mysticism: The Teaching of SS. Augustine, Gregory, and Bernard on Contemplation and the Contemplative Life* (New York: E. P. Dutton & Company, 1924), 236–37.

IV

Thirsting for the Beloved

Blessed are they that hunger and thirst after justice, for they shall have their fill.

Justice is love, serving God alone (St. Augustine).

1. A RETROSPECT AND A FORECAST

In the days of Confucius there was a current saying: "He who has freed himself from the love of mastery, vanity, resentment, and covetousness, may be called a perfect man." Commenting upon this saying, Confucius remarked: "Such a man has indeed accomplished what is difficult; as to whether he can be called perfect, I do not know."

In another passage of *The Analects*, we find Confucius making this significant remark: "In the pursuit of perfection, one has first to do what is difficult before one can expect results" (6.20).

In the first stage of the spiritual life, the Christian has, with the grace of God, accomplished what is difficult. He has detached himself, to a considerable degree, from worldly honors and riches, from the sinful dispositions and habits of his old self, and finally from his self-will. But this does not mean that he has already reached the heights of sanctity. No, he has only laid the foundations upon which the Divine Architect is to build a magnificent house for Himself. As Father Gabriel puts it: "Love makes us set our hand to the labors of detachment, but freeing the heart this detachment makes it capable of loving more and better; it even prepares it to be transformed by the Divine Love."[1]

Let us sum up what he has accomplished in the light of Psalms 1 and 23 (Vulgate 22). Being poor in spirit, he has not

---
[1] Gabriel of St. Mary Magdalen, *St. John of the Cross: Doctor of Divine Love and Contemplation*, trans. A Benedictine of Stanbrook Abbey (Cork: Mercier Press, 1946), 42.

followed the counsel of the ungodly; being mortified, he has not entered into the way of sinners; being meek, he has not sat in the company of the scornful. Thus it is clear that what he has achieved during the first stage is more negative than positive. However, this stage is at the same time one rich in consolations. For the Divine Physician is full of tact and tenderness in dealing especially with the beginners on the Way of Love. In the words of St. Bernard, "It is especially in the beginning of conversion that He anoints the ulcers with the oil of His pity, lest a man should be more aware than is desirable of the extent of his disease and of the difficulty of the cure" (*Of Conversion*). That is why "a certain facility of recovery smiles upon him" (Ibid.). There is no better description of the wondrous work of God in the first age of the interior life than the beginning verses of the Psalm of the Divine Shepherd:

> The Lord is my shepherd:
> I shall not want.
>
> He makes me lie down in green pastures;
> He leads me beside the refreshing waters.
> He restores my soul.

In other words, when one is meek, one's soul has been restored, and one enjoys spiritual health. But it must be remembered that one owes one's spiritual health entirely to the mercies of God. So it is about time for the Christian to ask gratefully, "What shall I render to the Lord for all the things that he hath rendered to me?" (115). It is time to requite the love of God by working for His glory. It is most significant, therefore, that immediately after the words "He restores my soul" comes the third verse: "He guides me in the paths of justice for his name's sake." With this verse begins the Illuminative Stage, or the Age of the Proficients, when love is blossoming forth. The great romance of love between God and the soul is commencing.

The truth is that only the meek and humble of heart could have the impetuous audacity of love without falling into the bottomless pit of presumption and pride. Each of us is a temple of the Holy Ghost; but this temple must be built upon the solid foundation of humility, and the deeper the foundation the higher the temple will rise.

The meekness of Moses is proverbial (Num. 12:3), and yet no man has prayed to God with greater audacity than he did when he said: "I beseech Thee: this people hath sinned a heinous sin, and they have made to themselves gods of gold. Either forgive them this trespass, or, if thou do not, strike me out of the book that thou hast written" (Exod. 32:31–32). St. Paul knew as well as anyone the humility of the heart, yet for the sake of his brethren he was so bold as to have wished himself to be anathema from Christ! (Rom. 9:1–5).

The organic relation between humility and magnanimity is best illustrated by the *Fiat* of Our Lady: "Behold the hand-maid of the Lord: be it done to me according to thy word." It was her humble and unquestioning obedience to the will of God that made her the Spouse of the Holy Spirit and the Mother of Christ, so that she could sing the Magnificat with-out the slightest echo of pride or vain glory. I cannot think of her *Fiat* without recalling to mind the Chinese proverb which says: "It is better to obey the order of the host than to stand on ceremony."

2. INFUSED LIGHTS: THE CAUSE OF THIRST

With the Beatitude of hunger and thirst for justice begin the lower degrees of infused contemplation. This hunger and thirst is not something that can be achieved by man's will and effort, but something infused into us by the grace of God. If we are humble and meek enough so that, like the publican, we dare not even lift our eyes toward heaven, there will come a day when we shall hear Him calling to us: "*Sursum corda!*" — Lift up your hearts! As soon as we hear this call, shall we not respond as promptly as we can, "Yes, Lord, we will lift up our hearts to Thee"? But no sooner do we lift up our hearts toward Him than we are vouchsafed some glimpses of His ravishing beauty. And the more glimpses we have, the more enamored we are of Him. He also gives us to drink of the Living Fountain; but the more we drink, the more thirsty we grow. It is true that a taste of the living waters should cure us of our inordinate desire for material

things; but at the same time it intensifies our thirst for things of
the spirit. For, as St. Thomas Aquinas puts it, "The least insight
that one can obtain into sublime things is more desirable than
the most certain knowledge of lower things" (*S. T.*, I, 1, 5 ad. 1).
What is more natural for the soul than to desire what she knows
and feels to be desirable?

In the meantime prayer and spiritual reading open the interior eye of the soul to a new heaven and a new earth. The soul
is like a bee which has entered into a garden where all kinds
of flowers grow. She cannot help singing with St. Clement of
Alexandria:

> Teacher, to thee a chaplet I present,
> Woven of words culled from the spotless mead,
> Where Thou dost feed Thy flocks, like to the bee,
> That skilful worker, which from many a flower
> Gathers its treasures, that she may convey
> A luscious offering to the Master's hand.[2]

One of the most penetrating and eye-opening passages in
the New Testament is St. Paul's magnificent prayer in his Epistle to the Ephesians, which was written during his first imprisonment in Rome. After begging his readers not to be disheart-
ened at his tribulations, which were their glory, he wrote:

> With this in mind, I fall on my knees to the Father of
> our Lord Jesus Christ, that Father from whom all father-
> hood in heaven and on earth takes its title. May he, out
> of the rich treasury of his glory, strengthen you through
> his Spirit with a power that reaches your innermost being.
> May Christ find a dwelling-place, through faith, in your
> hearts; may your lives be rooted in love, founded on love.
> May you and all the saints be enabled to measure, in all
> its breadth and length and height and depth, the love
> of Christ, to know what passes knowledge. May you be
> filled with the completion God has to give (Eph. 3:14–19).

What a tremendous prayer this is! In it the Apostle's love and
wisdom have burst forth in full splendor.

---

[2] H. A. Reinhold, ed., *The Soul Afire: Revelations of the Mystics* (New York:
Pantheon Books, 1944), 215.

With regard to the expression "the breadth and length and height and depth," Bible students throughout the ages have offered different interpretations. Some have thought that these dimensions refer to the Mystery of Redemption; others have maintained that they refer to Christ's love. But really there is not much material difference between the two, inasmuch as Christ's love is the very kernel of the Mystery of Redemption. So I am inclined to ask, with Father Charles J. Callan, "Is not that great mystery of the union of all peoples in Christ the effect or the fruit of divine love, and therefore ultimately to be resolved into that love?"[3] In God, love and wisdom are one.

Strictly speaking, Christ's love is beyond measure. Those dimensions are, however, useful as pointers to different directions, each of which melts into the infinite. With this preface, let us proceed lovingly to measure the measureless, in the hope that we may know something of that which surpasses knowledge.

(a) The Breadth

First, as to the breadth of Christ's love. In dealing with this, it is well to remember that Christ is the Word through Whom all things have been made, and that He is the true Light that enlightens every man who comes into the world. It is no wonder, then, that His love is universal in scope. How tenderly He spoke of the birds and flowers!

> Are not two sparrows sold for a farthing? And yet not one of them will fall to the ground without your Father's leave (Matt. 10:29).

> Behold the birds of the air: for they neither sow, nor do they reap, nor gather into barns; and your heavenly Father feedeth them (Matt. 66:26).

> Consider the lilies of the field how they grow; they labour not, neither do they spin. But I say to you, that

---

[3] Charles J. Callan, O. P., *The Epistles of St. Paul: With Introductions and Commentary for Priests and Students*, vol. 2 (New York: Joseph F. Wagner, 1922), 62.

not even Solomon in all his glory was arrayed as one of these (Matt. 6:28–29).

I know that all these words were addressed to His disciples to instill in them the virtue of trust in God. But the very words diffuse their tenderness upon all things in nature. Being the Creator, how could He help loving His creation? But among all His creatures, His delight is to be with the children of men, to the extent that "He is not ashamed to call them brethren" (Heb. 2:11). The Son of God condescended to be the Son of Man in order that the children of man might become children of God, and He showed us the Way in unequivocal terms:

> You have heard that it hath been said, Thou shalt love thy neighbour, and hate thy enemy. But I say to you, Love your enemies: do good to them that hate you, and pray for them that persecute and calumniate you: that you may be the children of your Father who is in heaven, who maketh his sun to rise upon the good and bad, and raineth upon the just and unjust (Matt. 5:43–45).

(b) The Length

Christ's love is not only infinitely broad, but infinitely long. Listen to the touching observation of St. John: "Before the festival day of the Pasch, Jesus, knowing that his hour was come that he should pass out of this world to the Father: having loved his own who were in the world, he loved them unto the end" (13:1).

And how comforting to all of us are His parting words: "Behold, I am with you all days, even to the consummation of the world" (Matt. 28:20). Any Christian worthy of the name should be able to testify how true He is to His word. To borrow the words of St. Paul: "Jesus Christ, yesterday, and today, and the same for ever" (Heb. 13:8). He was not now "Yes" and now "No," but only "Yes" was in Him (2 Cor. 1:19). The world will end some day, but His love never. For he is preparing a place for us, and will come again and take us to Himself; that where He is, there we also may be (14:3). Whose love can last longer than the love of Christ?

(c) The Height

The height of Christ's love can, perhaps, be gauged by the way He taught His disciples the science of love. He looked at them, He smiled, patiently He led them on, until their love was purified from all dross and completely spiritualized. They began by savoring the things of men; but ended by savoring the things of God. In the course of three years their transformation was complete. They underwent no less than three conversions. At the first conversion, which occurred when Christ called them, they gave up their material possessions to follow Him. At the second, which was evident after the Resurrection, they gave up their self-will and submitted to the will of God. At the third conversion, which took place on Pentecost Sunday, they entered into the unitive stage, in which they began to see eye to eye with Christ. Christ's love may thus be compared to Jacob's ladder, leading from earth to heaven and from heaven back to earth.

Christ is the Light. He enlightens us on all the essentials of the spiritual life. He teaches that the Kingdom of God is within us; that God prefers mercy to sacrifice; that we must worship God in spirit and in truth, not merely with our lips; that it is not what comes into the mouth, but what comes out of the mouth from the heart, that defiles a man; that we must not follow those blind guides who strain out the gnat but swallow the camel, for they make a fuss over trifles while neglecting the principal Commandments of God; that we must not imitate the self-righteous whose eyes are open to the slight faults of others but blind to their own heinous crimes; that a man's life does not consist in the abundance of his possessions, but in the interior peace and joy which He alone can give to us and no one will be able to take away from us. Without any doubt, Christ is the greatest Teacher, the only Teacher of humanity. Compared with Him, all other "teachers" are at most as candle-lights compared with the Sun. For He who comes from above is over all and speaks of the things of heaven; while they who are from earth belong to the earth, and of the earth they speak. He not only teaches these lofty doctrines, but gives us the grace to put them into practice. On this point no one has written better than St. John: "and of his fullness we have all received, and grace for grace. For the Law was given by Moses; grace and truth came by Jesus Christ. No man hath seen God at any time: the only-begotten Son who is in the bosom of the Father, he hath declared him" (1:16–18).

(d) The Depth

In dealing with the depth of Christ's love, we have to touch upon the mystery of mysteries: the Incarnation. Time does not allow nor my ability permit a probing into this great mystery. I wish only to say this: the Incarnation of the Word of God is the central event of human history. Without it there would have been no Revelation nor Redemption. The thoroughgoingness of Christ's love of God and of us baffles the imagination. He loves us unto folly. I have no words to describe this divine folly. I can only quote what St. Paul wrote to the Philippians: "Have this mind in you which was also in Christ Jesus, who though he was by nature God, did not consider being equal to God as a thing to be clung to, but emptied himself, taking the nature of a slave and being made like unto men. And appearing in the form of man, he humbled himself, becoming obedient unto death, even to death on a cross" (Phil. 2:5–8). (Confraternity Edition.)

In his treatise on *The Incarnation of the Word of God*, St. Athanasius said: "All these things the Savior thought fit to do, so that, recognizing his bodily acts as works of God, men who were blind to his presence might regain knowledge of the Father."

In his book *Human Destiny*, Lecomte du Noüy, a world-famous scientist, makes a similar remark: "Christ did not come too soon, for only the example of infinite perfection and total sacrifice could inspire men with the ambition to improve themselves and with the hope of resembling Him one day."[4]

---

[4] Pierre Lecomte du Noüy, *Human Destiny* (New York: Longmans, Green and Co., 1947), 124.

3. LOVE AND KNOWLEDGE

In fact, the more we come to know God, the more we wonder at His love and His wisdom and His works. One cannot
help exclaiming with the Psalmist: "O Lord, how great are thy
works! Thy thoughts are exceeding deep!" (Ps. 91).

> This knowledge is become wonderful to me: it is high,
> and I cannot reach it (Ps. 138).

But the interesting thing is that the unfathomability of the
Divine Wisdom and Goodness does not discourage us; it
rather draws us on. For, although we are in the dark, yet we
are encouraged by the thought that our Beloved Lord is in the
light, or rather He Himself is the Light:

> But darkness shall not be dark to thee, and night shall
> be light as the day: the darkness thereof and the
> light thereof are alike to thee (Ps. 138).

And we take consolation in the words of St. Thomas Aquinas
that "love of God is better than knowledge of God," and that
"we only know God truly when we believe that He is above all
that men can think about God." And Hugh of St. Victor writes:
"Love knocks and enters, but knowledge stands without."

This is why the same stage of the spiritual life which some
theologians call the "night of the senses" from the subjective
standpoint, is, from the standpoint of the subtle operations of
God's grace in us, also called the "illuminative way." For this is
the stage when the perfections of God are revealed more and
more to our interior vision. You begin to perceive, as St. John of
the Cross did, that, being omnipotent, He loves you with omnip-
otence; being wise, He loves you with wisdom; being good, He
loves you with goodness; being just and merciful, He loves you
with justice and mercy; and being the virtue of the greatest
humility, He loves you with the greatest humility, and with the
greatest esteem, making you His equal, joyfully revealing Himself
to you and saying to you: I am yours and for you, and I delight
to be such as I am that I may be yours and give Myself to you.

Having gradually perceived all this, you are overwhelmed with
wonder and gratitude. You realize what a profound meaning is

contained in these words of the *Gloria: We give Thee thanks for Thy great glory.* That is to say, "We are grateful to Thee for being what Thou art." If God were not what He is, there would have been no creation, no redemption, no sanctification. If a man is not aware of the wonders of creation, he has no rationality. If he is not aware of the wonders of redemption, he has no spirituality. If he is not aware of the wonders of sanctification, he has no part in divinity.

On the other hand, if once a man has some glimpses of the wonders of God, he cannot help thirsting after Him. He would say with the Psalmist:

> O God, my God, to thee do I watch at break of day.
> For thee my soul hath thirsted; for thee my flesh,
>   O how many ways!
> In a desert land, and where there is no way, and no
>   water (Ps. 62).
>
> As the hart panteth after the fountains of water; so my
>   soul panteth after thee, O God.
> My soul hath thirsted after the strong living God; when
>   shall I come and appear before the face of God?
> My tears have been my bread day and night, whilst it is
>   said to me daily: Where is thy God? (Ps. 41).

However, it is infinitely better to thirst for God than to be filled with things of the world. As St. Gregory the Great writes:

> There is this difference between spiritual and earthly plea-
> sures. So long as we do not yet enjoy them, earthly plea-
> sures are greatly desired; but when they are partaken to
> the full our liking for them soon begins to pall. Spiritual
> joys, on the other hand, are a matter of indifference to us
> when we do not possess them, but once we begin to expe-
> rience them, we are filled with desire; the more we enjoy
> them, the more we desire them. With pleasure of the
> body it is desire that delights us, realization which disap-
> points; with pleasures of the soul desire is weak but spir-
> itual experience is a source of the greatest joy.... When
> our souls are full of spiritual joy we long for more, since
> by tasting it we learn to desire it more eagerly.[5]

---

[5] Reinhold, *The Soul Afire: Revelations of the Mystics,* 189.

4. MUTUAL COURTSHIP BETWEEN GOD & THE SOUL

The word "justice" used in the fourth Beatitude means primarily Christ Himself. This is plain from the context. But in a secondary sense, it means the earnest and persistent desire on the part of the soul to requite the love of Christ by keeping His commandments, especially the first commandment: "Hear, O Israel! The Lord thy God is One God; And thou shalt love the Lord thy God, with thy whole heart, and with thy whole soul, and with thy whole mind, and with thy whole strength" (Mark 12:29–30).

In order to keep this commandment, it is well to recall to mind the four dimensions of Christ's love. We have seen how infinitely broad, long, high and deep His love is. To imitate Him well, your heart must be big enough to embrace the One and all; your soul should be filled with immortal longings and aspire after an ever closer union with God; your mind should try to understand the ways and thoughts of God, so that you may to some extent see eye to eye with God; and, finally, all your physical forces should be mobilized in the service of God, so that "with the instrument of the body, you may prove and exercise the virtues" (St. Catherine of Siena, *The Dialogue*).

Christ has loved us unto folly; shall we not love Him unto madness? St. Thérèse of Lisieux has written:

> It was folly indeed, for the King of Glory, who sitteth above the Cherubim, to seek out thrones for Himself in poor human hearts. Was He not supremely happy in the Company of His Father and the Holy Spirit of Love? Why, then, come down on earth in search of sinners to make of them His closest friends? Nay, our folly could never exceed the foolishness of Christ, and our deeds are quite within the bounds of reason by the side of His. The world may leave us alone. I repeat, it is the world that *is insane*, because it will not heed what Jesus has done and suffered to save us from eternal damnation.[6]

God has kissed us; shall we not kiss back? Ten years ago, I wrote something like the following: "When your mother kisses

---

[6] *The Collected Letters*, 349–350.

you, you do not say, 'Oh how wonderful is your art of kissing!' You simply love her and kiss her in return. The spiritual life is nothing but a kiss for a kiss, or rather a small kiss for a big kiss."

I still think these words are true. However, I have come to see that in a higher stage, the spiritual life is a big kiss for a small kiss. In a still later stage, we shall find that the two kisses are melted into one. But I do not want to anticipate.

In the classical anthology of ancient Chinese songs, there is a song which I have especially liked since my childhood days. Let me quote it to you:

Love for Love

She threw a quince to me;
I requited her with a girdle-gem.
No, not just as requital,
But as a pledge of eternal love.

She threw a peach to me;
I requited her with a greenstone.
No, not just as requital,
But as a pledge of eternal love.

She threw a plum to me;
I requited her with an amulet.
No, not just as requital,
But as a pledge of eternal love.

If we put this song into the mouth of the Divine Lover, we should have some idea of what is happening between Him and the soul, particularly during the period we are dealing with. The soul finds herself playing a losing game, for she can never beat her Beloved in the game of Love. But the more she loses, the more she gains; the more she is beaten the more she wins. Speaking in terms of Spanish chess, Teresa of Ávila said that the only way to checkmate the King is to use the Queen—that is, humility. The only way to conquer God is to be conquered by Him, and the only way to possess Him is to be possessed by Him.

St. Bernard, in answer to the question why and how God should be loved, said, "The reason for loving God is God Himself; the way is to love Him beyond measure."

This is certainly a large order. But we have no reason to be dismayed. In this tremendous romance of love, the soul is not left to her own resources. As St. John of the Cross says,

> . . . . if a soul is seeking God, its Beloved is seeking it much more; and, if it sends after Him its loving desires, which are as fragrant to Him as a pillar of smoke that issues from the aromatic spices of myrrh and incense, He likewise sends after it the fragrance of His ointments, wherewith He attracts the soul and causes it to run after Him. These ointments are His Divine inspirations and touches, which, whenever they are His, are ordered and ruled with respect to the perfection of the law of God and of faith, in which perfection the soul must ever draw ever nearer and nearer to God.[7]

From the foregoing it might seem that this period is marked only as an endless exchange of gifts. But the reality is not so simple. For God is not merely a generous Lover, but also the Divine Teacher. During this period of our pilgrimage, God often plays hide-and-seek with the soul. He is no sooner found than He disappears again. Every time He reappears, He presents Himself to her in a more ethereal light than before. This He does because He wants to spiritualize, step by step, her conception of Him and her love for Him, so that her delight becomes more and more pure and lasting. But each time He absents Himself from her, the soul is plunged into darkness and becomes restless. She is in the same state as the spouse in *The Canticle of Canticles* when she sang:

> In my bed by night I sought him whom my soul loveth;
> I sought him, and found him not.
> I will rise, and will go about the city:
> In the streets and the broadways I will seek him whom
>   my soul loveth:
> I sought him, and I found him not (3:1–2).

The fact is that He is not absent, but only hidden. As the author of *Scala Claustralium* observes, "He departs, so that He may be more vehemently desired; desired, that He may

---

[7] *Works*, 3:175.

be more avidly sought; sought, that He may be more happily found. He departs from us so that we may not consider this exile our fatherland. But take heed, O spouse. Thy Bridegroom is very sensitive and jealous. If He perceives that thou art inclined to some other lover; that is, to some consolation of this present life, He departs from thee and seeks another spouse." Christ Himself has said, "I go away, and I come unto you" (John 14:28). Indeed, it may be said that He comes to us by going away. What happened to the two disciples at Emmaus (Luke 24:13–32) happens to us from time to time. As soon as our eyes are opened and we recognize Him, He disappears from our sight that He may abide in the depths of our soul. But the soul does not realize it, and misses Him intensely, and says, with Teresa of Ávila, "I die because I do not die."

One has no idea of how many deaths and births one has to undergo before one's love is thoroughly purified, before one can truly say with St. Paul, "And I live now, yet not I; but Christ liveth in me" (Gal. 2:20). Those who believe in the transmigration of souls often say that to attain perfection one has to die and be reborn many times. We Christians do not believe in transmigration, but we do believe in dying daily and living every day anew in this very life, which furnishes our only chance to strive for perfection.

In conclusion, let me say that the Way of love is not all roses. No, there are thorns in it and highwaymen about it, especially on this step, when the soul is loaded with jewels. It takes a great deal of fortitude not to faint on the way. The pilgrim must gird his loins with truth, put on the breastplate of justice, have his feet shod with the readiness of the gospel of peace, and take with him the shield of faith, the helmet of hope, and the sword of the spirit (Eph. 6). Finally, he should have perfect confidence in the mercy and power of God, so that he can say with the Psalmist:

> For though I walk in the midst of the shadow of death,
> I will fear no evils, for thou art with me.
> Thy rod and thy staff: they comfort me.

V

The Practice of Fraternal Charity

Blessed are the merciful, for they shall find mercy.

1. CHRIST'S OWN COMMENTARY ON THE BEATITUDE

There can be no better exposition of this Beatitude than Christ's own words as recorded in the sixth chapter of St. Luke's Gospel. The words are familiar, but they constitute such a fundamental part of His teaching that I cannot afford not to quote them. I beg of you to listen to them with a freshness of loving attention, as if you were hearing them for the first time. In fact, if your spiritual life has been growing in the proper way, you will find that every time you reread the Holy Scriptures, especially the words of Christ, they taste fresher than before. Let me now present to you Christ's own exposition of this Beatitude:

> And now I say to you who are listening to me, Love your enemies, do good to those who hate you; bless those who curse you, and pray for those who treat you insultingly. If a man strikes thee on the cheek, offer him the other cheek too; if a man would take away thy cloak, do not grudge him thy coat along with it. Give to every man who asks, and if a man takes what is thine, do not ask him to restore it. As you would have men treat you, you are to treat them; no otherwise. Why, what credit is it to you, if you love those who love you? Even sinners love those who love them. What credit is it to you, if you do good to those who do good to you? Even sinners do as much. What credit is it to you, if you lend to those from whom you expect repayment? Even sinners lend to sinners, to receive as much in exchange. No, it is your enemies you must love, and do them good, and lend to them, without any hope of return; then your reward will be a rich

one, and you will be true sons of the most High, generous like him towards the thankless and unjust. Be merciful, then, as your Father is merciful. Judge nobody, and you will not be judged; condemn nobody, and you will not be condemned; forgive, and you will be forgiven. Give, and gifts will be yours; good measure, pressed down and shaken up and running over, will be poured into your lap; the measure you award to others is the measure that will be awarded to you (6:27–38).[1]

These words are easy to understand, but hard to practice. By his own efforts no man can practice them; but by the grace of God the saints throughout the ages have been able to live up to them more or less perfectly. Examples are innumerable. Let one suffice. When the first Christian martyr, St. Stephen, was being stoned to death, his dying words were: "Lord, do not lay this sin against them" (Acts 7:60). In this he was merciful up to the very end.

2. THREE DEGREES OF MERCY

If we study the words of Christ carefully, we find that there are three degrees of mercy. The first degree is represented by the words: "Judge nobody"; the second by "Forgive"; and the third by "Give." The first corresponds to the Golden Rule of Confucius: "Do not unto others what you do not want others to do unto yourself." Even this is hard enough for human nature. There is a tendency in human nature to exalt self and belittle others. To combat this tendency one has first to cultivate a sense of reverence towards one's fellow men. There is so much good in the worst of us and so much bad in the best of us that Confucius could say with all candidness: "When walking in a party of three, I can always be certain of learning from my companions as from my teachers. I just select their good qualities for imitation and note their unsatisfactory qualities for self-correction" (*Analects*, 7.21). When a man really possesses a deep self-knowledge and a broad knowledge of men, he will

---

[1] *The New Testament in English*, translated by Ronald Knox. Unless it is otherwise noted, the quotations from Scripture translated into modern English in this book are from the Knox translation.

naturally be mild in his judgment of others. Many sins against charity can thus be avoided. To counteract our inborn egoism, it would be good for us to form a habit of always seeing the good qualities of others and our own bad qualities. Then we should find everybody lovable, and life would be heavenly for us. This reminds me of a famous Confucian scholar in the old days, who felt ecstatic on coming back from a walk in a crowded city. Upon being asked by his friends why he was so happy, he said, "I saw the streets packed full of saints and sages." That is, every man is potentially a saint. So it is always a wise rule to judge yourself in the light of your rotten past, to judge others in the light of their golden future, and to judge everything in the light of God's infinite mercies. For as the Chinese proverb has it, "Who is narrow of vision cannot be big-hearted."

It was St. Bonaventure who said, "When you perceive in your brother anything worthy of reprehension, turn your eyes upon yourself; before you judge him, examine yourself well; and if you find you are guilty of the same fault, pronounce the sentence against yourself, and condemn that in yourself which you would have condemned in him, by saying with the royal prophet, 'It is I, I am he who has sinned, I have done wickedly'" (2 Kings 24:17). On the other hand, if you perceive in your brother a good quality, then, according to the advice of St. Bernard, you should see if you possess the same; "and if you have it, think how to preserve it: but if you have it not, endeavor to acquire it, and by this means you will make profit in all things." If you compare these quotations with the above quoted saying of Confucius, you will be struck by the similarity in their points of view.

To this degree of mercy also belong the words of St. Paul: "Charity does not envy." For, to love your neighbor as yourself requires that you should be delighted to see wisdom and virtues in others as if they were your own. In your heart, therefore, there will be no room for envy. In ancient China there was an exemplary ruler, Duke Mu (7th Century, B. C.). He was a man of generous and forbearing nature. In a speech addressed to his officers, he uttered some remarkable words which have a bearing on our present subject:

In reproving others there is no difficulty, but to receive reproof and allow it to have full course—this is difficult.

I have deeply reflected and reflected. I wish to see a single minister, who is plain and simple, without other ability, but having a sincere and liberal mind, and possessed of such a generous heart that he regards the talents of others as his own, and delights in the wisdom of others as if his own mouth had uttered it, really showing himself able to "contain" others. Such a minister would be able to protect my descendants and people, and would indeed be a giver of benefits (*Shu Ching*, Book of Chou, XXX).

If you are generous enough to "contain" others, then all their merits belong to you. But how many of us are being impoverished by our meanness of spirit and smallness of measure! How can God pour His superabundant gifts into a closed vessel?

Now we come to the second degree of mercy. It is harder to forgive other people's offences against us than not to commit offences against them. But Christ is so emphatic on this point that if we want seriously to follow Him, we have got to forgive any offences; for, as He says, "For if you will forgive men their offences, your heavenly Father will forgive you also your offences. But if you will not forgive men, neither will your Father forgive you your offences" (Matt. 6:14-15). Furthermore, on many occasions, what we regard as offences may not be offences in reality. It is only our hypersensitiveness that interprets them as offences. If we are truly steeped in the spirit of charity, we would put the best complexion on other people's words and actions, for Charity "thinks no evil." As St. Bernard says, "Excuse the intention if you cannot excuse the action: believe it proceeds from ignorance, or surprise; that it is the effect of the first motion, which he was not master of." A good stomach can digest many things, while a bad stomach, as St. Dorotheus says, "turns even the best meats into bile and bad humors." And even if people do hate us, what harm does it do to us so long as we do not hate back? As *The Dhammapada* puts it, "We live happily indeed, not hating those who hate us! among men who hate us we dwell free from hatred!" In the spiritual life, nothing is so desirable as a big heart. According to a Chinese proverb, a big heart is a great asset even in the world of politics, for, *In the heart of a Prime Minister, you can row a boat.*

As to the third degree of mercy, it ranges from giving a nickel to the poor to giving one's life in testimony to the Truth, so that others may be led to see the Light. Taken as a whole, this degree is also represented by the Golden Rule of Christ: "And even as you wish men to do to you, so also do you unto them." As you know, it is more blessed to give than to receive. I used to think that spiritual works of mercy were more important than corporal works of mercy; but upon deeper meditation I have come to the view that both are equally important. For everything depends upon the spirit of love with which you do them, and also upon the actual needs of others. In some circumstances, a kind word, so a Chinese saying goes, keeps one warm for three winters. On other occasions, kind words are not enough. Listen to what St. James has to say: "If a brother or a sister be naked and want daily food, and one of you say to them, Go in peace, be ye warmed and filled, yet give them not these things that are necessary for the body, what shall it profit? So faith also, if it have not works, is dead in itself" (2:15–16). And St. John: "And now, suppose that a man has the worldly goods he needs, and sees his brother go in want; if he steels his heart against his brother, how can we say that the love of God dwells in him?" (1 John 3:17). Perhaps no one has expounded better than St. Paul how corporal works of mercy redound to the glory of God.

> I would remind you of this, He who sows sparingly will reap sparingly; he who sows freely will reap freely too. Each of you should carry out the purpose he has formed in his heart, not with any painful effort; it is the cheerful giver God loves. God has the power to supply you abundantly with every kind of blessing, so that, with all your needs well supplied at all times, you may have something to spare for every work of mercy. So we read, He has spent largely, and given to the poor; his charity lives on for ever. He who puts grain into the sower's hand, and gives us food to eat, will supply you with seed and multiply it, and enrich the harvest of your charity; so

that you will have abundant means of every kind for all that generosity which gives proof of our gratitude towards God. The administration, remember, of this public service does more than supply the needs of the saints; it yields, besides, a rich harvest of thanksgiving in the name of the Lord. This administration makes men praise God for the spirit of obedience which you shew in confessing the gospel of Christ, and the generosity which you shew in sharing your goods with these and with all men; and they will intercede, too, on your behalf, as the abundant measure of grace which God bestows on you warms their hearts towards you. Thanks be to God for his unutterable bounty to us (2 Cor. 9:6–15).

From this you will see how matter can be spiritualized by the fire of love. To put it more plainly, material things can be transmuted into spiritual values in the furnace of divine love. On the other hand, spiritual riches can degenerate into worthless metal if they are spoiled by selfishness and possessiveness. Father Frederick William Faber hits the nail on the head when he says, in *All for Jesus*:

> The Gospel is a law of love, and the Christian life is a life of prayer. As the apostle tells us, we must make intercession for all sorts of men. Indeed, we shall never prosper with the work in our own souls, if we do not strive to advance the interests of Jesus in the souls of others. Many persons complain that they make no way in religion, and that they do not get on with the mortification of their evil passions, their sinful infirmities, and their tiresome self-love. They are just what they were a year ago, and this is disheartening. This often comes to pass, because they are selfish, because they only care to stand by themselves. They do not think they have anything to do with the souls of others, or with the interests of Jesus, or with intercessory prayer; and so they keep on a low level, because they do nothing to merit higher graces.

In the spiritual life as in the natural life, if you inhale you must also exhale. If you only inhale but do not exhale, your chest will soon be swollen into a balloon, and the natural process of respiration will cease. It is well, therefore, to remember, what Christ says, *"Freely have you received, freely give"* (Matt. 10:8). These words apply to all works of mercy, whether corporal or spiritual.

In this connection, I want to remind you again of St. Thérèse's philosophy of empty-handedness. Once a novice said to her, "We are often told that in God's sight the angels themselves are not pure enough. So how can you expect me to be otherwise than full of fear?" The saint replied, "There is but one means of compelling God not to judge us: we must take care to appear before Him empty-handed." "And how can I do that?" asked the novice. She answered, "It is quite simple: lay nothing by, spend your treasures as fast as you gain them. Were I to live to be eighty, I should always be poor, because I cannot economize. All my earnings are immediately spent on the ransom of souls."

Although the contributions of the contemplative to the welfare of mankind are invisible, they are among our greatest benefactors. In the first place, "any soul that uplifts itself uplifts the world," as Madame Leseur says. In the second place, they support with their powerful prayers all the apostolic activities going on in the world. Finally, we should take to heart Christ's words concerning the last days before the end of the world: "And unless those days had been shortened, no living creature would be saved. But for the sake of the elect those days shall be shortened" (Matt. 24:22). If we understood these words in the spirit of faith, we should be more grateful to the contemplatives for their intercessory prayers, for they are surely among the elect. They are not escapists. They are the levers that God designs to use for the uplifting of the world. As St. Teresa of Ávila has said, "To pray for those who are in mortal sin is the best kind of alms-giving."

3. THE MERCIFULNESS OF THE CONTEMPLATIVES

The value of the cloister is so little understood by the world that sometimes it is not regarded even as a charitable institution! I deem it fitting in this connection to reproduce parts of a speech which I made at New Brunswick, New Jersey, on "The Apostolic Mission of Carmel." Of course, what is said of the Carmel is true also of other cloistered orders.

It is not easy to talk about the apostolic mission of Carmel; because it is incidental to its principal mission. The principal mission of Carmel is to be the garden of delights for the Divine Lover, our Lord. The apostolic work is only an effect of the supreme romance between God and the soul in love with God. So long as it remains a garden of delights for the Divine Lover, it will necessarily continue to bear fruit; but as soon as it ceases to be a garden of delights, it will become a barren piece of ground.

The remarkable fruitfulness of the Carmelite apostolate is a spontaneous outflow of the plenitude of contemplation. It flows through hidden channels, and spreads through supernatural means.

Nothing illustrates the inseparable connection between sanctity and apostolic work better than the Canticle of Canticles. There, as you will recall, the Beloved was captivated by the single-heartedness of the Shulamite, who stands as a figure for the Church, for the Blessed Virgin, for the Carmelite, and for any soul in love with God. The beloved addresses the Shulamite in these terms:

> What a wound thou hast made, my bride, my true love, what a wound thou hast made in this heart of mine! And all with one glance of an eye, all with one ringlet straying on thy neck! Sweet, sweet are thy caresses, my bride, my true love; wine cannot ravish the senses like that embrace, nor any spices match the perfume that breathes from thee.... My bride, my true love, a close garden; hedged all about, a spring shut in and sealed! Well-ordered rows of pomegranates, tree of cypress and tuft of nard; no lack there whether of spikenard or saffron, of calamus, cinnamon, or incense-tree, of myrrh, aloes or any rarest perfume. A stream bordered with garden; water so fresh never came tumbling down from Lebanon (4:9–15).

No words can be more beautiful or more fitting than these inspired verses to describe the pure soul of a Carmelite, or any other soul on fire with love. But here is a significant thing: immediately following these verses are the words that the Beloved addresses to the winds:

Arise, north wind!
Come, south wind!
Blow upon my garden,
And let its perfumes be wafted abroad.[2]

From this it will be clear that the apostolic work of Carmel is initiated and receives its increase from the Divine Lover. It is because He is delighted with His garden that He commands the winds to arise and waft its perfumes abroad. One may be so bold as to remark with regard to the Carmelite, that the more exclusively she loves her Divine Lover for and in Himself, and the less she thinks of the fruits of her love, the more fruitful her love, or rather their love, will be. She has been thirsting for Him so intensely that He is bound to impart to her His own thirst, so that He and she will be thirsting with one mighty thirst — for the salvation of souls.

The secret root of the apostolic fruitfulness of the Carmel is, therefore, to be found in these words of St. John of the Cross: "On Mount Carmel God alone and I; God alone in my spirit to enlighten it; God alone in my acts to sanctify them; God alone in my heart to possess it."

In this age of ours, when pragmatism and activism seem to prevail, we cannot too often remind ourselves of what St. John of the Cross said: "An instant of pure love is more precious in the sight of God, and of the soul, and more profitable to the Church than all good works put together." To the ears attuned to the din of the world, these words may sound a little strange. But they constitute the quintessence of Christianity; they are an echo of St. Paul.

Certainly St. John of the Cross does not despise good works, still less apostolic work. Indeed, expressing his approval of it, he took the words of Denys the Areopagite: "Of all divine things, the most divine is to cooperate with God in the salvation of souls." It was because he was a sealed fountain that God made him into a living fountain of water for the irrigation of the gardens. He was such a dynamic apostle precisely because he was so thoroughly

---

[2] William Pouget and Jean Guitton, *The Canticle of Canticles*, trans. Joseph L. Lilly, C. M. (New York: Declan X. McMullen Company, 1948), 183.

detached from all creatures and so single-heartedly attached to God. There is a most touching and characteristic story about the saint related by his elder brother, Francisco de Yepes:

> When Father John of the Cross was in Segovia, and whilst he was Superior there, he sent for me. And I went to see him. When I had spent two or three days in his company, I asked him to let me go. He told me to remain for two or three days longer, that he did not know when we should meet again. It was the last time I saw him. One evening after supper, he took me by the hand and led me into the garden. When we were alone, he said to me: "I wish to tell you something that happened to me with Our Lord. We had a crucifix in the convent, and, one day, when I was standing in front of it, it occurred to me that it would be more suitable to have it in the church. I was anxious to have this crucifix honored not only by the religious, but also by the people. I carried out my idea. After I had placed it in the church as fittingly as I could, and whilst in prayer before it one day, Christ said to me: 'Brother John, ask me for what you wish, and I will give it you, for the service you have done me.' And I said to Him: 'Lord, what I wish you to give me are sufferings to be borne for your sake, and that I may be despised and regarded as worthless!'"[3]

This expresses the very essence of the Carmelite apostolate. The Carmelites love Christ so deeply that they are anxious to see Him loved widely by all. It also explains their love of suffering. They do not love suffering as an end in itself, but as a means. As St. Thérèse of Lisieux says, "When we want to attain an end, we must employ the means, and Jesus having made me understand that He would give me souls by means of the Cross, the more crosses I met with, the more did my attraction for suffering increase."

There is nothing morbid about this love of suffering. The means derive significance and even joyfulness from the end, which is the glory of God. This is why St. Teresa of Ávila could cry to Our Lord with all sincerity, "Let me suffer or let me

---

[3] Bruno de Jésus-Marie, O. C. D., *St. John of the Cross*, trans. Benedictines of Stanbrook (New York: Benziger Brothers, 1932), 133.

die." And because she was so willing to suffer for the love of Our Lord, He, not to be outdone in generosity, gave her the spirit of joy that no man could take from her.

When the mother of Sister Elizabeth of the Trinity was in great anguish at the thought of losing her, Sister Elizabeth wrote: "Your maternal heart should feel a divine joy when you think that the Master has deigned to choose your daughter, the fruit of your womb, to be associated with His great work of redemption, in order that He may suffer in her, as it were, an extension of His Passion. The bride belongs to the Bride-groom. Mine has taken me. He wishes me to be another humanity in which He can still suffer for His Father's glory, to help the needs of His Church."[4]

Not that the Carmelite is insensible to suffering; no, no heart can be more generous and more sensitive than the heart of a Carmelite. If she finds happiness in suffering, it is because she suffers for faith, she suffers in hope, she suffers with love. She knows that "the Cross is the heritage of Carmel," to quote Sister Elizabeth again.

The Carmelite is truly apostolic, and yet she takes to heart the words that Our Lord spoke to the seventy-two disciples when they returned elated from their first missionary trip: "But you, instead of rejoicing that the devils are made subject to you, should be rejoicing that your names are enrolled in heaven" (Luke 10:20). But the Carmelites are more especially privileged, for their names are not only enrolled in heaven, but are put as a seal on the heart and the arm of their Beloved (Cant. 8:6). For their love is "strong as death," and many waters cannot quench it. They are so generous that, having given Him every-thing, including themselves, they feel as though they had given nothing. Is it any wonder, then, that Christ should have given them in return many children throughout the ages? Well can they rejoice and sing with the Shulamite:

> My true love, I am all his; and who but I the longing
> of his heart? Come with me, my true love; for us the
> country ways, the cottage roof for shelter. Dawn shall find

---

[4] Marie-Michel Philipon, O. P., *The Spiritual Doctrine of Sister Elizabeth of the Trinity*, trans. A Benedictine of Stanbrook Abbey (Westminster, MD: Newman Press, 1947), 119.

us in the vineyard, looking to see what flowers the vine has, and whether they are growing into fruit; whether the pomegranates are in blossom. And there thou shalt be master of my love. The mandrakes, what scent they give! Over the door at home there are fruits of every sort a-drying; I put them by, new and old, for my true love to eat (Cant. 7:8–13).

In conclusion, let me remind you of an interesting event that happened when Céline, the beloved sister of St. Thérèse, was on the point of entering the Carmel, fifty-seven years ago. Certainly worldly relatives of theirs were carping at Céline's decision as being extravagant. In one of her most beautiful letters, the little saint wrote to Céline some unforgettable words:

> Nor are we the *lazy* ones, the thriftless ones. Jesus defended us, in the person of Magdalen. He was at table, Martha was waiting upon Him, Lazarus eating with Him and His disciples. Mary never gave a thought to her food, but only how she might give pleasure to One she loved; so she took a vessel filled with perfume of great price and breaking the vessel poured it upon Jesus' head, and all the house was filled with the odor of the ointment, but the Apostles murmured against Magdalen....
>
> It is very much the same with us, the most fervent Christians, the priests, consider that we are too extreme, that we ought to serve with Martha instead of consecrating to Jesus the vessels of our lives with the perfumes contained in them ... but after all, what matter that our vessels are broken, since Jesus is consoled, and since, in spite of itself, the world is forced to awareness of the perfumes they breathe forth, perfumes which serve to purify the poisoned air the world is ever breathing.[5]

Whether we are living in the cloister or in the world, so long as our heart remains a garden of delight for Our Lord, we are, in the words of St. Paul, "the good odour of Christ unto God, in them that are saved and in them that perish. To one indeed the odour of death unto death: but to the others the odour of life unto life" (2 Cor. 2:15–16). And for such offices,

---

[5] *The Collected Letters*, 240–41.

who is sufficient? The Little Flower of Jesus has answered it
for us: *"Tout est grace!"*

4. MERCY AS THE FULFILLMENT OF JUSTICE

When one realizes the great mission of a Christian, one's heart
cannot help leaping for joy and awe. To be a Christian is to be
another Christ, and to be another Christ is to bring good news
to the poor, to proclaim release to the captives, to give sight to
the blind, to set at liberty the oppressed, and to announce the
acceptable year of the Lord. When I think of the saints, I am
often reminded of the following verses of Psalm 83:

> Blessed is the man whose help is from Thee,
> When he has pilgrimages in his heart.
> Passing across a parched valley, they shall make it a
>   source of wells.
> And the first rain shall clothe it with blessings.
> They shall go from strength to strength:
> They shall see the God of gods in Sion.

Like another Christ, they pass through life doing good. Sister
Elizabeth of the Trinity uttered this prayer: "May I be another
humanity added to His own!" I think it is not far from the truth
to say that this has been the wish of all the saints throughout
the ages, and their lives have been marvelous fulfillments of this
single wish.

But this does not mean that their wish has been fulfilled by
dint of their efforts alone; the grace of God has aided them.
God had mercy on them for their mercifulness to others, and
this is why their mercifulness has blossomed forth into such
splendid flowers and borne such rich fruits. Even in this life,
only the saints are happy, because they alone have found the
home for their souls during their very pilgrimage. The more
they love others, the more they are loved by God. They alone
enjoy the life of prayer which is "a bath of love into which the
soul plunges," as St. John Vianney of Ars puts it. "God holds
the interior soul as a mother holds the head of her child in
her hand to cover it with kisses and caresses." Although externally they may suffer all kinds of hardships and afflictions,

internally they are being renewed every day. I can never forget this supremely beautiful expression: "good measure, pressed down, shaken together, running over, shall they pour into your lap." But who are "they"? Not human beings, but the Holy Trinity! The source of their blessings is inexhaustible. This is why it can truly be said of the saints that—

> The more they live for others, the more they have;
> The more they give, the more they receive
> (Lao Tse, 81).

There is a great deal of wisdom in the proverb: "To give to the poor is to lend to God." In fact, Christ has expressly identified Himself with each and every one of our neighbors, so that to serve our neighbor is, not figuratively but actually, to serve Christ Himself. In the remarkable words of St. John Chrysostom, every neighbor of ours is a living altar of Christ. "This altar you can see everywhere, in the streets and in the market-place, and at any hour you may offer sacrifice thereon; for it too is a place of sacrifice." To him, "the stone altar is august because of the Victim that rests upon it: but the altar of almsgiving is more so because it is made of this very Victim. The former is august because, though made of stone, it is sanctified by contact with the body of Christ; the latter, because it is the body of Christ."[6] A similar idea is expressed in the Chinese proverb: "It is better to be kind at home than to burn incense in a distant temple." In the Buddhist classic, *The Dhammapada*, I have found an aphorism which it is well for us to take to heart: "The thoughtless man, even if he can recite a large portion of the law, but is not a doer of it, has no share in the priesthood, but is like a cowherd counting the cows of others."[7]

The subtle and organic relations between love of God and love of our neighbor have been brought out in *The Dialogue* of St. Catherine of Siena, in which God is reported as saying to the saint:

---

[6] Reinhold, *The Soul Afire: Revelations of the Mystics*, 190–91.
[7] F. Max Müller, trans., *The Dhammapada: A Collection of Verses; Being One of the Canonical Books of the Buddhists*, in *The Sacred Books of the East*, vol. 10 (Oxford: Clarendon Press, 1881).

I require that you should love Me with the same love with which I love you. This indeed you cannot do, because I loved you without being loved. All the love you have for Me you owe to Me, so that it is not of grace that you love Me, but because you ought to do so. While I love you with grace, and not because I owe you My love. Therefore, to Me, in person, you cannot repay the love which I require of you, and I have placed you in the midst of your fellows, that you may do to them that which you cannot do to Me, that is to say, that you may love your neighbor as of free grace, without expecting any return from him, and what you do to him, I count as done to Me, which My Truth showed forth when He said to Paul, My persecutor—"Saul, Saul, why persecutest thou Me?" This He said, judging that Paul persecuted Him in His faithful.[8]

This is one of the highest flights in the firmament of Christian mysticism. The lesson is clearly brought home to us: that to be just to God, we must be merciful to men. Our fraternal charity is the fulfillment of our filial piety towards God. When a mother sees her children quarrel with one another, what is more natural than for her to say, "My dear children, if you love me, don't quarrel like this, for it rends my heart to see you hate each other." Now, the heart of God is more merciful than the heart of a mother. Did He not say through Isaias: "Can a woman forget her infant, so as not to have pity on the son of her womb? And if she should forget, yet will not I forget thee" (49:15).

How indispensable the practice of fraternal charity is to the attainment of union with the will of God is clearly brought out by St. Teresa in her treatment of the Fifth Mansions, which seem to me to correspond to the Beatitude of mercifulness. She says:

When I see people very diligently trying to discover what kind of prayer they are experiencing and so completely wrapt up in their prayers that they seem afraid to stir,

---

[8] St. Catherine of Siena, *The Dialogue of the Seraphic Virgin St. Catherine of Siena*, trans. Algar Thorold (Westminster, MD: Newman Bookshop, 1943), 155–56.

or to indulge in a moment's thought, lest they should lose the slightest degree of the tenderness and devotion which they have been feeling, I realize how little they understand of the road to the attainment of union. They think that the whole thing consists in this. But no, sisters, no; what the Lord desires is works. If you see a sick woman to whom you can give some help, never be affected by the fear that your devotion will suffer, but take pity on her: if she is in pain, you should feel pain too; if necessary, fast so that she may have your food, not so much for her sake as because you know it to be your Lord's will. That is true union with His will. Again, if you hear someone being highly praised, be much more pleased than if they were praising you; this is really easy if you have humility, for in that case you will be sorry to hear yourself praised. To be glad when your sisters' virtues are praised is a great thing, and, when we see a fault in someone, we should be as sorry about it as if it were our own and try to conceal it from others.[9]

5. ST. PAUL: THIRSTING WITH CHRIST

It is indeed one of the most wonderful events in the whole history of Christianity that Saul, who kicked against the goad, should after his conversion have been transformed into St. Paul, who was so united with Christ as to thirst with His thirst for the salvation of souls. He was so inebriated with the love of God that he became sober in his dealings with men, in order to be all things to all men. A true contemplative, he could not help being active. The same charity of Christ that made him such a great mystic made him a practical man.

No one, to my knowledge, has given us a truer insight into the character of St. Paul than Cardinal Newman. "There are saints," he said, "in whom grace supersedes nature; so it was not with this great Apostle. In him grace did but sanctify and elevate nature. It left him in the full possession, in the full exercise, of all that was human, which was not sinful. He who had the instant contemplation of the Lord and Saviour, as if he saw Him with his bodily eyes, was nevertheless as susceptible

---

[9] *Works*, 2:262–63.

of the affections of human nature and the influences of the external world, as if he were a stranger to that contemplation. Wonderful to say, he who had rest and peace in the love of Christ, was not satisfied without the love of man; he whose supreme reward was the approbation of God, looked out for the approval of his brethren."

The truth is, with St. Paul, the love of men flows spontaneously and continuously from the love of Christ, as a mighty river flows from a living source. The man who said, "It is now no longer I that live, but Christ lives in me," how could he help thirsting with Christ and feeling in the very depth of his heart: "Who is weak, and I am not weak? Who is scandalized and I am not on fire?" The integrality of his love comes from its sheer integrity. By embracing the One, he embraces all. St. Paul had no use for the "broken cisterns that can hold no water" (Jer. 2:13). He tenaciously kept his soul close to "the fountain of living water." All his apostolic activities flowed directly from the plenitude of contemplation.

Last year I hit upon a poem when I was waiting for the bus. I have outlined these as my ideals of life. Although I myself am very far from attaining these ideals, I think you may profit by the poem.

Ideals of Life

To see the cosmos in a flower;
To live Eternity in an hour;
To find the Transcendent in the ordinary,
    And the One in the many;

To drink the Tao in the cup of duty;
To realize that goodness is beauty.
To taste peace in activity,
    And joy in humility,

To meet Christ in your neighbor,
To feel refreshed in labor.
To be sober and drunk at the same time —
    Sublimely human and humanly sublime.

PART THREE

THE RIPENING OF LOVE

Anyone who has followed *The Spiritual Exercises* of St. Ignatius will be struck by the fact that all the graphic meditations on the Life of Our Lord lead to the prayer: "Take, O Lord, and receive all my liberty, my memory, my understanding, and my whole will, whatever I have and possess. Thou hast given to me all these things; to thee, O Lord, I restore them; all are Thine, dispose of them entirely according to Thy will. Give me Thy love and Thy grace, for these are enough for me." With this begins contemplation and true mysticism.

In the spiritual life, asceticism and mysticism form a continuous whole. In the first period, asceticism predominates, while mysticism lies dormant; in the second period, the two are combined; in the third, mysticism predominates and asceticism flows from it more or less spontaneously.

While in the second period you are more aware of your love for God, in the third you are more aware of God's love for you. Not that you cease to love Him. On the contrary, your love grows immensely; but you have come to see that there can be no comparison between His love and yours. Yours is like a little drop of water, while His is like a boundless sea. A Chinese poet sang of a mother's love:

> Who says that the inch-long heart of a grass
> Can ever requite the sunshine of a whole Spring?

If this is true of a mother's love, what can we say of God's love? This is why the mystics are so overwhelmed by the love of God that they can no longer think of their own love, still less of their other virtues.

In the Canticle of Canticles thrice did the Shulamite announce her love, each time differently. First she said "My beloved to me, and I to my beloved" (2:16). The second time she said, "I to my beloved, and my beloved to me" (6:2). The third time she said, "I to my beloved, and his turning is toward me" (7:10).

As her love grew, she became less and less possessive, more and more possessed. Unless you can say with her, "I to my beloved, and his turning is toward me," your love is not perfect. Formerly you were happy in your own happiness, now you are happy in His happiness. There is no more *tuum* and *meum*, for you are one spirit with Him.

How the mind of a mystic works can be illustrated by an anecdote about St. Thérèse, related by her sister Céline who was one of the novices under her direction:

> I was grieving bitterly over a fault that I had committed. "Take your crucifix," she said, "and kiss it." I kissed the feet.
> "Is that how a child kisses its father? Throw your arms at once around His neck and kiss His face." When I had done so, she continued: "That is not sufficient—*He must return your caress.*" I had to press the crucifix to both my cheeks, whereupon she added: "Now, all is forgotten."[1]

One may wonder how a person can be so audacious and yet remain humble. The answer, perhaps, lies in simplicity. But simplicity is a quality that you can never achieve by your own conscious effort; for it is the work of the Holy Spirit. The Spirit alone can bring to a harmony strains which, humanly speaking, are discordant. Speaking of St. Augustine, Bérulle said, "Consider this great saint; he has, through a singular power from Jesus Christ and by His grace, privileges which are humanly speaking incompatible: he is very learned and very humble, which is rare; he is very speculative and very affective, which is not less rare; and, whereas in most doctors we meet with nothing but knowledge, in this one we find a certain spice of wisdom which gives relish to all he says and has the unusual gift of making the truth pass from the mind to the heart."[2]

The Holy Spirit that dwells in a saint transmutes all his learning, knowledge, virtues and talents into fuel for the fire of love. It is only where the fire is weak that it is liable to be smothered by the fuel. But where the fire is intense, as in a saint, no amount of fuel is too much for it to consume. On the contrary, the more the fuel, the brighter will be the flame.

---

[1] Sainte Thérèse de l'Enfant-Jésus, *Conseils et souvenirs* (Lisieux: Carmel de Lisieux, 1952), 40.
[2] Pourrat, *Christian Spirituality*, 3:341.

But before one can reach such a state, one has to pass through what the spiritual writers call "the dark night of the soul" or "the passive purification of the spirit." This corresponds to that phase of the metamorphosis of the silkworm in which it buries itself in the cocoon and becomes a chrysalis. The Old Man must die completely before the New Man can be formed in you. You must be nailed to the cross with Christ, before you can say with St. Paul, "And I live, now not I; but Christ liveth in me" (Gal. 2:19–20).

Now, to be nailed to the cross is to be suspended between heaven and earth. The Apostles must have felt like that between the Ascension and Pentecost. Christ is gone, and the Holy Ghost has not come, and God is in the clouds.

St. Augustine was probably in this state when he uttered the prayer: "Lord, burn, cut, do not spare on this earth, that Thou mayest spare in eternity." This is virtually Purgatory on earth. But, as nothing stained can enter heaven, and as there are still so many stains in the depths of the soul, it is certainly better to be purified here with merit than hereafter without merit. Egoism and intellectual pride gnaw at the root of our soul like a canker. We have the tendency to become self-righteous and censorious. We are excessively attached to our personal judgment, to our own way of seeing, feeling and willing. We have received so many favors from God that we are tempted to the sin of presumption. St. Teresa of Ávila wrote in her *Interior Castle* (Fifth Mansions, Chapter III):

> A person who takes care not to offend the Lord and has entered the religious life may think he has done everything. But oh, there are always a few little worms which do not reveal themselves until, like the worm which gnawed through Jonas's ivy, they have gnawed through our virtues. Such are self-love, self-esteem, censoriousness (even if only in small things) concerning our neighbours, lack of charity towards them, and failure to love them as we love ourselves. For, although late in the day we may fulfill our obligations and so commit no sin, we are far from attaining a point necessary to complete union with the will of God.[3]

---

[3] *Works*, 2:260–61.

What she says about religious applies to lay apostles as well. "If these stains be not removed by the soap and strong lye of the purgation of this night, the spirit will be unable to come to the purity of the divine union."[4] Therefore, if God sends you great trials, you must endure them patiently and gratefully, trusting blindly that it is for your good that He has sent them. In the meantime, you can cooperate with Him in this purification in an oblique way, by practicing more intensely the virtue of fraternal charity:

> You must do violence to your own will, so that your sister's will is done in everything, even though it may cause you to forgo your own rights and forget your own good in your concern for theirs, and however much your physical powers may rebel. If the opportunity presents itself, too, try to shoulder some trial in order to relieve your neighbour of it. Do not suppose that it will cost you nothing or that you will find it all done for you. Think what the love which our Spouse had for us cost Him, when, in order to redeem us from death, He died such a grievous death as the death of the Cross.[5]

Your fraternal charity will not serve to abate your sufferings. God will sometimes permit even your friends to misunderstand you and scoff at you, to the end that you may no longer seek after human consolations but set your hope on Him alone. But he will never try you beyond your strength, for He will give you the gift of understanding, so that you may perceive the meaning of all that is happening to you and deeply appreciate the ineffable favor of being treated like His Son. St. Teresa was not exaggerating when she wrote in the "Sixth Mansions" of her *Interior Castle:* "The soul is fortified rather than daunted by censure, for experience has shown how great are the benefits it can bring; and it seems to the soul that its persecutors are not offending God, but that His Majesty is permitting this for its great advantage. Being quite clear about this, it conceives a special and most tender love for them and thinks of them

---

[4] *Works,* 1:400.
[5] *Works,* 2:263

as truer friends and greater benefactors than those who speak well of it."[6] Whatever happens, the soul recalls the words of Jesus: "It is I, fear not." It makes no difference whether you only recall these words or actually hear them by way of locution; for visions and locutions and elevations belong to graces *gratis datae*, and are not essential to your sanctification. The essential thing is a perfect confidence in Our Lord. To quote St. Teresa again: "When Our Lord is pleased to have pity upon this soul, which suffers and has suffered so much out of desire for Him, and which He has now taken spiritually to be His bride, He brings her into this Mansion of His, which is the seventh, before consummating the Spiritual Marriage. For He must needs have an abiding-place in the soul, just as He has one in Heaven."[7] Needless to say, where the Son is, there also is the Father, and the Spirit of Love. When the Holy Trinity takes up His abode in you, then you will have peace that surpasses understanding, and joy that no man can take away from you. Furthermore, your devotion to the Sacred Humanity of Christ and to the Blessed Virgin will deepen beyond measure, for no one can truly be united with the Holy Trinity without being convinced of the eminent appropriateness and necessity of the Incarnation. This is the surest sign of true mysticism.

---

[6] *Works*, 2:271.
[7] *Works*, 2:330.

VI

The Dark Night

Blessed are the pure of heart, for they shall see God.

1. THE NEED OF THE PASSIVE PURIFICATION OF THE SPIRIT

In the ultimate sense, our whole pilgrimage here below is but a prelude to heaven. As Frank Sheed has pointed out in his *Theology and Sanity*, this life is a preparation for the next "in the way in which pre-marital purity is a preparation for marriage. At the time it may seem pointless and dreary and even painful: its perfection as preparation is seen only when marriage comes. So with this life as a whole in relation to the next. In a sense we may think of it as the tuning of the instruments, so that it gives only a hint of the glory of the symphony when all instruments are tuned and all are obeying the conductor."[1]

In a relative sense, however, an earlier stage of our spiritual life may be regarded as a tuning up for a later stage. Thus we have seen how the purgative stage prepared for the illuminative; and now we are at the end of the illuminative stage and on the threshold of the unitive, to which belong the three last Beatitudes, namely Purity of Heart, Peace, and Joy. It is on the step of Purity of Heart that occurs what spiritual writers call "Spiritual Betrothal," while "Spiritual Marriage," or "Transforming Union," takes place on the last two steps.

In a way, the Beatitude of Purity of Heart recapitulates all the preceding steps, by refining and intensifying them and bringing them into an organic unity. It is here that your multiplicities are simplified, your stiffness is softened, your love becomes disinterested and sincere, and your self-distrust and trust in God are perfected.

In the first stage, the Christian was awakened from the erring ways of the world and from his own sins. In the second,

---

[1] Frank Sheed, *Theology and Sanity* (London: Sheed & Ward, 1946), 325.

he has been going from virtue to virtue. Now the time has come for him to be awakened from the sense of virtuousness. To be awakened from "virtuousness" does not mean to cease to practice virtues. No, it means that you no longer practice them as onerous duties or as meritorious actions, but as something incidental to Love; for you have come to an experimental knowledge of Christ's words: "My yoke is sweet, and My burden light." The truth is, He is our yoke-fellow, and bears the greater path of our burden.

The Beatitude of Purity of Heart, with which we are dealing now, covers two phases: the first is the "passive purification of the spirit," which is a painful phase; the second is the beginning of the unitive life, which is a sweet phase.

You may be wondering how it is that, having advanced as far as the step of mercifulness, and having already produced so much fruit, you have again to undergo a period of intensive purification, walking through, as it were, the valley of the shadow of death, before you can attain the unitive stage, where your Beloved will feast you before the eyes of your foes. The answer is to be found in the words of Christ: "I am the true vine, and My Father is the vine-dresser. Every branch in Me that beareth no fruit He will take away; *and every vine that beareth fruit He will purge it, that it may bring forth more fruit*" (John 15:1-2). Thus, it is not because you are not lovable or have not borne fruit that you need purification, but rather because you are lovable and have borne fruit that God prunes you in order to make you more lovable and more fruitful. In the earlier stages you have been purged of your mortal sins and venial sins so far as you could see. But there are still a great deal of superfluities, imperfections and hidden faults in you, which only God can see and only He can uncover one by one to your interior eye.

You delight in goodness, but you have still too strong a desire that good be done by you or in your way. You are still attached to your own judgment, to your particular good works and devotions. Your manner of seeing, willing and acting is still excessively personal. When God sends you trials, at first you feel as though you were plunged into icy water without a forewarning. You could easily understand when He chastised you for your sins. But this time you seem to be chastised for your virtues! Has not your apostolic work been prospering? Have you not borne fruit for God? Do you not love Him with your whole heart and with your whole soul? How is it that God seems to be frustrating His own work? At times you even fear that you are forsaken by God and you are tempted to despair. Even your friends have deserted you; the very souls whom you have led to God turn against you. You are *like a pelican in the wilderness, like an owl in the ruins. You are sleepless and you lament like a bird all alone on the housetop* (Ps. 101). You cry with the Psalmist:

> Save me, O God: for the waters are come in even unto
>   my soul.
> I stick fast in the mire of the deep: and there is no sure
>   standing.
> I am come into the depth of the sea: and a tempest
>   hath overwhelmed me.
> I have laboured with crying: my jaws are become
>   hoarse: my eyes have failed, whilst I hope in my
>   God (Ps. 68).

You do not, of course, rebel against God. In your past experience God has shown such tenderness to you that you cannot doubt for a single moment His goodness. Even now you feel at the depth of your heart that all that is happening to you is for your good, that the fault must be yours, although you do not understand exactly what your fault is. With the Psalmist you say:

> Yet who can know his faults?
> From my hidden offences cleanse me.

Like a patient who feels sick to death but who does not know exactly what ails him, you set your hope on the Divine Physician. Willy-nilly, you will find yourself echoing the *De Profundis:*

> Out of the depths I have cried to thee, O Lord: O Lord,
>   hear my voice.
> Let thy ears be attentive to the voice of my supplication.

If thou, O Lord, wilt mark iniquities: Lord, who shall
stand it?

For with thee there is merciful forgiveness: and by reason of thy law, I have waited for thee, O Lord.

My soul hath relied on his word: my soul hath hoped
in the Lord.

From the morning watch even until night, let Israel
hope in the Lord (Ps. 129).

This period is truly like a nightmare; in fact, the Divine
Physician is cleansing you of your hidden faults and preparing
you for union with Him. By the gift of understanding which
He infuses into you, He makes you realize many secret truths
of which you had no idea before, especially two main lessons.
First, with regard to your past, He wants you to understand
that all your interior attainments and exterior accomplishments
are due to His grace rather than to your own merit. You must
understand, as Bishop Sheen puts it, "that even the desire for
God came from God and that the fires that burned within itself
were kindled from the hearth of God." It is not enough for
you to have just a nodding acquaintance with this truth; you
must be utterly convinced of it and feel it in your very bones.
Even the great Apostle St. Paul, whose apostolic work was for
the most part carried out after he had reached the unitive state,
had to learn this lesson before he reached it, and in the very
heart of his works of mercy. As he said in his Second Epistle to
the Corinthians, "Make no mistake, brethren, about the trial
which has been befalling us in Asia; it was something that
overburdened us beyond our strength, so that we despaired of
life itself. Indeed, for ourselves we could find no outcome but
death; so God would have us learn to trust, not in ourselves,
but in him who raises the dead to life." (1:8-9).

Secondly, with regard to your future, God wants you to
understand once for all and never to forget that no one can
be pure enough to be united to Him, so that, if you are admitted to the state of union, it will be a sheer gift from Him, just
as all your virtues and your good works have been sheer gifts
from Him. On this point again St. Paul has spoken in the spirit
of absolute denudation:

And lest the greatness of the revelations should exalt me, there was given me a sting of my flesh, an angel of Satan, to buffet me. For which thing, thrice I besought the Lord that it might depart from me. And He said to me: My grace is sufficient for thee: for power is made perfect in infirmity. Gladly therefore will I glory in my infirmities, that the power of Christ may dwell in me. For which cause I please myself in my infirmities, in persecutions, in distresses, for Christ. For when I am weak, then am I powerful (2 Cor. 12:7–10).

2. SOME ILLUSTRATIONS
(a) The Elder Brother of the Prodigal Son

Many understand the conversion of the prodigal son; but few have ever thought about the need of a more radical conversion on the part of the elder son. You remember how, when the elder son returned from the field, he heard music and dancing in the house, how after he had learned the reason for this feasting he was angered and would not go in, and his father came out to entreat him to come in and he answered: "Behold, for so many years do I serve thee and I have never transgressed thy commandment: and yet thou hast never given me a kid to make merry with my friends. But as soon as this thy son is come, who hath devoured his substance with harlots, thou hast killed for him the fatted calf. But he said to him: Son, thou art always with me and all that I have is thine. But it was fit that we should make merry and be glad: for this thy brother was dead and is come to life again; he was lost and is found" (Luke 15:29–32).

From this it is clear that the elder son's love for his father was far from being pure. By his words he revealed unconsciously how mercenary his love was, and how little he prized the company of his father. He thought more of the fatted calf than of his father! Outwardly he was as pure as the angels, inwardly he was as proud as the devil! The younger brother has returned; when will the elder brother return? The younger brother has awakened from his sins; when will the elder brother awaken from his "virtues"? In this connection I am reminded of a passage in Cardinal Newman's *The Church of the Fathers*, which embodies such a wonderful flash of insight that I want to share it with you:

> When sinners repent and turn to God, and, by way of showing sorrow and amendment, subject themselves to voluntary mortifications, the memory of what they were, and the prospect of judgment to come, are likely, it is hoped, to keep them from spiritual pride. But when a young and innocent girl, whose baptismal robe the world has not sullied, takes up a self-denying life in order to be nearer to God, and to please Him more entirely, who does not see the danger she is in of self-importance and self-conceit — the danger of forgetting that she is by nature a sinner, as others, and that whatever she has of spiritual excellence, and whatever she does praiseworthy, is entirely of God's supernatural grace?[2]

For such a soul, it is well to remember what Lao Tse said:

> High virtue is unaware of its virtuousness,
> Therefore it has virtue.
> Low virtue is never free from virtuousness,
> Therefore it has no virtue.

His greatest disciple Chuang Tze has expounded the idea more fully:

> The truly great man does not injure others, but does not credit himself with charity and mercy. He seeks no gain, but does not despise the servants who do. He strives not for goods, but does not pique himself on modesty. He asks for help from no man, but is not proud of his self-reliance, neither does he look down upon the greedy. He acts differently from the vulgar crowd, but does not set store by his own eccentricities (Chapter 17).

(b) The Sorrows of the Shulamite

You remember that, in the last chapter, it was stated that it is more blessed to give than to receive. At the present step, we

---

[2] John Henry Newman, *The Church of the Fathers* (London: Burns and Lambert, 1842), 272.

no longer think in terms of giving, because we have come to understand that our very giving is a receiving, for every perfect gift comes from above, and we have really given nothing, since nothing actually belongs to us. This is what Christ meant when He said: "Let not thy left hand know what thy right hand has done"; for the right hand knows very well that it has given nothing of its own. Love is enlightened by truth, and becomes pure. "If man should give all the substance of his house for love, he shall despise it as nothing" (Cant. 8:7).

But it is not easy to arrive at this state, even if you are far advanced in the practice of virtues. In fact, your very attachment to your virtues may be an impediment to your complete union with your Beloved. As an illustration take the following verses of the Canticle of Canticles:

> I lie asleep; but oh, my heart is wakeful! A knock on the door, and then my true love's voice: Let me in, my true love, so gentle, my bride, so pure! See, how bedewed is this head of mine, how the night rains have drenched my hair! Ah, but my shift, I have laid it by: how can I put it on again? My feet I washed but now; shall I soil them with the dust? Then my true love thrust his hand through the lattice, and I trembled inwardly at his touch. I rose up to let him in; but my hands dripped ever with myrrh; still with the choicest myrrh my fingers were slippery, as I caught the latch. When I opened, my true love was gone; he had passed me by. How my heart had melted at the sound of his voice! And now I searched for him in vain; there was no answer when I called out to him. As they went the city rounds, the watchmen fell in with me, that guard the gates; beat me, and left me wounded, and took away my cloak. I charge you, maidens of Jerusalem, fall you in with the man I long for, give him this news of me, that I pine away with love (5:2–8).

Now here is an interesting case worth our study. There can be no question that she loved him with her whole heart. But when he came knocking and begging her to open to him, for his head was filled with dew and his locks with the drops of the night, she hesitated, and her reasons were:

Ah, but my shift, I have laid it by:
how can I put it on again?
My feet I washed but now;
shall I soil them with the dust?

This shows that she had her own precious ideas about purity and other virtues which were not those of her Beloved. That is why she had to go through a painful period of purification called the "passive Night of the Spirit" in order that she might see eye to eye with her Beloved.

(c) Mary and Martha

Another case in point is that of Martha. The one thing necessary to our spiritual life is union with Christ. But Martha was impeded from that union by her preconceived ideas of virtue.

> Now it came to pass as they went, that he entered into a certain town: and a certain woman named Martha received him into her house. And she had a sister called Mary, who, sitting also at the Lord's feet, heard his word. But Martha was busy about much serving. Who stood and said: Lord, hast thou no care that my sister hath left me alone to serve? Speak to her therefore, that she help me. And the Lord, answering, said to her: Martha, Martha, thou art careful and art troubled about many things: but one thing is necessary. Mary has chosen the best part, which shall not be taken away from her (Luke 10:38–42).

Why did Christ rebuke Martha? Certainly not for her serving! Christ would have been an ungrateful guest indeed if He was angry at the hospitality of Martha. No, it was not for her hospitality but for her uncharitable attitude towards Mary that Christ dealt her the gentle rebuke. To serve Him is a commendable thing; but to be absorbed in one's service in such a way as to be anxious and troubled about many things is to prefer the means to the end, the end being always to please the guest. There are many ways of pleasing the guest; and it was Martha's fault to think that her own way was the only way, and that her sister was wasting her time by sitting idly at the Lord's feet and listening to His word. By her complaint against her sister, her very hospitality became the height of inhospitality. Thus, her love was not yet pure. Christ's words must have awakened her from the lethargy of self-virtuousness, they must have broadened her mental horizons immensely by uplifting her from the cave of narrow prejudice. She continued to render the same services, but with a different spirit. She continued to cook the same dishes for her Lord, but they must have tasted infinitely better than before, because they were now prepared with the sauce of pure love. While doing her work, she must have felt grateful to her sister for keeping Him company and thus making Him feel at home. And her sister Mary would feel all the more grateful to her for making her contemplative life possible.

I wish all active workers for Christ would take to heart the words I have already quoted of St. John of the Cross: "An instant of pure love is more precious in the sight of God and of the soul, and more profitable to the Church than all good works put together." For love is the end of everything. On the other hand, let the contemplatives remind themselves of their indebtedness to the active workers. They must remember that they can eat oats because other members of the Mystical Body of Christ are eating a lot of hay. Let them ponder the following quotation from St. Gregory the Great:

> There are some, who if they have made ever so small a beginning in spiritual conversation, on observing that their rulers fix their thoughts only on worldly and temporal objects, begin to blame the disposition of supreme Providence as if they were improperly appointed to rule, since they set an example of worldly conversation. But because the power of office cannot be exercised without our engaging in worldly cares, therefore Almighty God frequently imposes the burden of rule on hard and laborious hearts, in order that the tender minds of spiritual men may be released from worldly cares: in order that the one may be more safely concealed from the bustle of the world, the more willingly the others employ themselves in worldly anxieties.

And how properly this is ordered in the Church by divine appointment is signified by the very construction of the tabernacle. For Moses is commanded by the voice of God to weave curtains of fine linen and scarlet and blue, for the covering of the Holy of Holies within. And he was ordered to spread, for the covering of the tabernacle, curtains of goats' hair and skins, to sustain the rain and wind and dust. What then do we understand by the skins and goats' hair, with which the tabernacle is covered, but the gross minds of men, which are sometimes hard though they be placed on high in the Church by the secret judgements of God? And because they are not afraid of being employed in worldly concerns, they must needs bear the winds and storms of temptation which arise from the opposition of this world. But what is signified by the blue, scarlet, and fine linen, but the life of holy men, delicate, but brilliant? And while it is carefully concealed in the tabernacle under goats' hair and skins, its beauty is preserved entire. For in order that the fine linen may shine, the scarlet glitter, and the blue be resplendent with azure brilliance, the skins and the goats' hair endure the rains, the winds, the dust from above. They then who advance in great excellence within the bosom of holy Church, ought not to despise the doings of their rulers, when they see that they are engaged in the business of the world. For that they penetrate in safety into secret mysteries, is owing to the help of those who buffet with the storms of this world from without. For how would the fine linen retain the grace of its brightness, if the rain were to touch it? Or what splendour or brightness would the scarlet or blue display, should the dust light on and defile them? Let the strong texture of the goats' hair, then, be placed above, to resist dust; and the brightness of the blue, fitted for ornament, be placed beneath. Let those who are engaged in spiritual pursuits alone, adorn the Church. Let those guard her, who are not wearied with the labours of the world. But let not him who now gleams with spiritual brightness within holy Church, murmur against his superior, who is employed in worldly business. For if thou glitterest securely within, like scarlet, why dost thou blame the goats' hair with which thou art protected? (Mor. XXV 38, 39).[3]

There is no question that contemplation constitutes the kernel of spiritual life, but it takes more than the kernel to make the whole fruit.

According to St. Catherine of Siena, a man whose love for God is pure and generous finds joy in everything; he does not make himself judge of the servants of God or of any rational creature, "but rejoices in every condition and in every manner of holiness which he sees, saying: 'Thanks be to Thee, Eternal Father, Who hast in Thy House many mansions.' And he rejoices more in the different ways of holiness which he sees, than if he were to see all travelling by one road, because, in this way, he perceives the greatness of (God's) Goodness become more manifest, and thus rejoicing, draws all the fragrance of the rose."[4]

I have laid so much emphasis on this point, because it is of paramount importance to understand that one is only a part of the whole, that just as "each of us has one body, with many different parts, and not all these parts have the same function; ... so we, though many in number, form one body in Christ, and each acts as the counterpart of another" (Rom. 12:4). Unless the mind is made to understand this and other secrets of Divine dispensation, the heart cannot be pure. In one word, unless you have the mind of Christ, you will not possess His heart. And I may add that the mind of Christ is nowhere better expressed than in the liturgy of the Church. The earmark of genuine mysticism is its catholicity, which means that it must include three elements, namely, the Institutional, the Rational, and the Intuitive-Emotional.[5] Unless the soul sees herself as a member of the Mystical Body of Christ, she will not be whole.

---

[3] Butler, *Western Mysticism*, 236–37.
[4] St. Catherine of Siena, *The Dialogue*, 216–17.
[5] Baron Friedrich von Hügel, *The Mystical Element of Religion as Studied in Saint Catherine of Genoa and Her Friends*, vol. 2 (New York: E. P. Dutton, 1923), 387–96.

3. THE SPIRIT OF CATHOLICITY

The heart cannot be perfectly pure unless the mind sees clearly.
It was Evelyn Underhill who said:

> The greatest mystics have not been heretics but Catho-
> lic saints. In Christianity the "natural mysticism' which,
> like "natural religion," is latent in humanity, and at a
> certain point of development breaks out in every race,
> came to itself; and attributing for the first time true and
> distinct personality to its Object, brought into focus the
> confused and unconditioned God which Neoplatonism
> had constructed from the abstract concepts of philos-
> ophy blended with the intuitions of Indian ecstatics,
> and made the basis of its meditations on the Real. It
> is a truism that the chief claim of Christian philosophy
> on our respect does not lie in its exclusiveness but in
> its Catholicity: in the fact that it finds truth in a hun-
> dred systems, accepts and elucidates Greek, Jewish, and
> Indian thought, fuses them in a coherent theology, and
> says to speculative thinkers of every time and place,
> "Whom therefore ye ignorantly worship, Him declare I
> unto you."[6]

The mysticism of the Catholic saints is so comprehensive
and profound, because it is not composed of irresponsible
fancies of isolated individuals, but is rooted in theoretical
and moral theology, and is constantly nourished by the Spirit
through the living channels of grace. In other words, it is not
purely intuitive-emotional, but is balanced and supported by
the institutional and rational elements.

(a) Institutional Element

Concerning the institutional element, let it be remembered
that a Christian is an integral member of the Mystical Body of
Christ. It is said that blood is thicker than water; but the Blood
of Christ is thicker than the blood of man. If, therefore, we
love Christ, we must necessarily love each other, being of the
same Blood. In His Priestly Prayer, Christ prayed not only for

---

[6] Underhill, *Mysticism*, 105–6.

His disciples, but for all of us who believe in Him. To quote
His own words:

> And not for them only do I pray, but for them also who
> through their word shall believe in me: that they all may
> be one, as thou, Father, in me, and I in thee: that they
> also may be one in us: that the world may believe that
> thou hast sent me. And the glory which thou hast given
> me, I have given to them: that they may be one, as we
> also are one: I in them, and thou in me: that they may
> be made perfect in one: and the world may know that
> thou hast sent me, and hast loved them, as thou hast also
> loved me (John 17:20–23).

Certainly no relation can be closer than that of Christians
to one another. They are bound to one another by a triple tie.
As St. Paul says, "Now there are diversities of graces, but the
same Spirit; and there are diversities of ministries, but the
same Lord; and there are diversities of operations, but the
same God, who worketh all in all" (1 Cor. 12:4–6). Since they
form one body, it is little wonder that "if one member suffer
anything, all the members suffer with it, or if one member
glory, all the members rejoice with it" (1 Cor. 12:26).

It is most important to note that to be a member of the
Mystical Body does not obliterate your personality. On the contrary, you will realize your personality only in the community.
As Christ says, "He that abideth in me, and I in him, the same
beareth much fruit; for without me you can do nothing. If
anyone abide not in me, he shall be cast forth as a branch, and
shall wither, and they shall gather him up, and cast him into
the fire, and he burneth" (John 15:5–6).

In his Encyclical Letter *Mystici Corporis Christi*, Pope Pius XII
has brought out the distinction between the Mystical Body and
a physical body:

> Whereas in a physical body the principle of unity joins
> the parts together in such a way that each of them com-
> pletely lacks a subsistence of its own, on the contrary in
> the Mystical Body the cohesive force, intimate though it
> is, unites the members with one another in such a way

that each of them wholly retains his own personality. A further difference is seen if we consider the mutual relation between the whole and each individual member; for in any living physical body the sole final purpose for which each and every individual member exists is for the benefit of the whole organism, whereas any social structure of human beings has for its ultimate purpose, in the order of utilitarian finality, the good of each and every member, inasmuch as they are persons. Therefore—to return to our subject—as it was for the eternal salvation of us all that the Son of the Eternal Father came down from heaven, so it was in order to obtain and secure the beatitude of immortal souls that He founded the Body of the Church and enriched it with the divine Spirit, according to the words of the Apostle: "All things are yours; and you are Christ's; and Christ is God's." For as the Church is fashioned for the benefit of the faithful, so it is destined for the glory of God and Jesus Christ whom He has sent.

It is only as a member of the Mystical Body of Christ that one becomes fully a person, in whom the Holy Spirit makes His abode. For the reception of the Spirit, so essential to the inner life, is conditioned on faith in Christ and on incorporation in His Body, of which He is the Head and the Holy Spirit is the Heart. As Father John Oesterreicher has said:

All that the mystics are, they are through the Church, as rivulets drawing from that mighty stream whose fountainhead is Christ. They could not know the incomprehensible and ineffable God were it not for Him, the "revelation which has a definite date," and Him they could not hear were it not for the Church, who is His voice resounding till the end of time. It is she who communicates to them aspiration for the union with God, as it is her dogma which—far from stifling the inner life—enkindles it. Because their path is beaconed by the light of faith, the mystics can proceed on their arduous journey to direct experience of God.... The beginning and growth of their inner life is owed, they themselves attest, to the sacraments, those

vessels of love in which matter, otherwise retarding the
movements of the Spirit, becomes His chariot.[7]

If we grasp this point, we can easily see the important function that the Liturgy plays in the development and enrichment
of our inner life. The Holy Spirit breathes in the liturgical
prayers, so they are your own prayers in the degree in which
He breathes in you. Thus, they do not lose their freshness
and spontaneity, no matter how many times they have been
repeated. It is only where love and understanding are lacking
that your prayers become mechanical and lifeless. Then your
silence is awkward, your speech nothing but lip-service, and
liturgical prayers become so many vexatious repetitions. All
depends upon your interior dispositions. For sincerity is the
soul of prayer. When you are sincere, the dictates of your
heart become liturgical, and the liturgical prayers flow from
your heart, so that whenever you hear the priest say, *Sursum
corda,* you will joyfully answer, *Habemus ad Dominum;* and
whenever he says, *Gratias agamus Domino Deo nostro,* you will
be ready heart and soul to respond, *Dignum et justum est.* To
my mind the highest prayer consists in an understanding and
wholehearted *Amen* to all the prayers of the Church. Who but
the Holy Ghost could ever have suggested such a prayer as:
"O God, who in a wonderful manner didst create and enno-
ble human nature, and still more wonderfully hast renewed
it; grant that by the mystery of this water and wine, we may
be made partakers of His divinity who vouchsafed to become
partaker of our humanity, Jesus Christ Thy Son, our Lord"?
And who but the Spirit of Love could have uttered a *Felix culpa?*
We need not multiply instances; we need only say that anyone who does not recognize the voice of the Holy Spirit in the
prayers of the Church cannot be of the Spirit and therefore
cannot be a genuine mystic. As Romano Guardini remarks
in *The Spirit of the Liturgy,* "Only a system of life and thought
which is truly Catholic—that is to say, actual and universal—
is capable of being universally adopted, without violence to the

---

[7] John M. Oesterreicher, *Walls Are Crumbling* (New York: Devin-Adair
Company, 1952), 40.

individual. Yet there is an element of sacrifice in such adoption. Each one is bound to strive within himself, and to rise superior to self. Yet in doing so he is not swallowed up by, and lost in, the majority; on the contrary, he becomes more independent, rich, and versatile."[8] We may add that an individual becomes a person only by being a member of a community. No one can acquire universality except by accepting limits. It was by incarnation that God became man; so it is by incarnation — that is, incorporation in His Mystical Body — that a man can be deified. As Christ is the Way of God to man, so is He the Way of man to God. The realization of this truth is the beginning of all mystical insights.

(b) Rational Element

Theology is to contemplation what the scaffolding is to a building. In the words of Fr. Garrigou-Lagrange:

> The more theology progresses, the more, in a sense, it has to conceal itself; it has to disappear very much as St. John the Baptist disappears after announcing the coming of our Lord. It helps us to discover the deep significance of divine revelation contained in Scripture and Tradition, and when it has rendered this service, it should stand aside. In order to restore our cathedrals, to set well-hewn stones into their proper place, it is necessary to erect a scaffolding; but when once the stones have been replaced, the scaffolding is removed and the cathedral once more appears in all its beauty. In a similar way theology helps us to demonstrate the solidity of the foundations of the doctrinal edifice, the firmness of its construction, the proportion of its parts; but when it has shown us this, it effaces itself to make place for that supernatural contemplation which springs from a faith enlightened by the gifts of the Holy Spirit, from a faith that penetrates and savours the truths of God, a faith that is united with love.[9]

---

[8] Romano Guardini, *The Spirit of the Liturgy* (London: Sheed and Ward, 1930), 67–68.
[9] Réginald Garrigou-Lagrange, O. P., *The Three Ways of the Spiritual Life* (Westminster, MD: Newman Press, 1948), 47.

If we think that we can dispense with the scaffolding in the early stages of our spiritual life, we shall never be able to erect the cathedral. On the other hand, if we mistake the scaffolding for the cathedral, our spiritual life will be stultified. It should be noted, however, that the disappearance of the scaffolding does not mean the disappearance of rationality; it should rather mean that whatever rationality there is in the scaffolding has been absorbed into the cathedral. For example, a contemplative does not, certainly, forget about the Credo. On the contrary, he penetrates more deeply into the mysteries, so that every iota of the Credo becomes in his mind vibrant with meaning. In fact, originality in the spiritual life does not so much consist in the discovery of new truths as in the sounding of new depths of old truths. One's spiritual life is an organism, of which dogmatic theology constitutes the skeleton and mystical life forms the flesh and blood. Without reason and dogma, mysticism is apt to be a monster. Without mysticism and contemplative, affective life, dogmatic theology and discursive reasoning are apt to be like a sapless tree. We are too prone to forget that St. Thomas himself was one of the greatest mystics of all times.

The airplane can fly precisely because it is built according to the laws of physics. A mystic can be truly united with God only if he follows strictly the laws of reason and the principles of metaphysics. This may be called *intellectual asceticism*, which, together with *moral asceticism*, must be passed through *before one can hope to be a temple of the Holy Spirit or a sanctuary of the Blessed Trinity*. Only an unleavened bread can be fully leavened by the Holy Spirit. In mystical parlance, you must tame the Green Lion before you can give it wings.

When one is a true mystic, one is no longer afraid of reason; on the contrary, one realizes the important function that reason performs in the whole of the spiritual life. Reason fulfills a negative function in an active way, while contemplation fulfills a positive function in a passive way. Both the negative and the positive, the active and the passive, are equally indispensable to our spiritual perfection, which is a joint enterprise between God and ourselves, between grace and nature.

There is a close analogy between the spiritual life and the art of poetry. It was the mystical poet Coventry Patmore who said, "The quality of all emotion which is not ignoble is to boast of its allegiance to law."[10] Alice Meynell has likewise remarked, "Those who have nothing to say clamor for large license in which to say it, and hence the *vers libre*. Those who have something to say cling to the order and discipline of bonds valuing that voluntary obedience which is the force of art, literature, morals, religion and politics."[11] There is a deep meaning in these words. In every field of human endeavor, superlative excellence is attained only by the harmonious cooperation of reason and intuition. In jurisprudence, for instance, nothing is more interesting than to study how law and equity, justice and mercy, rigidity and fluidity, complement each other in the formation of any living juridical order. So in the spiritual life, there is also an orderly subordination of passions and emotions to reason, and of reason to grace. As Patmore observes, "the spirit of man is like a kite which rises by means of those very forces which seem to oppose their rise; the tie that joins it to the earth, the opposing winds of temptation, and the weight of earth-born affections which it carries with it into the sky" (*Aurea Dicta*, XII).

(c) The Intuitive-Emotional Element

The intuitive-emotional element of our spiritual life belongs, by way of appropriation, especially to the Holy Spirit. Where the Spirit of Love is, there is the liberty and wisdom of the children of God. All virtues are reduced to Love. "Temperance is love surrendering itself wholly to Him who is its object; fortitude is love bearing all things gladly for the sake of Him who is its object; justice is love serving only Him who is its object, and therefore rightly ruling; prudence is love making wise distinctions between what hinders and what helps itself" (St. Augustine, *De Moribus Eccl.* XV). So far, you have cultivated these virtues in order to discipline your heart and your mind

---

[10] Coventry Patmore, *Mystical Poems of Nuptial Love*, ed. Rev. Terence L. Connolly, S. J. (Milwaukee: Bruce Publishing Company, 1949), 155.
[11] Ibid.

and to prepare yourself for pure love. Now you are in a position to follow the counsel of St. Augustine, "Love, and do anything you like." Formerly, you had to struggle upstream until you should reach the source; now, having got at the source, you can glide downstream, although you must always be alert and hold the rudder fast. Formerly you had to acquire with persevering efforts the moral habits; now these habits are engrafted on love and are enlivened by the Spirit. You begin to understand the deep meaning of St. Paul's eulogy of love: "Love is patient, is kind: love envieth not, dealeth not perversely, is not puffed up, is not ambitious, seeketh not her own, is not provoked to anger, thinketh no evil: rejoiceth not in iniquity, but rejoiceth with the truth: beareth all things, believeth all things, hopeth all things, endureth all things" (1 Cor. 13:4–7).

One of the surest signs that you are possessed by the Holy Spirit is that every experience puts you in mind of the words of Christ and of the Holy Scripture. When you see a flower, your heart will leap for joy and echo the words of Christ: *"not even Solomon in all his glory was arrayed as one of these"* (Matt. 6:28). When you hear the song of a bird, you will probably say: "I wish I could sing so beautifully of the mercies of God." When you see the sunrise, you will probably remember some such words as: "Who is she that cometh forth as the morning, fair as the moon, bright as the sun, terrible as an army set in array?" (Cant. 6:9). Thus you will be thinking of the Blessed Virgin. When you are so fortunate as to lead a sinner back to Christ, so that you weep for joy and gratitude, you will be reminded of His words that "there shall be joy before the angels of God upon one sinner doing penance" (Luke 15:10). You will also be comforted in the thought that the joy that you are feeling now is akin to that of the angels. When you have done a good turn to your neighbor, and met with nothing but ingratitude, you will probably say, "This serves me right, O Jesus. I am but an unprofitable servant." When you see a man of weak faith, you will deal with him patiently and with delicate hands, remembering: "A bruised reed he will not break, and a smoking flax he shall not extinguish" (Matt. 12:20). When you read the accounts of the heroic martyrdoms, which are happening even now in

China and other countries, can you help recalling the promise of Christ: "But when they shall deliver you up, take no thought how or what you are to say; for it shall be given you in that hour what you are to speak. For it is not you that speak, but the Spirit of your Father that speaketh in you" (Matt. 10:19–20).

In short, if everything lifts your heart to God and recalls to your mind the words of Christ, you may be sure that the Holy Spirit is dwelling in you. Whether in prosperity or adversity, you will rejoice in God: in the former, because it probably gives you more scope for glorifying Him and leading more souls to Him; in the latter, because it certainly makes you resemble His Son, the Man of Sorrows. Thus you are practically emancipated from all the vicissitudes of life. Then you can truly say with Paul, "For I have learned, in whatsoever state I am, to be content therewith. I know both how to be brought low, and I know how to abound (everywhere and in all things I am instructed): both to be full and to be hungry: both to abound and to suffer need. I can do all things in him who strengtheneth me" (Phil. 4:10–13). Truth alone has made you free.

4. THREE DEGREES OF PURITY OF HEART

The first degree of purity of heart consists in utter sincerity in our thoughts, words, and actions. "Let your speech be yea, yea: no, no" (Matt. 5:37). This sincerity comes from the realization that although we may deceive men and even ourselves, we can never deceive God, who is omnipresent and omniscient. Christ said: "Beware ye of the leaven of the Pharisees, which is hypocrisy. For there is nothing covered that shall not be revealed: nor hidden that shall not be made known" (Luke 12:1–2). One of the most beautiful psalms sings of the omniscience and omnipresence of God:

> Lord, Thou hast proved me, and known me,
> Thou hast known my sitting down and my rising up.
>
> Whither shall I go from thy spirit?
> Or whither shall I flee from thy face?
>
> If I ascend into heaven, thou art there:
> If I descend into hell, thou art present (Ps. 138).

Speaking of Christ as the Second Person of the Holy Trinity, St. Paul wrote a magnificent passage in his Epistle to the Hebrews: "For the word of God is living and effectual and more piercing than any two-edged sword and reaching into the division of the soul and the spirit, of the joints also and the marrow: and is a discerner of the thoughts and intents of the heart. Neither is there any creature invisible in his sight: but all things are naked and open to his eyes, to whom our speech is" (4:12–13). To know this and to act in the light of this knowledge is to walk in the presence of God. If we reach this degree of purity of heart, we shall see God in all things. In the words of Garrigou-Lagrange: "Even here on earth, the Christian will, in a sense, see God in his neighbor, even in souls that at first seem opposed to God. The Christian will see God in Holy Scripture, in the life of the Church, in the circumstances of his own life, and even in trials, in which he will find lessons on the ways of Providence as a practical application of the Gospel. Under the inspiration of the gift of understanding, this is the true contemplation which prepares us for that by which, properly speaking, we shall see God face to face, His goodness and His infinite beauty. Then all our desires will be gratified, and we shall be inebriated with a torrent of spiritual delights."[12]

The second degree consists in the candid acknowledgement of our own impurity and an entire trust in the power of God to cleanse us within and without. David certainly knew how to pray when he said:

> Create a clean heart in me, O God,
> And renew a right spirit within me (Ps. 50:12).

One of the most touching scenes in the Gospel is the cure of a leper: "And when he was come down from the mountain, great multitudes followed him. And behold, a leper came and adored him, saying: Lord, if thou wilt, thou canst make me clean. And Jesus stretching forth his hand, touched him, saying: I will. Be thou made clean. And forthwith his leprosy was cleansed" (Matt. 8:1–3). If only we had the faith of the

---

[12] Garrigou-Lagrange, *Three Ages*, 1:170.

leper and besought him to cleanse our heart, our heart would be made clean.

However, let us always remember what St. Paul says: "For God, who commanded the light to shine out of darkness, hath shined in our hearts, to give the light of the knowledge of the glory of God, in the face of Christ Jesus. But we have this treasure in earthen vessels, that the excellency may be of the power of God and not of us" (2 Cor. 4:6–7).

The third degree consists in our single-hearted and loving attention to the Holy Trinity dwelling in the center of our soul. This may be called the contemplation of Divine Immanence, whereas the first degree is that of Divine Transcendence. As Louis Lallement says, "When the heart is thoroughly cleansed, God fills the soul and all its powers, the memory, the understanding and the will, with His holy presence and love. Thus purity of heart leads to union with God, and no one ordinarily attains thereto by other means."[13] This seems to be the meaning of what the Psalmist says:

> Light springs forth for the just,
> And gladness for the upright of heart.

Christ Himself has said to us, "The light of your body is your eye. If your eye be single, your whole body shall be lightsome." The right interpretation of this passage seems to be this: if your interior eye contemplates with singleness of purpose the Divine Guest within you, your whole personality will be radiant with His glory. In fact, this is what St. Paul says: "The Spirit we have been speaking of is the Lord; and where the Lord's spirit is, there is freedom. It is given to us, all alike, to catch the glory of the Lord as in a mirror, with faces unveiled; and so we become transfigured into the same likeness, borrowing glory from that glory, as the spirit of the Lord enables us" (2 Cor. 3:17–18). Here is a mystery. We do not see God; but we reflect Him as in a mirror. In this life, to see God is to be looked upon by God and to be happy for it. Now the soul can sing to her Spouse:

---

[13] Lallemant, *Spiritual Doctrine*, 81.

Despise me not,
For, if thou didst find me swarthy,
Now canst thou indeed look upon me,
Since thou didst look upon me
And leave me in grace and beauty.[14]

Christ Himself has clearly indicated the signification of seeing Him during our life on earth. During the Last Supper, Christ spoke to His disciples some words which mystified them. He said: "A little while and you shall behold me no longer; and again a little while and you shall see me, because I go to the Father." The disciples were puzzled by these words. "We do not know," they said among themselves, "what He is saying." But Christ knew that they wanted to ask Him, and He said to them: "You inquire about this among yourselves because I said, 'A little while and you shall not behold me, and again a little while and you shall see me.' Amen, amen, I say to you, that you shall lament and weep, but the world shall rejoice; and you shall be made sorrowful, but your sorrow shall be turned into joy. A woman, when she is in labour, hath sorrow, because her hour is come; but when she hath brought forth the child, she remembereth no more the anguish, for joy that a man is born into the world. So also you now indeed have sorrow; but *I will see you again, and your heart shall rejoice; and your joy no man shall take from you*" (John 16:16–22).

I would like to bring out two points for your special attention. First, there is a difference between "beholding" and "seeing." In the original Greek text, the word for "beholding" is θεωρεπέ, while that for "seeing" is ὄχεσθέ. The former has to do exclusively with physical vision, while the latter has a more general connotation, including spiritual insight and interior experience. So the whole sentence may be paraphrased as "A little while and you will no longer see me physically, and again a little while you will see me spiritually." This leads us to the second point. The words: "but I will see you again, and your heart shall rejoice, and your joy no man shall take from you"—these words are meant to explain the clause: "and

---

[14] *Works*, 2:367.

again a little while you shall see me." From this it is as clear
as daylight that, during this life, to see Him means to be seen
and looked upon by Him and to be filled with interior joy.
In other words, to see Him does not mean to have a vision,
either physical or mental, of Him; it means rather to have an
experimental knowledge of Him.

Let us go a step further. We must remember that Christ
is not only True Man, but also True God. So you cannot see
Him without at the same time seeing also the Father and
the Holy Spirit. This is indeed the Mystery of mysteries. We
must again let the Divine Word speak for Himself, for no one
can speak as well. "I will not leave you orphans," He said, "I
will come to you. Yet a little while and the world seeth me
no more. But you shall see me: *because I live, and you shall live.*
In that day you shall know that I am in my Father: and you
in me and I in you. He that hath my commandments and
keepeth them; he it is that loveth me. And he that loveth me
shall be loved of my Father: and I will love him and manifest
myself to him." At this point, one of His disciples, St. Jude,
raised an appropriate question. "Lord," he said, "How is it
that thou wilt manifest thyself to us, and not to the world?"
The answer of Christ was: "If anyone love me, he will keep my
word. And my Father will love him: and we will come to him
and make our abode with him. . . . These things have I spoken
to you, abiding with you. But the Paraclete, the Holy Ghost,
whom the Father will send in my name, he will teach you all
things, and bring all things to your mind, whatsoever I shall
have said to you" (John 14:18–26).

To keep His word is to see Him. And here is the tremendous
word of this tremendous Lover: "This is my commandment,
that you love one another, as I have loved you" (15:12). So, my
dear friends, love is the essence of contemplation, which in
turn reinforces love. "Love knocks and enters," writes Hugh
of St. Victor, "but knowledge stands without."

We do not see God in this life as the blessed in heaven see
Him. But neither do we see our own souls; and He is the Soul
of our souls, He is your *You*, and my *Me*. The pure soul, even
while on earth, is like the heavenly city that "hath no need

of the sun nor of the moon, to shine in it. For the glory of God hath enlightened it: and the Lamb is the lamp thereof" (Apoc. 21:23).

The beatitude of purity of heart is the most crucial stage in our spiritual pilgrimage. It marks the transition between the second stage and the third. It is the age of what Dionysius calls "translucent darkness." St. John of the Cross was referring to this when he said that "one of the great favours that God grants fleetingly [to the soul] in this life is to give it to understand so clearly and to feel so deeply concerning God, that it is able to understand clearly that it cannot understand or feel at all; for in some manner the soul is like those who see Him in Heaven, where those that know Him the best understand the most distinctly the infinitude that they still have to understand, while those that see Him least perceive less clearly than those that see most how much they have yet to see."[15] The soul no longer understands anything distinctly, but it "approaches God more nearly by not understanding than by understanding." It has been plunged into a dark night. It no longer sees the near objects, but it sees the stars on the firmament not visible during the day. In this way its faith, hope and love are purified and strengthened. When this happens, one may be sure that the Holy Spirit is already dwelling in the center of his soul. One is reminded of the promise of Christ: "He who believes in Me, as the Scripture says, *From within him shall flow rivers of living water.*" Compared with this living water, all particular kinds of knowledge and acts of understanding are like so many broken cisterns that can hold no water.

---

[15] *Works*, 2:227.

VII

Peace of Soul

Blessed are the peacemakers, for they shall be called the children of God.

1. PEACE AND THE SWORD

Christ is the Prince of Peace. At His birth a multitude of the heavenly host was heard praising God and saying: "Glory to God in the highest, and on earth peace among men of good will" (Luke 2:13–14). On the eve of His Passion, He said to His disciples: "Peace I leave with you, my peace I give unto you; not as the world giveth do I give unto you" (John 14:27). And yet Christ also said: "Do not think that I came to send peace upon earth; I came not to send peace, but the sword" (Matt. 10:34). This is one of the greatest paradoxes of Christianity, and we have to deal with it before we can understand the Beatitude of the Peacemakers.

Peace is not compromise. It is based upon Truth, and no one who adulterates Truth or the word of God can ever attain real peace. The life of a Christian is a continual warfare against his three enemies: the worldly philosophy of life, the temptations of Satan, and the inborn evil inclinations of the old self. So long as we live, we can never be absolutely immune from these influences. We must always watch and pray, that we may not enter into temptation (Matt. 26:41). In this life, then, only relative peace can be attained; and even this can only be maintained on the condition of our ever-watchfulness. Like a soldier on the battlefield, a Christian should sleep with his armor on and with the sword for a pillow. And the better armed he is, the more soundly and peacefully he can sleep. This, I think, is the reason why Christ, who has given us His peace, has also furnished us with His sword, the sword of Truth. These two things are so far from contradicting each other that the sword is actually an indispensable means toward the attainment and maintenance of true peace.

Peace cannot be sought after directly, for it is the fruit of perfection. And since, as St. Bernard says, "Man's perfection does not consist in being perfect, but in constantly striving to be perfect," it is clear that the peace of soul that we enjoy on earth can only be a relative thing, and that its degrees correspond to the degrees of perfection, that is to say, to the degrees of Love and Wisdom. On the other hand, so long as we are constantly striving to be perfect, Christ will never fail to give the peace which He promised. Seek God, and you will have peace; seek peace apart from God, and you will have war upon war.

The peace that Christ has promised us is not a dead peace but a living peace. Speaking of the Roman soldiers, Tacitus wrote: "*Solitudinem faciunt et pacem appellant*" — they make a desert and call it peace. This is certainly not the kind of peace that Christ has given us. No, the peace that we receive from Him is like a river, full, overflowing, and rising from the very depths of our hearts. In the Apocalypse, St. John saw "a river of the water of life, clear as crystal, coming from the throne of God and of the Lamb." Interpreted with reference to our spiritual life, the throne of God and of the Lamb may be said to be our soul, and the river of the waters of life, clear as crystal, coming from that throne, may be taken as a symbol of the interior peace which the Holy Spirit has infused into us. Christ Himself has said: "He who believes in me, from within him there shall flow fountains of living water, as the Scripture says." Apropos of this, St. John commented: "Now this he said of the Spirit, which they should receive, who believed in him" (John 7:38-39). The Holy Spirit is the Spirit of peace, and where He is, there is peace.

2. CHRIST THE PEACEMAKER

We can now deal with the Beatitude: "Blessed are the peacemakers, for they shall be called the children of God."

In the absolute sense, there is only one Peacemaker, and that is Christ. In the first place, He makes peace between God and man. "Because," as St. Paul says, "in him, it hath well pleased the Father, that all fulness should dwell: and through him to reconcile all things unto himself, making peace through the blood of his cross, both as to the things that are on earth, and the things that are in heaven" (Col. 1:19-20). In one of the most splendid of the Messianic Psalms (84), we find the following verses:

> I will hear what the Lord God will speak in me:
>> for he will speak peace unto his people:
> And unto his saints: and unto them that are
>> converted to the heart.
> Surely his salvation is near to them that fear
>> him: that glory may dwell in our land.
> Mercy and truth have met each other: justice
>> and peace have kissed.
> Truth is sprung out of the earth: and justice
>> hath looked down from heaven.
> For the Lord will give goodness: and our earth
>> shall yield her fruit.
> Justice shall walk before him: and shall set his
>> steps in the way (9-14).

It is only in the Word Incarnate that mercy and truth have embraced each other, and justice and peace have kissed each other. It is only in Him that heaven and earth have united. It is only in the way of His steps that salvation is to be found.

In the second place, He not only reconciles man to God, but also reconciles all races of mankind with one another. This double reconciliation, one vertical and the other horizontal, is perfectly symbolized by the Cross. As St. Paul says, "He is our bond of peace; he has made the two nations one, breaking down the wall that was a barrier between us, the enmity there was between us, in his own mortal nature. He has put an end to the law with its decrees, so as to make peace, remaking the two human creatures as one in himself; both sides, united in a single body, he would reconcile to God through his cross, inflicting death, in his own person, upon the feud" (Eph. 2:14-16).

No peacemaking can be so thoroughgoing as that of Christ. This is not the job of a man but that of a God. Just as He is the only-begotten Son of God, He is the only Peacemaker, cosmically speaking. It is only by virtue of the fact that He gives us His peace that we can make peace, just as it is only by virtue of the fact that He gave us the power of becoming sons of God that we can partake of the divine nature.

3. THE SOURCE OF PEACE

Nothing conduces to peace more than self-abandonment to the good pleasure of God. In *The Imitation of Christ* there is a conversation between Christ and the Disciple. Christ says: "Son, suffer Me to do with thee what I will: I know what is best for thee." The Disciple answers: "Lord, what Thou sayest is true; Thy care over me is greater than all the care I can take of myself…. If Thou wilt have me to be in darkness, be Thou blessed; and if Thou wilt have me to be in light, be Thou again blessed; if Thou vouchsafest to comfort me, be Thou blessed; and if it be Thy will I should be afflicted, be Thou always equally blessed" (III, 17).

When King David was in danger of death, he could still sing as if he were in the greatest security and prosperity:

> Many say: "Who will show us good things?"
> Lift up the light of Thy countenance upon us, O Lord!
> Thou hast given greater joy to my heart
> Than that of men who abound in corn and wine.
> As soon as I lie down, I fall asleep in peace.
> For thou alone, O Lord, makest me to dwell in security
>   (Ps. 4:7–9).

Is it not clear that his inward peace flowed from his absolute confidence in God?

Christian peace is rooted in faith, nourished by hope, and perfected by love. It is a peace which is not achieved directly by man, but given by God to those who are disposed to receive it. It issues from the indwelling of the Holy Trinity in the center of the soul. When you realize that God has found a home in your spirit, which is the apex of your soul, you feel a security which the world can neither give nor take away. Perfect love casts out fear, as St. John says; and the reason is that "God is love and he who abideth in love abideth in God, and God in him" (1 John 4:16). If God abides in you, you have nothing to fear any longer, seeing that "Greater is he that is in you, than he who is in the world" (1 John 4:4). Then you will feel with St. Paul: "If God be for us, who is against us?" "Who then shall separate us from the love of Christ? Shall tribulation? or distress? or famine? or nakedness? or danger? or persecution? or the sword?.... For I am sure that neither death, nor life, nor angels, nor principalities, nor powers, nor things present, nor things to come, nor might, nor height, nor depth, nor any other creature shall be able to separate us from the love of God, which is in Christ Jesus our Lord" (Rom. 8:31–39). Not even the atom bomb or cosmic rays can separate us from the love of God. Teresa of Ávila wrote:

> You know that God is everywhere; and *this is a great truth*, for, of course, wherever the king is, or so they say, the court is too: that is to say, wherever God is, there is Heaven. No doubt you can believe that, in any place where His Majesty is, there is fulness of Glory. Remember how St. Augustine tells us about his seeking God in many places and eventually finding Him within himself. Do you suppose it is of little importance that a soul which is often distracted should come to understand this truth and to find that, in order to speak to its Eternal Father and to take its delight in Him, it has no need to go to Heaven or to speak in a loud voice? However quietly we speak, He is so near that He will hear us: we need no wings to go in search of Him but have only to find a place where we can be alone and look upon Him present within us. Nor need we feel strange in the presence of so kind a Guest; we must talk to Him very humbly, as we should do to our father, ask Him for things as we should ask a father, tell him our troubles, beg Him to put them right, and yet realize that we are not worthy to be called His children.[1]

It is all as simple as that. But you say, How do I know that God is delighted with me? Well, if you have anything on your conscience, go to Confession immediately and begin

---

[1] *Works*, 2:114.

anew. Don't be afraid of the priests. They are, every one of them, potentially great sinners like you and me. A holy priest, Msgr. John Murphy, who died not long ago, said in a speech on the occasion of his Golden Jubilee something to the following effect: "Those of you who have known me well during these years must think that you are witnessing a miracle today!" The holier you are, the greater glory you give to God; for His power is revealed in the very distance between your present attainment and what you might have been without His grace.

The point I am driving at now is that we must have full confidence in God and His priests, who are endowed with the power to bind and to loosen. God cannot abide in your soul when you are in mortal sin. He is, of course, still present in other modes, but *abide* in you He can not. And if He is not at home in you, you will not be at home with yourself nor anywhere else. You make a hell for yourself and for others who have to live with you. Get up as quickly as you fall, and you will recover all your past merits. You will not have to start the journey all over again; you will continue from the point where you fell. According to St. Thomas and other theologians, grace may even revive in the soul in a higher degree than before its loss, provided the contrition is fervent enough. This is the way to peace, because it will restore the indwelling of the Holy Trinity within us.

For those of us who are of scrupulous conscience, I want to quote the words of Father Alfred Wilson, C. P., in his *Pardon and Peace*: "Love of God is the most effective antidote to sin. If we love God intensely, we shall hate sin effectively. If you desire to hate and conquer sin, try to forget all about yourself for a time, and study instead and ponder the goodness and lovableness of God, so that your soul may be refreshed by basking in the sunshine of His love. Get out into the fresh air of God's love and away from the fetid atmosphere of the repulsive and depressing dungeons of self and sin."[2]

---

[2] Alfred Wilson, C. P., *Pardon and Peace* (London: Sheed and Ward, 1946), 55.

Nothing pleases God like a contrite heart coupled with a loving confidence in His mercy. If our conscience accuses us, then be sorry, go to Confession, and resolve to do better hereafter. Thus our peace of mind is restored. If we have the testimony of a good conscience, then, as St. John says, "we have confidence towards God, and whatsoever we shall ask, we shall receive of him, because we keep his commandments, and do those things which are pleasing in his sight" (1 John 3:21–22).

Obviously, it is foolish to think that sins need not be repented of and absolved, that they will dissolve themselves in the course of time. The longer they stay on your conscience, the worse trouble they will make, leaving you no peace and nagging at you constantly like a shrewish housewife. Can you enjoy peace of mind with a buzzing bee in your ear? But it is even worse to entertain a mean idea of God, as though He were not a forgiving Father. I have come across a very significant story in Father Mateo Crawley-Boevey's book *Jesus, King of Love*. As it has helped me, it may also help some of my readers:

> One of the many souls who regard Jesus as a tyrant was preparing to make a general Confession for the hundredth time. Restlessly, she spent the days of her retreat writing down the sins of her whole life. She neither meditated nor prayed, she was entirely absorbed in an examination which stifled her. At last she went into the Confessional. She read out the list of her sins, repeating and explaining over and over again, in fear and trembling. When at length she thought she had finished, a voice was heard which gently and very sadly said: "You have forgotten something very important."
>
> "I thought I must have," she answered, terror-stricken, and hastily prepared to read it all again.
>
> "Your sin is not in your notes," continued the Voice, "and it offends me much more than all that you have said. Accuse yourself of *lack of trust*."
>
> The voice moved her to the depths and she sought to ascertain if it was really her confessor's. The Confessional was empty! Jesus had come to give her a supreme lesson.[3]

---

[3] Mateo Crawley-Boevey, *Jesus, King of Love* (Fairhaven, MA: National Center of Enthronement, 1933), 123.

The reason why I have tarried so long on this theme of sin is that it alone separates us from God and makes us unhappy. A psychiatrist once told me that psychiatry arises in the wake of the failure of religion to hold the modern mind. I am one of those who believe that a right cooperation between the priest and the psychiatrist will produce most salutary results. (See on this subject Father James H. VanderVeldt and Dr. Robert P. Odenwald, *Psychiatry and Catholicism*, and Father John S. Kennedy's review of the book in *The Advocate*, July 5, 1952.) Our hearts are made for God, and they will know no peace until they rest in Him. This fundamental insight of St. Augustine should form the starting-point for psychiatry. To repeat Léon Bloy's dictum: "There is but one sorrow, and that is to have lost the Garden of Delight, and there is but one hope and one desire, to recover it." But just because the true goal of life is missed and some other goals have been set up in its stead, the soul of man has created for itself a veritable maze of by-paths and dead ends, in which it is lost. Therefore, it is highly desirable for the priest to know something about complexes, fixations, neuroses, conflicts, parataxes, in order to help to lead the soul back from where it has lost itself to the Main Road to happiness or, as the case may require, recommend his penitent to a reliable psychiatrist. More important still, the priest may prevent the soul, by timely advice, from straying from the Way of Love into the labyrinth of self-analysis.

So far, we have dealt only with the conditions for peace. Now we can try to learn something about the actual state of peace from the writings of the saints who speak to us from their experience. We are now dealing with the summit of the Mount of Love; but, I am still far, far away from that sublime state, may God help me in re-telling what I have learned from the saints themselves.

In the Beatitude of peace we find the consummation of our adopted sonship *vis*-à-*vis* God. The power to be children of God was given us at Baptism by virtue of sanctifying grace. As our knowledge and love grow, and thanks to the infused virtues and the gifts of the Holy Spirit, this power is increasingly actualized in us, until we are ready to receive the spirit of adoption

whereby we cry "Abba, Father," so that the Spirit Himself testi-
fies that we are children of God (Rom. 8:14). As Christ Himself
has said, "If anyone love me, he will keep my word, and my
Father will love him, and we will come to him and will make
our abode with him" (John 14:23). This "we" apparently means
the Father and the Son. But just before that, He had also said,
"If you love me, keep my commandments. And I will ask the
Father and he will give you another Paraclete, that he may abide
with you for ever: the Spirit of Truth, whom the world cannot
receive, because it seeth him not, nor knoweth him. But you
shall know him; because he shall abide with you, and shall be
in you" (John 14:15–17). It is clear from the two passages that
it is on the condition that we love Christ and keep His word,
actively and contemplatively, that God will be delighted with us,
and will send the Holy Spirit into us; and that it is only when
we possess the Holy Spirit that the Father and the Son come to
us and make Their abode in us. Now, making Their abode in us
means more than the transitory visits we used to receive from
Them in the earlier stages; it means Their permanent dwelling
in us. God is at home in us, and we are at home in God. Only
then do we feel true security and that peace which surpasses
understanding, together with that joy that no man can take
away from us. Because of the element of permanence, the saints
like to speak of this state in terms of Spiritual Marriage, seeing
that it belongs to marriage to be indissoluble — "for better, for
worse, for richer, for poorer, in sickness and in health." The
only difference is that in the case of Spiritual Marriage it is
always for the better, and never for the worse, and that instead
of saying "till death doth us part," we should say "till death
doth us truly unite." On this point Henri Bergson has written something which shows a profound insight: "When critics
reproach mysticism with expressing itself in the same terms as
passionate love, they forget that it was love which began by pla-
giarizing mysticism, borrowing from it its fervor, its raptures, its
ecstasies: in using the language of a passion it had transfigured,
mysticism has only resumed possession of its own."[4]

---

[4] Henri Bergson, *The Two Sources of Morality and Religion*, trans. R. Ashley
Audra and Cloudesley Brereton (New York: Macmillan, 1935), 30–31.

This state is so wonderful that, according to St. John of the Cross, no one ever enters it without being confirmed in grace. St. Teresa is less positive, but even she, speaking of herself in the third person, has this to say: "She has great confidence that God will not leave her, and that, having granted her this favour, He will not allow her to lose it. For this belief the soul has good reason, though all the time she is walking more carefully than ever, so that she may displease Him in nothing."[5]

It will be interesting to study how St. Teresa was brought into this state. As is well known, she compares the soul to a castle that has seven groups of mansions. The seventh represents the innermost center of the soul, where the Blessed Trinity dwells. The first three groups of mansions correspond in the main to the first three Beatitudes, although she did not consciously think of them and did not refer to them. The fourth and the fifth correspond to the Beatitudes of justice and mercifulness. The sixth corresponds to the Beatitude of purity of heart; and the seventh to the Beatitudes of peace and joy in the midst of sufferings. I have been struck by this correspondence, but I am not surprised, because Christ is the source of all wisdom, and no spiritual book which attempts to sketch the growth of love can deviate widely from the order that He Himself has outlined. The doctrine of the indwelling of the Blessed Trinity is also based upon His own teachings.

According to St. Teresa, the seventh is God's own mansion; and in order to be admitted to this mansion and to enjoy the Divine friendship, you have to pass through all the outer mansions, beginning with the first: for all the mansions lead to the center. After a most stormy period (in the Sixth Mansions), the soul is brought finally to the haven. St. Teresa tells us how it happened to her:

> Our good God now desires to remove the scales from the eyes of the soul, so that it may see and understand something of the favour which He is granting it, although He is doing this in a strange manner. It is brought into this Mansion by means of an intellectual

---

[5] *Works*, 2:332.

vision, in which, by a representation of the truth in a particular way, the Most Holy Trinity reveals Itself, in all three Persons. First of all the spirit becomes enkindled and is illumined, as it were, by a cloud of the greatest brightness. It sees these three Persons, individually, and yet, by a wonderful kind of knowledge which is given to it, the soul realizes that most certainly and truly all these three Persons are one Substance and one Power and one Knowledge and one God alone; so that what we hold by faith the soul may be said here to grasp by sight, although nothing is seen by the eyes, either of the body or of the soul, for it is no imaginary vision. Here all three Persons communicate Themselves to the soul and speak to the soul and explain to it those words which the Gospel attributes to the Lord—namely, that He and the Father and the Holy Spirit will come to dwell with the soul which loves Him and keeps His commandments.[6]

It is important to note that here was no vision, properly speaking, but an intuitive insight and awareness. In other words, faith borders on knowledge and conviction. "Each day,' she continues to tell us, "this soul wonders more, for she feels They have never left her, and perceives quite clearly, in the way I have described, that They are in the interior of her heart— in the most interior place of all and in its greatest depths. So although, not being a learned person, she cannot say how this is, she feels within herself this Divine companionship."[7]

But at this point it may be asked, since God is omnipresent, what is the difference between His "Indwelling" and presence in the ordinary sense. This may be answered in the words of St. Thomas:

> For God is in all things by His essence, power, and presence, according to His one common mode, as the cause existing in the effects which participate in His goodness. Above and beyond this common mode, however, there is one special mode belonging to rational nature wherein

---

[6] *Works*, 2:331–32.
[7] *Works*, 2:332.

> God is said to be present as the object known is in the
> knower, and the beloved in the lover. And since the ratio-
> nal creature by its operation of knowledge attains to God
> Himself, according to this special mode God is said not
> only to exist in the rational creature, but also to dwell
> therein as in His temple (*S. T.*, Ia, Q. 43, A.3).

St. Thomas further says that the reason why the Divine Person
is in the rational creature in a new mode is none other than
sanctifying grace. In short, God is present in all things as their
preserving cause; but He is present, really and substantially, in
the just soul in a new and higher manner because of sanctifying grace. He is not like a beloved friend who is absent, but
really present and united to the substance of the soul, which
St. Teresa calls "the spirit."

It may further be asked: Since the Holy Trinity dwells in
the soul in the state of grace, why do the spiritual writers not
talk about Their indwelling in connection with beginners, but
only when they deal with the unitive state? The explanation
is to be found in what St. Teresa writes about the First Mansions of *The Interior Castle*. "You must note," she says, "that the
light which comes from the palace occupied by the King hardly
reaches these first Mansions at all; for, although they are not
dark and black, as when the soul is in a state of sin, they are to
some extent darkened, so that they cannot be seen (I mean by
anyone who is in them); and this not because of anything that
is wrong with the room, but rather because there are so many
bad things—snakes and vipers and poisonous creatures—
which have come in with the soul that they prevent it from
seeing the light."[8] This underlines the necessity of purifications
and of our continuous progress toward the innermost mansion,
so that we may come closer and closer to the light. It is only
when we arrive at the center of our soul where God abides that
we shall be perfectly happy, because this is our ultimate goal
on earth, which is the normal prelude to heaven.

No one has sung better of the happiness of this state than
St. John of the Cross:

---

[8] *Works*, 2:210.

How gently and lovingly thou awakenest in my bosom,
Where thou dwellest secretly and alone!
And in thy sweet breathing, full of blessing and glory,
How delicately thou inspirest my love.[9]

Of course, as St. John has pointed out, it is not God that has awakened, it is the soul who has been awakened to the presence of God within her. This is the third and final awakening of the soul as a wayfarer. The effects of this awakening are so wonderful that no words can describe them adequately.

But one sure effect of this awakening is that the soul is granted some glimpse of the providential plan of redemption and of the mystery of the Incarnation. In the first stage of our spiritual life, Christ led us back to the Father; in the second stage, we tried our best to follow Christ as our exemplar; in this stage, the Holy Spirit imprints on us the likeness of that exemplar. If, then, we are really conformed to His image, we should possess His interior dispositions toward the Father and His boundless love for humanity. We should pray with Sister Elizabeth of the Trinity, "May I be another humanity added to His own"; and utter the great vow in the words of the Little Flower that we shall spend our heaven by doing good on earth. So long as we see a single human being who has not found his way home, the Spirit of Love will not permit us to rest. It is only by working unceasingly for the benefit of souls that we can keep the peace that Christ has given us. So long as we remain wayfarers, let us spend our *haven*, so to speak, by serving as life-boats on the tempestuous ocean of the world. For where Christ is, there is our haven.

4. SPIRITUAL MARRIAGE AS A SYMPHONY

(a) Fire and Water

In the state of Spiritual Marriage, the soul burns inwardly and sweetly through love and wisdom. Love is like fire and wisdom is like water. The soul that has entered into this state is at once fiery and watery. It is like a hot spring where, as Tu Fu writes,

---

[9] *Works*, 3:207.

A hidden fire is constantly warming up a crystal spring,
Bubbling forth its waters to swell a quiet crevice.

For, as Shakespeare says,

Love's fire heats water, water cools not love.

St. Teresa of Ávila has spoken of four degrees of prayer in
terms of the different ways of watering the garden of the soul.
Let me quote an interesting passage from her *Life*:

> The beginner must think of himself as of one setting out
> to make a garden in which the Lord is to take His delight,
> yet in soil most unfruitful and full of weeds. His Majesty
> uproots the weeds and will set good plants in their stead.
> Let us suppose that this is already done — that a soul has
> resolved to practise prayer and has already begun to do so.
> We have now, by God's help, like good gardeners, to make
> these plants grow, and to water them carefully, so that they
> may not perish, but may produce flowers which shall send
> forth great fragrance to give refreshment to this Lord of
> ours, so that He may often come into the garden to take
> His pleasure and have His delight among these virtues.
>
> Let us consider how this garden can be watered, so
> that we may know what we have to do, what labour it
> will cost us, if the gain will outweigh the labour and for
> how long this labour must be borne. It seems to me that
> the garden can be watered in four ways: by taking the
> water from a well, which costs us great labour; or by a
> water-wheel and buckets, when the water is drawn by a
> windlass (I have sometimes drawn it in this way; it is less
> laborious than the other and gives more water); or by a
> stream or a brook, which waters the ground much better,
> for it saturates it more thoroughly and there is less need
> to water it often, so that the gardener's labour is much
> less; or by heavy rain, when the Lord waters it with no
> labour of ours, a way incomparably better than any of
> those which have been described.[10]

You will note that the first two ways correspond to the first
two stages of the spiritual life, while the third and fourth

---

[10] *Works*, 1:65.

belong to the unitive stage. It should also be noted that the Lord sends the sunshine of love as well as the showers of wisdom.

(b) Senses and Spirit

The soul in peace is a divine symphony, where all kinds of counterpoints are harmonized. Even "the lower and sensual part of the soul has now been reformed and purified and has been brought into conformity with the spiritual part, so as not only not to be hindered from receiving spiritual blessings, but rather to be prepared for them, for, according to its capacity, it is already a partaker of these which it now has" (St. John of the Cross).[11] Although "this sensual part with its faculties has not the capacity to taste essentially and properly of the spiritual blessing, either in this life or in the next" yet "through a certain overflowing of the spirit they receive in the senses refreshment and delight therefrom, whereby these senses and faculties of the body are attracted into that interior recollection wherein the soul is drinking of spiritual blessings."[12] These words from St. John of the Cross are but a commentary upon the following verses of the Psalm of the Good Shepherd:

> Thou anointest my head with oil;
> My cup brims over.

It is because God showers upon the soul His choicest blessings so as to fill its inmost part, that they overflow even to the outmost parts of the body. Then the soul can indeed say with David: "My heart and my flesh have rejoiced in the living God" (Ps. 83). This corresponds to loving God with one's whole strength, the last degree of love.

There is an interesting parallel to this happy condition even in the purely moral and rational sphere. Take, for instance, what Mencius said:

> What belongs by his nature to the superior man cannot
> be increased by the largeness of his sphere of action,

---

[11] *Works*, 2:404.
[12] Ibid., 406.

nor diminished by his dwelling in poverty and retire-
ment....What belongs to his nature are love, justice,
propriety and knowledge. These are rooted in his heart;
they manifest themselves as a mild harmony appearing
in the countenance, a rich fullness in the back. They
spread even to the four limbs; and the four limbs seem
to understand without being told (*Works*, Book VII, Part
I, Chapter 21).

(c) Action and Contemplation

The soul in the state of peace is Mary and Martha in one. St.
Paul wrote to the Corinthians: "For whether we be transported
in mind, *it is* to God: or whether we be sober, it is for you. For
the charity of Christ presseth us..." (2 Cor. 5:13). Happy are
the saints who joyfully drink sober inebriation of the Spirit!
They can be quiet without being quietists, and active without
being activists; for there is activity in their quiet and quiet
in their activity. They are quiet because even when they find
themselves in a crowd, they are still aware of the Holy Trinity dwelling in the very center of their souls. They are active
because souls on fire with love can never remain inactive. In
such souls love and reason work together harmoniously. As St.
Gertrude said, "O most loving Lord, if it is true that my love
can keep place near Thee, I hope that reason will suffice to
guide my exterior conduct, that I may love Thee more freely."
I can think of no better words to describe such a happy soul
than the third verse of the first Psalm:

> And he is like a tree which is planted near the running
>   waters
> Which shall bring forth its fruit in due season, and his
>   leaf shall not fall off,
> And whatsoever he shall do shall prosper (1:3).

How is it that "whatsoever he shall do, shall prosper"? Because
he does nothing by his own will, but always according to the
will of God, so that what he does is really the doing of God,
and what he prays is really the prayer of the Holy Spirit within
him.

Brother Lawrence of the Resurrection has shown us how

one can be contemplative and active at the same time. "The time of action," he said, "does not differ at all from that of prayer; I possess God as tranquilly in the bustle of my kitchen—where sometimes several people are asking me different things at one time—as if I were on my knees before the Blessed Sacrament."[13]

(d) Sweetness and Bitterness

It is written that perfect love casts out fear; but it does not cast out pain in this life. Commenting on the last line of the following stanza of his *Spiritual Canticle*:

> The breathing of the air,
> The song of the sweet philomel,
> The grove and its beauty in the serene night,
> *With a flame that consumes and gives no pain—*

St. John of the Cross remarks, "This cannot be save in the beatific estate." As for the transformed souls in this life, "although they have become perfected by the fire, it has nevertheless consumed them and reduced them to ashes. This comes to pass in the soul that in this life is transformed with perfection of love; for, although there is conformity, still the soul suffers some degree of pain and detriment; first, because of the beatific transformation which the spirit still lacks; and secondly, because of the detriment which is suffered by weak and corruptible sense from its contact with the fortitude and loftiness of love that is so great."[14]

Nor does perfect love cast out sorrows. The soul in this state bears within her bosom the sorrows of all ages and the joys of eternity. The soul is feasting, as it were, upon a delicious dish which is composed of a wonderful assortment of sweetness and bitterness. They thus give savor to each other. In *The Dialogue of St. Catherine of Siena*, God is reported as saying to her:

> Oh, best beloved daughter, how glorious is that soul who
> has indeed been able to pass from the stormy ocean to

---

[13] Brother Lawrence, *The Practice of the Presence of God*, trans. Sister Mary David, S. S. N. D. (Westminster, MD: Newman Press, 1949), 48.

[14] *Works*, 2:402–3.

Me, the Sea Pacific, and in that Sea, which is Myself, the Supreme and Eternal Deity, to fill the pitcher of her heart. And her eye, the conduit of her heart, endeavours to satisfy her heart-pangs, and so sheds tears. This is the last stage in which the soul is blessed and sorrowful.

Blessed she is through the union which she feels herself to have with Me, tasting the Divine love; sorrowful through the offenses which she sees done to My goodness and greatness, for she has seen and tasted the bitterness of this in her self-knowledge, by which self-knowledge, together with her knowledge of Me, she arrived at the final stage. Yet this sorrow is no impediment to the unitive stage, which produces tears of great sweetness through self-knowledge, gained in love of the neighbour, in which exercise the soul discovers the plaint of My divine mercy, and grief at the offences caused to her neighbour, weeping with those who weep, and rejoicing with those who rejoice — that is who live in My love.[15]

As St. Paul says, "Who is weak and I am not weak? Who is scandalized and I am not on fire?" And yet he did not lose his peace of mind. Christian peace is rather a living equilibrium than an unfeeling imperturbability. Besides, grief and sorrow are given to the soul lest it should come to a state of presumption, "induced by the subtle breeze of love of her own reputation, and should fall at once, vomited from the heights to the depths."[16]

(e) The Soul and the Cosmos

The soul in peace with God and with itself lives harmoniously with the whole universe and with the spirit of the liturgy, being perfectly attuned to the rhythms of life and to the liturgical cycles of the Church. There is a parallel of this harmony even in the natural sphere, for natural contemplation attunes one's spirit to the Cosmos. For example, here is a poem by Lu Yun, a recluse of ancient China:

---

[15] St. Catherine of Siena, *The Dialogue*, 192–93.
[16] Ibid.

The Valley Wind

Beyond the dusty world,
I enjoy solitude and peace.
I shut my door,
I close my window.
Harmony is my Spring,
Purity my Autumn.
Thus I embody the rhythms of life,
And my cottage becomes a Universe.

Another poem, by Chen Hao, a great philosopher of the eleventh century:

When leisure comes, I take everything easy.
I sleep until my east window is radiant with the sun.
Quietly I observe all creatures enjoying themselves.
Heartily I join my fellowmen in seasonal festivities.

My contemplation transports me beyond the visible
    universe;
While my thoughts enter into changes of wind and cloud.
To keep pure in prosperity and happy in poverty,—
This is the way of true manhood.

Both of these poems are of pantheistic inspiration. But there is room in the Christian soul for all that is beautiful, good and true in pantheism; for who is one with God is one with His whole creation. As Father James says in *The Music of Life*, "Francis saw Nature for what it is, a creature of God like himself, and in their common creaturehood, Francis could fraternize with all creation." If a Christian does not love Nature, he is worse than a pantheist; but if he does, he will drink all the joys of a pantheist at their very Source.

"*To be one with the Word,*" Mother Mary of St. Austin writes, "is to be one with the Divine Artist by whom all things were made. Think what it means to have within us the mind that paints the dawn, the noons, the sunsets; that shades with a thousand colors these great earth waves called mountains, and these great sea-waves of the deep. We shall be with the Master who makes His masterpiece every leaf of a tree and every feather of a bird. 'I shall know,' said little Thérèse, 'how He

made the roses, the winds and the birds.' More than that, we
shall see all those marvels according to His creative mind and
with a participation in the rapture of the Divine Artist Himself."[17] She was speaking, it is true, of the blessed in heaven;
but it is equally true that for a soul in the transforming union
heaven has already begun on earth. To her:

> The heavens show forth the glory of God: and the fir-
>   mament declareth the work of his hands.
> Day to day uttereth speech: and night unto night
>   showeth knowledge (Ps. 18).

A truly profound spirit can never rest contented in the
bosom of Nature; for in God alone can it find its peace. Before
he had found God, Francis Thompson sought solace in Nature,
but could find none:

> I triumphed and I saddened with all weather,
>   Heaven and I wept together,
> And its sweet tears were salt with mortal mine;
> Against the red throb of its sunset-heart
>   I laid my own to beat,
>   And share commingling heat;
> But not by that, by that, was eased my human smart.

Chesterton has observed that

> . . . only the supernatural has taken a sane view of Nature.
> The essence of all pantheism, evolutionism, and modern
> cosmic religion is really in this proposition: that Nature
> is our mother. Unfortunately, if you regard Nature as
> a mother, you discover that she is a stepmother. The
> main point of Christianity was this: that Nature is not
> our mother: Nature is our sister. We can be proud of
> her beauty, since we have the same father; but she has
> no authority over us; we have to admire, not to imi-
> tate. This gives to the typically Christian pleasure in this
> earth a strange touch of lightness that is almost frivolity.
> Nature was a solemn mother to the worshippers of Isis
> and Cybele. Nature was a solemn mother to Wordsworth
> or to Emerson. But nature is not solemn to St. Francis

---

[17] Nageleisen, *Divine Crucible of Purgatory*, 133.

of Assisi or to George Herbert. To St. Francis, Nature is a sister, and even a younger sister: a little sister, to be laughed at as well as loved.[18]

In studying the nature-poets, one often wonders if they had ever heard Nature's answer as St. Augustine did, "I am not He, but He made me."

A Chinese poet of the eighth century, Wang Wei, wrote a quatrain which every Chinese scholar has loved to recite:

> Beneath the bamboo grove, alone,
> I seize my lute and sit and croon;
> No ear to hear me, save my own:
> No eye to see me — save the moon.[19]

He is as happy as a pantheist can be. But this happiness belongs to a different order from that of Sister Madeleva, who sings:

My Windows

> These are my two windows; one
> Lets in the morning and the sun,
> Lets in tranquility and noon,
> Lets in all magic and the moon.
>
> One, looking on my garden, shows
> Me miracles: a sudden rose,
> A poppy's flame, a tulip's cup,
> A lily's chalice lifted up.
>
> Wonder-windows! who could guess
> The secret of their loveliness?
> Beyond transfigured sky and clod
> My two windows show me God.[20]

Nor can the lyrical ecstasy of a pantheist compare with the interior landscape and joy of St. John of the Cross, who, having passed beyond Nature, rediscovers her in God:

---

[18] G. K. Chesterton, *Orthodoxy* (New York: Dodd, Mead, 1908), 205.
[19] Giles' version. Wang Wei, "Title of Poem," in *Chinese Poetry in English Verse*, trans. Herbert A. Giles (London: Trübner & Co., 1898).
[20] Sister Madeleva, *Collected Poems* (New York: Macmillan, 1947).

My Beloved in the mountains,
The solitary wooded valleys,
The strange islands,
The roaring torrents,
The whisper of the amorous gales;
The tranquil night
At the approaches of the dawn,
The silent music
The murmuring solitude
The supper which revives, and enkindles love.

(f) Light and Darkness

The soul in peace harmonizes light and darkness. She knows that God is incomprehensible, but she also knows that He has condescended to show us the bright way to lead us to Him:

Clouds and darkness are round about him;
   justice and judgment are the establishment of his
   throne (Ps. 96:2).

The first line represents mysticism proper, while the second represents moral life. All true mysticism must be founded upon solid virtues, which in turn depend upon mysticism for their full development. The soul in the unitive stage does not cease to purify herself and to practice the virtues. For in the spiritual life, to cease to advance is to fall back. But such a soul continues to practice the virtues and to purify herself with a greater facility than before. This is due to her progress in the life of prayer, which is the chief means for spiritual growth.

The point I am stressing is that Christian mysticism employs what the Oriental philosophers call the negative method, as well as the positive. In Chinese Zen Buddhism, the positive method is represented by a poem written by Shen Hsiu, who was the founder of the northern school:

The body is like a Bodhi-tree,
And the mind to a mirror bright;
Carefully we cleanse them hour by hour
Lest dust should fall on them.

The negative method is represented by the poem of Hui-neng, the founder of the southern school:

> Originally there was no Bodhi-tree,
> Nor was there any mirror;
> Since originally there was nothing,
> Whereon can the dust fall?

The two schools have never been reconciled. But both of the methods work harmoniously in Christian mysticism, the positive method being used in the purgative and illuminative stages and the negative in the unitive. As the soul draws nearer and nearer to God, she begins to realize the truth of what St. Thomas Aquinas said: "This is the final knowledge of God: to know that we do not know God." For, "the more perfectly do we know God in this life, the more we understand that He surpasses all that the mind comprehends" (*S. T.*, IIa, IIae, Q.8, Art. 8). A few days before he died, the saint ceased to dictate or write. His companion, Reginald, urged him to continue, but the saint replied: "Reginald, I can do no more; such things have been revealed to me that everything I have written seems to me like straw."

And yet we can conceive of people who, even if they had attained an intuition of the inexpressible, could still find a profound delight in the writings of St. Thomas and other saints. One can even surmise that such persons would enjoy and appreciate them far more profoundly than others less advanced in contemplation. The reflections of St. Thomas and other great theologians should be regarded as a prism through which the invisible white light of Divine Truth is objectively refracted and broken in an orderly manner into visible hues. If the differentiations are viewed against the background of the Undifferentiated, their beauty and significance is charged with the grace of the Infinite. This point is near the incommunicable; we can only borrow the symbolic language of a poet to suggest it:

Beata

> Of infinite Heaven the rays,
> Piercing some eyelet in our cavern black,
> Ended their viewless track
> On thee to smite
> Solely, as on a diamond stalactite,
> And in mid-darkness lit a rainbow's blaze,

Wherein the absolute Reason, Power, and Love,
That erst could move
Mainly in me but toil and weariness,
Renounced their deadening might,
Renounced their undistinguishable stress
Of withering white,
And did with gladdest hues my spirit caress,
Nothing of Heaven in thee showing infinite,
Save the delight.

—Coventry Patmore

To realize that the expressed is also the inexpressible, that the known is also the unknown, that the immanent is also the transcendent, is to move beyond image and logic, and this is the essence of contemplation.

St. Teresa says that in this state ecstasies cease, but St. Bernard understood the word ecstasy in a different sense. St. Bernard spoke of ecstasy as a sheer absorption of the mind in God without any psycho-physical concomitants. In this sense, ecstasy certainly belongs to Spiritual Marriage. It is a very high degree of contemplation, and it is quite normal and open to all sincere lovers of God. In his 52nd Sermon on the *Canticle of Canticles*, he describes two forms of mystical death. The first form is a death which delivers the soul from the snares of life:

> For in this life we proceed in the midst of snares; which, however, are not feared as often as the soul, by some holy and vehement thought, is carried away out of itself, provided that it so far departs in mind and flies away that it transcends its usual way of thought. For how should impurity be feared, where there is no consciousness of life? For when the soul is transported, though not from life, yet from a consciousness of life, the temptations of life cannot be felt. It is a good death which does not take away life, but changes it into something better, by which the body does not fall, but the soul is elevated.
>
> This is still the lower form of death, the death of men. Besides this, the soul must also experience "the death of angels," which happens when, departing from the memory of things present, it divests itself not only of the desires but of the images of things below and corporeal.

Such transports alone, or in the highest degree, is named contemplation. For while alive not to be held by the desires of things is the part of human virtue; but in the processes of thought not to be enveloped by the images of bodies is the part of angelic purity. Both are by divine gift, both are "to be transported," both are to transcend yourself; but one a long way, the other not long. You have not yet gone a long way unless you are able by purity of mind to fly over the phantasmata of corporeal images that rush in from all sides.[21]

This degree of supernatural contemplation corresponds to the degree attained by Hui-neng in the sphere of natural contemplation.

Lao Tse said: "If Tao could be described in words, it would not be the eternal Tao." The Christian mystics, too, are profoundly impressed with the thought of the transcendence and incomprehensibility of God:

So transcendent is His infinite Being that no human words are able to describe him. We may take all the highest words of human language and apply them to God; but we do not express his Being. We may go further and speak of him as the super-Good, the super-Beautiful, the super-True; but still we fall short. And, in fact, we reach more nearly to him when, pursuing the "negative way," we say that he is neither good, nor beautiful, nor true — as we understand those words. And what is true of language is true also of thought. Let us form the noblest conceptions we may of goodness, and beauty, and truth, we still must fail to comprehend God; let us take these conceptions and raise them to their highest power, we are yet far from God. But if we cease from this effort, recognize our limitations and the infinite transcendence of God, and, accepting the darkness of our ignorance, reach out in a way above mind to him who is above mind, then (like Moses on Sinai) we pass within the cloud, we enter the "divine dark," and are united in a way that

---

[21] Butler, *Western Mysticism*, 169. See, for another translation, Terence L. Connolly, *St. Bernard on the Love of God* (Westminster, MD: Newman Press, 1951), 189–90.

surpasses reason and cannot be expressed by language
to the incomprehensible and inexpressible God.[22]

All language, therefore, is "like a man calling the attention
of another man to the moon by pointing his finger toward it.
The other man ought to look at the moon. If instead of looking at the moon, he looks at the finger, he will not only miss
the moon, but also miss the finger. And why? Because he has
taken the finger to be the moon. Not only that, he has failed
to notice the difference between darkness and brightness. And
why? Because he takes the dark finger for the moon's brightness" (*The Surangama Sutra*).

(g) Speech and Silence

This reminds me of what is said in Ecclesiasticus: "Glorify the
Lord as much as ever you can, for he will yet far exceed and
his magnificence is wonderful. Blessing the Lord, exalt him as
much as you can: for he is above all praise. When you exalt
him put forth all your strength, and be not weary: for you can
never go far enough" (43:32–34).

Not that we cannot keep silence. But even silence will never
fathom the depth of God. Neither silence nor speech nor silence
and speech combined will ever be able to exhaust the infinite
qualities of the Holy Trinity. So long as there is love and wisdom, there is silence in speech and speech in silence. The true
mystic moves beyond silence and speech, the negative and the
positive, the east and the west, the south and the north, the old
and the new, beyond all the universes and creatures visible and
invisible; for he can never rest until he rests in the Triune God.
Even then he will not rest, for he must spend his heaven, actual
or anticipatory, on earth, such being the will of God, whose
delight is with the children of men. For His will is our peace.

(h) Peacemaking and the Children of God

In conclusion, let me say some words about peacemaking. We
really do not make peace by ourselves. If we lead any soul to

---

[22] Dom Justin McCann, introduction to *The Cloud of Unknowing*, trans.
Justin McCann (London: Burns, Oates, 1952).

God, it is because God loves us as little children and places some of His own flowers in our hands so that we may offer them to Him as though these flowers were our own. Every service that we are able to render to God is a sign of His love for us more than of our love for Him. Every virtue is a pure gift from Him. The diamond is good, although the setting, which is our soul, is defective. But defective as it is, it too is His gift. Then what do we possess? Nothing! But we are made His children, and to be the children of God is to be the heirs of all things. As St. Paul says:

> "For whosoever are led by the Spirit of God, they are the sons of God. For you have not received the spirit of bondage again in fear; but you have received the spirit of adoption of sons, whereby we cry: Abba, Father. For the Spirit himself giveth testimony to our spirit, that we are the sons of God. And if sons, heirs also; heirs indeed of God, and joint heirs with Christ: yet so, if we suffer with him, that we may be also glorified with him" (Rom. 8:14–17).

We cannot attain peace until our destiny is fully realized; and our destiny will not be fully realized until we are perfectly transformed in Christ by the Holy Spirit into children of God. "For ye are gods!" These are the words of Christ.

VIII

The Joy of Love

Blessed are they that suffer persecution for justice' sake, for theirs is the kingdom of heaven.

Put me as a seal upon thy heart, as a seal upon thy arm, for love is strong as death, jealousy as hard as hell: the lamps thereof are fire and flames. Many waters cannot quench charity, neither can the floods drown it. If a man should give all the substance of his house for love, he shall despise it as nothing (Canticle of Canticles 8:6–7).

1. DEGREES OF JOY

The last Beatitude, which we shall call the Beatitude of Joy, is the consummation of all the preceding steps and the immediate prelude to heaven.

Joy grows with love. The degrees of love are also the degrees of joy. At the very start of our spiritual pilgrimage, the soul experienced the joy of the discovery of herself and of a new universe. The initiation into the life of grace is full of thrills. The new convert feels something of the joy that Columbus must have felt when he first sighted land. In the words of St. Paul: "When a man becomes a new creature in Christ, his old life has disappeared, everything has become new about him" (2 Cor. 5:17). Upon St. Paul's conversion, there fell from his eyes something like scales and he recovered his sight. What actually happened to St. Paul happens spiritually to every convert; for conversion means, as we have seen, a radical transvaluation of all values. At the next step, the Christian tries to mortify the habits of his old self, and he experiences joy in proportion to the degree of his self-conquest. At the step of meekness, he experiences the joy of recovery.

At the step of thirst for justice, he feels the thrill of pursuit. At the step of mercifulness, he feels the joy of action, somewhat like the joy experienced by the seventy-two disciples, who returned joyfully and reported: "Lord, even the devils are made subject to us in thy name" (Luke 10:17).

At the step of purity of heart, the soul experiences the joys of contemplation. She has said the final "yes" to her Beloved, and she is betrothed to Him. She is given the joy of single-hearted integrity. In the state of peace, she enjoys the habitual presence of God in her innermost center. Like the bride in the Canticle, she is "become in his presence as one finding peace" (8:10). In the words of St. Teresa of Ávila, "He has been pleased to unite Himself with His creature in such a way that they have become like two who cannot be separated."[1] Being joined to the Lord, she is one spirit with Him. You can easily imagine what deep interior joy she must feel in such a happy state. This is only one step from the last Beatitude, where joy is consummated.

The important thing to remember is that joy is a function of love. If you have one ounce of love, you have one ounce of joy. If you have a ton of love, you have a ton of joy. If your love is beyond measure, so will be your joy.

2. PEACE AND JOY

You may wonder what is the difference between the joy of the seventh Beatitude and that of the eighth. Both of them are within the same state of transforming union. The difference is one between fire and flame. St. John of the Cross uses a very appropriate analogy in elucidation of this point. "When a log of wood has been set upon the fire, it is transformed into fire and united with it; yet as the fire grows hotter and the wood remains upon it for a longer time, it glows much more and becomes more completely enkindled, until it gives out sparks of fire and flame."[2]

Let us take one stanza from his *Spiritual Canticle* and another from *The Living Flame*. By comparing them with each other, we shall see something of the difference between two phases of the same state. I will first quote a stanza from *The Spiritual Canticle*:

---

[1] *Works*, 2:335.
[2] *Works*, 3:115.

> Let us rejoice, O my Beloved!
> Let us go forth to see ourselves in thy beauty,
> To the mountain and the hill,
> Where the pure water flows;
> Let us enter into the heart of the thicket.

Here the love and its concomitant joy are intense enough. Besides, there is a beauty that comes from a leisurely and restful atmosphere. The soul feels like a bride enjoying a honeymoon with her beloved. However, the last line: *Let us enter into the heart of the thicket,* seems to pave the way for the final step. In his exposition of this line, St. John says that "thicket" signifies the multitude of God's marvelous works and profound judgments. The soul greatly desires to be immersed in these wonders and judgments and to have a deeper knowledge of them; "and to that end it would be a great consolation and joy for her to pass through all the afflictions and trials of the world, and through all else that might be a means to her thereto, howsoever difficult and grievous it might be; and through the agonies and perils of death, that she might enter more deeply into her God."[3] She understands perfectly well that she "cannot attain to the thicket and wisdom of the riches of God, which are of many kinds, save by entering into the thicket of many kinds of suffering." She desires even to enter into the thicket of the Cross. For her, suffering is wisdom, and wisdom is suffering.

Now let me quote a stanza from *The Living Flame of Love*:

> Oh, sweet burn! Oh, delectable wound!
> Oh, soft hand! Oh, delicate touch
> That savours eternal life and pays every debt!
> In slaying, thou hast changed death into life.[4]

You find here a *vehemence* that was lacking in the other stanza. St. John comments that the happy soul that attains to this state of burning love knows everything, tastes everything, does all that she desires, and prospers, and none prevails against her and nothing touches her.[5] For the more it wounds, the more it

---

[3] *Works,* 2:383.
[4] *Works,* 3:140.
[5] *Works,* 3:142.

heals. The saint comments further that "This burn of love has the property that, when it touches a soul, whether this soul be wounded by other wounds, such as miseries and sins, or whether it be whole, it leaves it wounded with love."[6] The soul is completely cauterized and turned into one wound of love. Indeed, love consumes a multitude of sins. But here is the wonderful thing: she is altogether healthy, precisely because she is altogether wounded! The Lord wounds but to heal, and slays but to give life. When a soul reaches such a state, it no longer makes any difference to her whether she actually undergoes martyrdom or not, for in her spirit she has already tasted the joy of the Cross. She is like those generous volunteers in the Chinese Revolution of 1911, who went to fight after they had been injected with some deadly poison which was sure to take effect in a week. They called themselves "the corps of the already dead." There was another group of volunteers who formed "the corps of death-bravers." Both groups of volunteers were heroic; but the former was even more so than the latter; because while the latter had still a chance of surviving, the former were virtually dead.

3. LOVE AND THE CROSS

The way of love is the way of the cross. "It is not sufficient to suffer in order to follow Jesus Christ. It is necessary to die a mystical death, which is the starting of a merciful glorification. The ideal of man is the divine Crucified. All the saints without exception have been crucified, but willingly so. It was their one aspiration. The cross of Christ was the object of their desires. Privileged souls, in whom grace has already triumphed over nature, have no difficulty entering upon this divine plan of voluntary suffering as into a palace resplendent with love."[7]

Christ says to us, "Come to Me, all you who labor and are burdened, and I will give you rest." Then He calls us to take His yoke upon us, for His yoke is sweet and His burden light. These words must have mystified many a beginner. Certainly no burden could be heavier than the cross of Christ. And yet

---

[6] Works, 3:143.
[7] Marie de Saint Jean Martin, *Ursuline Method in Education* (New York: Quinn and Boden, 1931), 273.

He calls it sweet and light! This again is one of the great paradoxes of Christianity; and like all the others it can only be explained in terms of *love*. For love "carries a burden without being burdened, and makes all that is bitter sweet and savoury" (*Imitation of Christ*, III, 5). "Love feels no burden, it does not mind labours, it would willingly do more than it can, it complains not of impossibility, because it believes that it may and can do all things" (Ibid.). As St. Paul says, "Love beareth all things, believeth all things, hopeth all things, endureth all things" (1 Cor. 13). "Nothing is sweeter than love, nothing stronger, nothing higher, nothing more generous, nothing more pleasant, nothing fuller or better in heaven or on earth; for love is born of God, and cannot rest but in God, above all things created" (*Imitation*, III, 5). Therefore, the lover flies, runs and rejoices; he enjoys the spirit of liberty which belongs to the children of God. Many know "the free man's worship"; but few know the worshipper's freedom.

O the magical power of love! Love is the Alpha and the Omega; love is also the Way. Love separates; love purifies; love tames. Love makes you thirst for God. Love unites you with Him and with His whole creation. Love gives simplicity to your heart and peace to your soul. Love enables you to suffer with joy. Love binds together in one volume all the loose leaves "that the universe holds scattered through its maze." Even the eight Beatitudes are but steps on the Way of Love.

Love impels you to renounce the pride of life and the pomps of the devil. Love urges you to advance unceasingly toward God. Love makes you perfect.

Love transmutes action into contemplation, and causes contemplation to overflow into action. Love initiates you into the secret of being actively contemplative and contemplatively active. Love inebriates you; love sobers you; love makes you taste the sweetness of sober inebriation.

Love causes you to weep for your sins, for it is your sins that estrange you from the object of your desires. Love presses you to ornament yourself with virtues in order to win the heart of your Beloved. Love makes you despise your own beauty, because you can never be beautiful enough for Him. Love puts you at the mercy of your Beloved, and emboldens you to beg for His love in spite of your unworthiness. Finally, love initiates you into the joy of the cross, and gives you a foretaste of eternal bliss.

O the mystery of love! It began by separating, and ends by embracing all. It began by loving nothing but God; it ends by loving all things in God. What a wonder it is that the same "love that moves the sun and the other stars" has drawn the Son of God down to the earth and the sons of man up to heaven!

4. LOVE AND JOY

A man in love with God has begun his heaven on earth. Life is a continual feast and a perpetual spring to him. He finds God within and without. To him the whole universe is a hymn to God. God is singing in the birds, smiling in the flowers, shining in the sun, twinkling in the stars, showering blessings in the rain, rejoicing with the happy, weeping with the prisoners. He is the Father of the orphans, the Friend of the lonely, the Hope of the forlorn, the Music of life. He fills the air with gladness; the earth is full of His glory. He dances to the rhythm of your heart, and causes your cup of joy to brim over. The true lover of God "always swims in joy, always keeps holiday, and is always in a mood of singing" (St. John of the Cross). He dances with Christ in the bosom of the Father to the tunes of the Holy Spirit. He is still a wayfarer, it is true. But he already feels like a river about to pour its waters into the ocean. To borrow the words of Tagore, "In the music of the rushing stream sounds the joyful assurance, 'I shall become the sea'"[8] How can a lover of God refrain from singing:

Let the heavens rejoice, and let the earth be glad (Ps. 95).

In fact, such a soul is like a flying fish. Flying fish stay most of the time in the sea; but when a ship passes, leaving two beautiful chains of waves behind it, they will be seen leaping over the crests of the waves one after another like a group of athletes. To my mind, these hilarious leapings symbolize the brief transports of love and joy which the saints have

---

[8] Rabindranath Tagore, *Sadhana: The Realisation of Life* (New York: The Macmillan Company, 1913), 156.

experienced even while they were still on earth. Those ecstasies, brief as they were, prepared them for entering into the ethereal atmosphere of heaven. They were in the world, but not of the world. They lived in time, but enjoyed moments of eternity. In the valley of tears, they served as the heralds of the dawn:

> Night's candles are burnt out, and jocund day
>   Stands tip-toe on the misty mountain-tops.

The worldly people are dreamers; the saints alone are awake. The worldlings are miserable; the saints alone are happy. For them:

> The spring seasons are hidden in the autumns,
> And the autumns are charged with springs.[9]

When the fire of love is burning intensely in the soul, every action and every mortification acquires an infinite value. Each of her little sacrifices is "like a grain of incense which seems nothing in itself but, when thrown into fire, becomes a fragrant perfume. When grace and love take hold of everything in our life, then our whole life becomes a perpetual hymn to the glory of the Heavenly Father; it becomes for Him, through our union with Christ, like a censer from whence arise perfumes that rejoice Him."[10] For we are Christ's incense offered to God" (2 Cor. 2:15).

In the Apocalypse we read that St. John saw an angel who "came and stood before the altar, having a golden censer; and there was given to him much incense, that he should offer of the prayers of all saints, upon the golden altar which is before the throne of God. And the smoke of the incense of the prayers of the saints ascended up before God from the hand of the angel" (8:3–4). This is one of the most beautiful passages in the New Testament. The only comment I wish to make is that the saints' whole is a life of prayer. Their prayers are actions and their actions are prayers.

The true lover of God is a living "praise of His glory." For him, to live is Christ, and to die is gain. This means that to live is to be crucified with Christ, and to die is to be glorified with Him.

---

[9]   F. Hadland Davis, *The Persian Mystics: Jalálu'd-Dín Rúmí* (London: John Murray, 1920), 74.
[10] Marmion, *Christ the Life of the Soul*, 24.

5. JOY AND SUFFERING

I have found no better presentation of the subtle relations between suffering and rejoicing in the true lover of God than in *The Dialogue* of St. Catherine of Siena. The soul who finds herself in the unitive state, according to the saint, desires infinitely to leave the barren earthly state in order to unite herself completely to God. It is easy to understand this desire; for, as St. Paul points out, we groan in this earthly house which is our body, yearning for that "dwelling not made with hands, that will last eternally in heaven." "Yes, if we tent-dwellers here go sighing and heavy-hearted, it is not because we would be stripped of something; rather, we would clothe ourselves afresh; our mortal nature must be swallowed up in life" (2 Cor. 5:1–4). And we have a foretaste of it even now, because God has given the Holy Spirit as its pledge. So it is easy to understand the desire of all the saints is to be dissolved in Christ.

> Nevertheless [God has revealed to St. Catherine] as their will is not their own, but becomes one with Mine, they cannot desire other than what I desire, and though they desire to come and be with Me, they are contented to remain, if I desire them to remain, with their pain, for the greater praise and glory of My name and the salvation of souls. So that in nothing are they in discord with My will; but they run their course with ecstatic desire, clothed in Christ crucified, and keeping by the Bridge of His doctrine, glorifying in His shame and pains. *Inasmuch as they appear to be suffering they are rejoicing, because the enduring of many tribulations is to them a relief in the desire which they have for death, for oftentimes the desire and the will to suffer pain mitigates the pain caused them by their desire to quit the body.*[11]

This is the secret reason why the more they suffer, the more they rejoice;—a phenomenon beyond the comprehension of natural reason.

---

[11] *St. Catherine of Siena, The Dialogue*, 180–81.

6. THE JOY OF MARTYRDOM

In the light of the foregoing discussions, we should be able to understand the joy of the saints. How joyous are the Epistles that St. Paul wrote from his imprisonment! I like especially the Epistle to the Philippians, which is permeated with the spirit of joy. He addressed them as "sharers in my joy." He told them that some were preaching Christ out of envy and contentiousness, while others were doing it out of good will. "What matter," he went on to say, "so long as either way, for private ends or in all honesty, Christ is proclaimed? Of this I am glad now; yes, and I shall be glad hereafter" (1:18). "Rejoice in the Lord always; again I say, rejoice" (4:4). What a happy man who could say: "For I have learned, in whatsoever state I am, to be content therewith. I know both how to be brought low, and I know how to abound (everywhere and in all things I am instructed): both to be full and to be hungry: both to abound and to suffer need." And mark the sentence that follows: "*I can do all things in him who strengtheneth me*" (4:11–13). And what is the secret of all this joy and all this power? Here it is "*With Christ I am nailed to the cross. And I live, now not I: but Christ liveth in me*" (Gal. 2:20). In this sense all the saints have been martyrs, nailed with Christ to the cross. It was because of the stigmata of Christ that St. Francis could sing such joyful canticles. He was singing even on his deathbed.

Peter and the apostles were brought before the Sanhedrin; and the high priest said to them, "We commanded you that you should not teach in this name. And behold, you have filled Jerusalem with your doctrine: and you have a mind to bring the blood of this man upon us." To this Peter and his friends answered, "We ought to obey God rather than men." Finding that they were such hard nuts to crack, and following the wise counsel of Gamaliel, the members of the Sanhedrin, calling in the apostles and having them scourged, charged them once more not to speak in the name of Jesus, and then let them go. "And they indeed went from the presence of the council, *rejoicing that they were accounted worthy to suffer reproach for the name of Jesus*" (Acts 5:41). Now, these words set the tone to the feelings of the martyrs throughout all the centuries. I have read the lives of many martyrs in the Roman days. The Roman rulers tried to force them to sacrifice to the idols; their answers were practically uniform, couched in some such words as the following: *"I am a Christian, and will not sacrifice to the idols."* They were at once the meekest and stubbornest of men. They realized what a supreme privilege it was to be a Christian and to die for Christ. It has been said of St. Agnes, who was a girl of barely thirteen, that she went to the place of execution more cheerfully than others go to their wedding. In the trial of St. Eusebius, the governor said, "These Christians are a hardened race, it seems to them more desirable to die than to live." The fact is that they see what the world cannot see. The same story is being repeated in China and other parts of the world today. The stories of our martyrs like Beda Chang, John Tung, Bishop Francis X. Ford, and many others will form a glorious chapter in the history of Christianity.

One of the most touching scenes I have read about is the martyrdom of St. Julitta and her three-year-old son, Quiricus. Brought up for trial, Julitta appeared before the court leading her child by the hand. She was of noble lineage, but when questioned as to her name and position she would give no other reply than that she was a Christian. She was condemned to be racked and scourged, and her son Quiricus was separated from her in spite of his tears and protestations. The governor tried to pacify him by fondling him, but the boy had eyes and ears only for his mother. Piteously he held out his hands towards her as she was being racked, and when she exclaimed: "I am a Christian!" he cried out: "I am a Christian too!" In a desperate struggle to release himself in order to get to his mother, he kicked the governor and scratched his face with his little nails. This aroused the governor to ungovernable fury. Seizing Quiricus by the foot, he hurled him down the steps, fracturing his skull and killing him on the spot. Julitta was filled with joy and exultantly thanked God for granting to her child the crown of martyrdom. Finally, she was beheaded.

St. Ignatius of Antioch was condemned to be thrown to the wild beasts during the persecution of Trajan and sent in chains to Rome. Afraid that some of his influential disciples might intervene to change the sentence, he wrote several epistles on his way to Rome. I need only to quote one paragraph which has touched me deeply:

> The farthest bounds of the universe shall profit me nothing, neither the kingdoms of this world. It is good for me to die for Jesus Christ rather than to reign over the farthest corners of the earth. Him I seek who died on our behalf; Him I desire who rose again (for our sake). The pangs of a new birth are upon me. Bear with me, brethren. Do not hinder me from living; do not desire my death. Bestow not on the world one who desireth to be God's, neither allure me with material things. Suffer me to receive the pure light. When I am come thither, then shall I be a man. Permit me to be an imitator of the passion of my God. If any man hath Him within himself, let him understand what I desire, and let him have fellow-feeling with me, for he knoweth the things which straiten me.... Then shall I be truly a disciple of Jesus Christ, when the world shall not so much as see my body.[12]

Indeed, in the case of the martyrs, we may say, "Death is swallowed up in victory! O grave, where is thy victory? O death, where is thy sting?" (1 Cor. 15:55).

7. ALL SAINTS ARE MARTYRS

All the saints were martyrs. This does not mean that all underwent physical martyrdom, but that they all had the spirit of martyrdom. The Blessed Virgin is called the Queen of Martyrs, because she suffered her com-passion with Christ. When she was standing beside the cross, her sufferings were beyond our utterance. In fact, at the Presentation, the prophet Simeon had said to her, "And thy own soul a sword shall pierce, that out of many hearts, thoughts may be revealed" (Luke 2:35). Now, all the saints were co-sufferers with Christ. Their hearts were transfixed with the same sword that had transfixed the heart of Mary, although to a lesser degree. This is why she is called the Queen of Martyrs.

---

[12] Reinhold, *The Soul Afire: Revelations of the Mystics*, 201–2.

Physical martyrdom is a privilege given to a few; but to live in the spirit of a martyr is open to all. On this point, St. Francis de Sales has written:

> Be ready then, Philothea, to suffer many great afflictions for our Lord, and even martyrdom; resolve to give all that is most precious to you, should it please him to take it — father, mother, brother, husband, wife, children, even your eyes and your life, for you ought to make ready your heart to endure all such things. But so long as his divine Providence does not send you such painful and such great afflictions, and does not demand of you your eyes, at least give him your hair — I mean bear patiently the little injuries, the little inconveniences, the losses of trifling importance, which befall you daily; for by means of these little occasions made use of with love and dilection, you will entirely win his heart, and make it wholly yours. These little daily acts of charity, this headache, this toothache, this inflammation, this ill-humour of a husband or of a wife, this breaking of a glass, this contempt or this pouring, this loss of gloves, of a ring, of a handkerchief, this little inconvenience of going to bed betimes and of rising early to pray, to communicate, this little feeling of shame at doing certain acts of devotion in public — in a word, all these little sufferings, when accepted and embraced with love, are extremely pleasing to the goodness of God, who for a glass of water has promised the sea of perfect happiness to his faithful.[13]

Apropos of this, I have only one remark to make: "the sea of happiness" is none other than God Himself. Did He not say to Abraham, *"Fear not, Abraham, I am thy protector and thy reward exceeding great"*? (Gen. 15:1). They are mistaken who say that we Christians are mercenary workers, because we talk of reward. They should know that the reward we are hoping for is not extrinsic but intrinsic, for it consists in the union with the Source of our being. A lover is not mercenary when he desires to be united with the object of his love. Nor can a fish

---

[13] St. Francis de Sales, *Introduction to the Devout Life*, ed. and trans. Allan Ross (New York: Benziger Brothers, 1943), 196–97.

in shallow waters be said to be a mercenary fish when it yearns for its home in the deep.

Happy are the saints, for their sorrows are the sorrows of the Sacred Heart of Christ, and their joy is identical with His joy. The sorrows are temporal and human, the joy is eternal and divine. The sufferings and tribulations of the saints are many, but they can be measured. Who can ever measure the joy of the saints? Who can ever recount all the tender caresses and attentions that God lavishes upon a soul in union with Him? The joy of the saints is not their joy, but the joy of Christ.

For, as St. Thomas Aquinas says: "Since the enjoyment of God, deservedly due to His excellence, surpasses the power of all creatures, it follows that this complete and perfect joy does not enter into man but rather man enters into it. *Enter into the joy of thy Lord*" (Matt. 25:21).

The secret of the joy of the saints seems to lie in their love of the Cross. Perhaps, no one has known this secret better than St. Francis of Assisi, whose words on the nature of perfect joy reveal in a graphic way the mind of all the great lovers of Christ. The meaning of his words will grow deeper and fresher every time you ponder them. However familiar they may be, I cannot resist the urge to quote:

> One day when St. Francis came from Perugia to St. Mary of the Angels (Portiuncula) with Brother Leo in winter, and the great cold was tormenting him, he called Brother Leo, who was walking ahead of him, and said:
>
> "O Brother Leo, although God is pleased that the Brothers Minor give a great example of saintliness and edification in all lands, nevertheless you must write down and note diligently that not in that consists perfect joy."
>
> And going a little further, St. Francis called out a second time:
>
> "O Brother Leo, even if a Brother Minor should give sight to the blind, make straight the crooked, cast out the devils, give back their hearing to the deaf and make the lame to walk and the dumb to speak, and even more, resuscitate a man dead four days, write that not in that consists perfect joy."

And going on again, St. Francis called out loudly: "O Brother Leo, if a Brother Minor possessed every language and every science and the whole of the Scriptures, even if he could prophesy and reveal not only the future but the secrets of the conscience and the soul, write that not therein consists perfect joy."

Passing on a little further, St. Francis again called out loudly: "O Brother Leo, little lamb of God, even if a Brother Minor should speak with the tongue of an angel and know the course of the stars and the virtues of the herbs, even if all the treasures of the earth had been revealed to him and he knew the qualities of the birds, the fish and all the animals, of men and of trees and stones and roots and waters — write that not therein consists perfect joy."

And thus he spoke for the best part of two miles, until Brother Leo in great amazement questioned him, saying:

"Father, I beseech you for God's sake, tell me wherein consists perfect joy!"

And St. Francis answered him thus:

"When we come to Saint Mary of the Angels drenched by the rain, numbed with cold, covered with mud and tormented by hunger, and knock at the gate, and the porter comes and asks: 'Who are you?' and we answer: 'Two of your brothers,' and he says: 'You are lying, you are a pair of scoundrels who go around deceiving people and robbing alms from the poor, go away!' and refuses to open and leaves us standing outside in the snow and the rain, shivering and hungry until night-time: then if we endure so much abuse and cruelty patiently and calmly and without murmuring, thinking with humility and charity that this porter knows us as we really are, and that God makes him turn against us thus, O Brother Leo, write that therein consists perfect joy. And if we persevere and go on knocking, he will come out angrily and chase us away like importunate louts with insults and blows, saying: 'Get away from here, you good-for-nothing thieves, get you gone to the workhouse! for here there is neither lodging nor food for you.' To endure this patiently, with gladness and good humour, therein, O Brother Leo, consists perfect joy. And if we, constrained by hunger and cold and darkness, go on knocking and weeping loudly, entreat him for the love of God to open the door and let us in, he will be even more enraged and say: 'These are importunate scoundrels, I will give them what they deserve!' and rush out with a knotted stick and, seizing us by our hoods, throw us down and roll us in the snow and beat us with all the knots of his stick: if we endure all these things patiently and with gladness, thinking of the sufferings of our blessed Lord, which we must bear for love of Him: O Brother Leo, write that therein consists perfect joy. And now listen to the conclusion, Brother Leo. Above all grace and all gifts of the Holy Spirit which Christ vouchsafes to His friends, is that of overcoming one's self, and for the love of Christ gladly bearing pain, insults, disgrace and hardship. For we cannot glory in any of the other gifts of God, as they are not ours but God's. Therefore the Apostle says: 'What hadst thou, that thou didst not receive? now if thou didst receive it, why dost thou glory, as though thou hadst not received it?' (1 Cor. 4:7). But we may glory in the cross of tribulation and of affliction, for that is ours, wherefore the Apostle says: 'For God forbid that I should glory, save in the cross of our Lord Jesus Christ' to whom be honour and glory, world without end, Amen."[14]

---

[14] *Saint Francis of Assisi*, ed. Otto Karrer (New York: Sheed and Ward, 1931), 184–86.

EPILOGUE

Christ the Living Way

1. THE WAY HOME

During his last illness, Bishop Henry Valtorta of Hong Kong, from whom I had received Confirmation, wrote me a most touching letter, dated May 27, 1951, ending with these words: "Goodbye! I don't think I will see you again but will await you *Home!*"

This brought to my mind a Chinese prose poem called "Return Home," which used to fascinate me when I was a child. It opens this way: "Homeward I bend my steps. My fields, my gardens, are choked with weeds: should I not return? My soul has led a bondsman's life: why should I remain to pine? But I will waste no grief on the past; I will devote my energies to the future. I have not wandered far astray. I feel that I am on the right track once again. Lightly, lightly speeds my boat along, my garments fluttering in the gentle breeze. I inquire my way as I go. I grudge the day the slowness of its dawning. From afar I descry my old home, and joyfully press onwards in my haste." Somehow I have always felt that there is more to the poem, and to my liking of it, than the mere description of the joy of homecoming on the temporal plane. At any rate, in me it has evoked an indescribable homesickness of a higher order.

So long as we remain pilgrims on earth, there is always a longing for Home. It is God Himself who draws us towards Him, lest we should forget our true destiny. In the words of Father Poulain, S. J., "With a loving cruelty He may quite well enkindle a great craving for eternal blessedness, breathing into us a homesickness for the Divine Essence, that true country of our souls."[1]

In order to reach that Home, we must begin our journey on earth. We journey neither eastwards nor westwards, but inwards; because in the center of our soul dwells the Divine Essence, which is our true home. We must, by the help of

---

[1] Augustin Poulain, S. J., *The Graces of Interior Prayer*, trans. Leonora L. Yorke Smith (London: Kegan Paul, Trench, Trübner & Co., 1910), 211.

grace, make ourselves fitting homes for God, if we want ultimately to find our Home in God. Thus, grace is the seed of glory; our spiritual life is a continuous process which begins here below and finds its consummation in heaven.

It is only by the Way of God that we can reach God. There can be no mistake in following Christ, who is the Way of God. But in order to follow Him intelligently, it is necessary to know and assimilate His mind.

2. CHRIST'S PARTING WORDS TO ST. PETER

To me, one of the most touching and revealing scenes in the whole New Testament is found in the last chapter of St. John's Gospel:

> When therefore they had breakfasted, Jesus said to Simon Peter, "Simon, son of John, lovest (ἀγαπᾷς) thou Me more than do these?" He saith to Him, "Yea, Lord, Thou knowest that I have affection (φιλῶ) for Thee." He saith to him, "Feed My lambs" (Βόσκε τὰ ἀρνία μου).
>
> He saith to him a second time, "Simon, son of John, lovest (ἀγαπᾷς) thou Me?" He saith to Him, "Yea. Lord, Thou knowest that I have affection (φιλῶ) for Thee." He saith to him, "Shepherd My sheep" (Ποίμαινε τὰ προβάτιά μου).
>
> He saith to him a third time, "Simon, son of John, hast thou affection (φιλεῖς) for Me?" Peter was grieved because He said to him the third time, "Hast thou affection for Me?" And he said to Him, "Lord, Thou knowest all things; Thou knowest that I have affection for Thee." Jesus saith to him, "Feed My sheep" (Βόσκε τὰ προβάτιά μου).

This passage is so pregnant with meaning that the more you ponder it, the more revelations it will make to you. In the first place, it confirms the primacy of St. Peter among all the Apostles. So much has been written on this point that we need not dwell upon it here. Secondly, the three affirmations of St. Peter set off, in a wonderful way, his three denials of Our Lord. Thirdly, it brings out in the clearest way possible the organic relation between the love of God and the love of our neighbor. Christ is here saying to every one of us, "Love Me, love My sheep." And as all men and women, at least potentially, are His lambs and sheep, we are commanded to love all mankind, but especially the actual members of the Mystical Body, for the love of Christ. It is really touching when we consider these words as the parting words, the last testament, of Christ the Man. They remind me of some verses of an ancient Chinese song about a virtuous widow:

> Mindful of her late lord,
> Making provision for his helpless ones.

This is exactly what the Catholic Church, the Spouse of Christ, has been doing and is still continuing to do.

These three points are interesting enough. But there is a fourth which is even more so. If you read the above passage carefully, you will find that each time Our Lord asks His question of Peter, the wording of His command to him is somewhat different. First He says "Feed My lambs," then "Shepherd My sheep," and finally, "Feed My sheep." Did Our Lord do this for literary effect? I do not think so. There is a deep meaning in all His words. It seems to me certain that Christ means here to indicate the three ways of our spiritual life, or better, the three stages of the Way of Love. "Feed My lambs" represents the stage of the beginners; "Shepherd My sheep," the stage of the proficients; and "Feed My sheep," the unitive stage.

There can be no better commentary on this than the Psalm of the Good Shepherd:

> The Lord is my shepherd;
> I shall not want.
> He makes me lie down in green pastures;
> He leads me beside refreshing waters.
> He restores my soul.

This describes the Dawn of Love, in which Our Lord feeds us with sensible consolations. Then follows the Flowering of Love:

> He guides us along the right paths for His name's sake.
> Although I walk in a darksome valley, I shall fear no evil,
> For Thou art with me.
> Thy rod and thy staff: they comfort me.

Does this not correspond to "Shepherd My sheep"? For the lambs have grown into sheep; they can now feed themselves; but they must be guided along the right paths, and be made to walk through desert land and dark valleys in order that they may grow in strength, fortitude and purity. They need protection, but they also need discipline. Hence the rod and the staff. But in the meantime the sheep evidently have grown in knowledge and spiritual insight, for they realize that adversities are blessings in disguise, and they have no fear because they have confidence in the Shepherd.

Finally comes the Ripening of Love, symbolized by the following magnificent verses:

> Thou preparest a table for me before the eyes of my foes;
> Thou anointest my head with oil;
> My cup brims over.

> Goodness and kindness will follow me all the days of
>   my life,
> And I shall dwell in the house of the Lord days without
>   end.

This is how the Divine Shepherd feeds, or rather feasts, His sheep after they have struggled through the desert and the valley. I am quite aware that the simile of the shepherd and the sheep has been dropped here, to give place to that of the host and the guest. But it must be remembered that we are dealing with the spirit that gives life, not with the letter that kills. In spirit, at any rate, these verses correspond exactly to what is indicated by the words, "Feed My sheep."

What is important to note is that, whether it is a case of feeding the lambs, or of shepherding the sheep, or of feeding the sheep, it is clearly the intention of Christ that it should be done by St. Peter, who represents the Catholic Church with all her priests, with all her invaluable heritage of the Holy Scriptures and the spiritual teachings of her Doctors and Saints, with all her life-giving Sacraments and refreshing sacramentals and devotions, with all her wonderful liturgy, and finally with the Holy Spirit working through her and guiding her in her growth and development throughout the ages.

It is vain to seek the Truth outside of Christ. It is equally vain to seek Christ outside the Church that He Himself has founded to carry on His mission to the consummation of the world. For only a loving submission to the Truth can make us free; and only by the Way of God can we reach God.

There is still another point, which has a special bearing on our present theme, the growth of love. In the above-quoted passage Our Lord used the word *agapas* in the first two questions, but used *phileis* in the third question. Now, *agapas* is a less endearing term than *phileis*. The former indicates a love that is benevolent, but more or less detached, if not impersonal; while the latter denotes a love that is more intimate and warm, like affection between friends. It may not be too farfetched to say that Our Lord intends to tell us that only in the unitive stage does our love ripen into friendship. As He has said elsewhere, "You are my friends, if you do the things that I command you. I will not now call you servants; for the servant knoweth not what his lord doth. But I have called you friends: because all things whatsoever I have heard of my Father, I have made known to you" (John 15:14). In the first two stages, we were not yet prepared for the intimate love of friendship; therefore it was incumbent upon us to cultivate a kind of rational and estimative love. It is only after we have carefully done what He has commanded us to do that He will admit us into intimate friendship with Him. Such then is Christ's idea of the threefold way of love.

3. THE WAY OF THE BEATITUDES

The Mind of Christ is nowhere more clearly revealed than in the Beatitudes which He announced on the Mount. They may be familiar to every Christian; but they never become commonplace. For, the more you ponder them in your heart, the deeper and fresher are the meanings revealed to your mind, until you are inebriated with them. The Beatitudes comprehend all the conceivable types of sanctity. It is not for nothing that the Church should have appointed them to be read on the Feast of All Saints. But here we envisage them not as types of sanctity, but as the ascending degrees of love.

The more I have studied the growth of the spiritual life, the simpler it appears to me. The whole process can be presented in a simple formula: *Avoid evil and pursue goodness, and you will be united with God.* There is only one way to God, the way of Love; and there is only one Teacher, and that is Christ. Christ has not only shown us the way, but marked out, by precept and example, the definite steps and stages on the way. The Beatitudes are "the way of His steps" (Ps. 84). If we follow Him step by step, we are not only assured of our life of bliss hereafter, but of the indwelling of God and of the Divine friendship even during this life. Grace is the seed of glory. There is a continuity between our life on earth and our life in heaven. Heaven, therefore, must in some way begin on earth if we are to know heaven at all. The rewards as stated in the Beatitudes, such as "they shall be comforted," "they shall find mercy," "they shall see God," "they shall be called children of God," and "theirs is the kingdom of heaven," refer primarily to our ultimate goal; but they refer also to the inchoate happiness of the spiritually ripe. It is true that we cannot enjoy the beatific vision, so long as we are living in the body. As St. Paul says, "For now we see through a mirror, in a dark manner; but then face to face. Now I know in part; but then shall I know even as I am known" (1 Cor. 13:12). But it is no less true that our seeing in a mirror, obscure as it may be, is a necessary preparation for our seeing in full light, just as the gleams of twilight before dawn are pregnant with the light of day. Furthermore, so long as we keep close to Christ and follow Him step by step, even night is like day. For Christ has assured us, "*He that followeth me, walketh not in darkness*" (John 8:12). Even before the coming of Christ, the Psalmist had sung:

> Thy word is a lamp to my feet, and a light to my paths.
> Thy justifications were the subject of my song,
>   in the place of my pilgrimage,
> In the night, I have remembered thy name, O Lord:
>   and have kept thy law (Ps. 118).

Is it, then, nothing to us, that we have been born after the Incarnation, that we live in the era of grace, when Christ has opened for us "a new and living way" to the bosom of God

and taught us how to walk, to run in it? Can we not sing, with
St. John of the Cross:

> In that happy night,
> In secret, seen of none,
> Seeing nought myself,
> Without other light or guide
> Save that which in my heart was burning,
>
> That light guided me
> More surely than the noonday sun
> To the place where He was waiting for me,
> Whom I knew well,
> And where none but He appeared.
>
> O, guiding night;
> O, night more lovely than the dawn;
> O, night that hast united
> The Lover with His beloved,
> And changed her into her Love.

4. CHRIST & THE BEATITUDES OF PURIFICATION

As our redeemer, Christ has given us the power to become the
children of God, to be gods. As our Teacher, He has shown
us the way to actualize the power; He has set us an example
by living out all the Beatitudes in their plenitude. Was He not
poor? "The foxes have holes, and the birds of the air nests: but
the Son of Man hath not where to lay his head" (Luke 9:58).
Well has St. Paul said of Him: "For you know the grace of our
Lord Jesus Christ, that being rich, he became poor for your
sakes: that through his poverty you might be rich" (2 Cor. 8:9).

He was the Man of Sorrows, weeping, not over His own
sins, because He had none, but over the sins of mankind. What
a touching scene St. Luke has recorded for us on the entry
into Jerusalem: "And when he drew near, seeing the city, he
wept over it, saying, If thou hadst known, and that in this thy
day, the things that are to thy peace!" (Luke 19:41–42). What
infinite tenderness is revealed in these words: "Jerusalem, Jerusalem! thou that killest the prophets and stonest them that are
sent unto thee, how often would I have gathered together thy
children, as a hen doth gather her chickens under her wings,

and thou wouldst not!" (Matt. 23:37). Not only did He suffer vicariously for our sins, but in His human nature He knew many temptations and trials. "For," in the words of St. Paul, "we have not a High Priest who is unable to realize in himself our weaknesses, but rather one who has been tried in every way like ourselves, short of sin" (Heb. 4:15).[2] We have a High Priest who knows that "The spirit indeed is willing, but the flesh is weak," and therefore urges us with a maternal solicitude to watch and pray, lest we should enter into temptation.

On the meekness of Jesus no one has written better than St. Peter. St. Peter did not write intentionally about Him. He was advising servants to subject themselves to their masters, "not only to the good and moderate, but also to the severe." The image of Christ rose spontaneously in Peter's mind as the pattern of meekness. Here is what he wrote:

> For this is thankworthy: if, for conscience towards God, a man endure sorrows, suffering wrongfully. For what glory is it, if, committing sin and being buffeted for it, you endure? But if doing well you suffer patiently: this is thankworthy before God. For unto this you are called: because Christ also suffered for us, leaving you an example that you should follow his steps. *Who did no sin, neither was guile found in his mouth.* Who, when he was reviled, did not revile: when he suffered, he threatened not, but delivered himself to him that judged him unjustly. Who his own self bore our sins in his body upon the tree: that we, being dead to sins, should live to justice: by whose stripes you were healed. For you were as sheep going astray: but you are now converted to the shepherd and bishop of your souls (1 Pet. 2:19–25).

But is it not truly wonderful that this great Shepherd of ours should have been willing to be the Lamb of God, who takes away the sins of the world?

These three virtues: the spirit of poverty, mortification and meekness flow spontaneously from the personality of Christ. By the help of His grace, we must acquire them one by one with the utmost effort. We can only enter the royal way to happiness "by the narrow gate." If one desires to become a temple

---

[2] Lattey's version.

of the Holy Spirit, one must begin by a painstaking cleansing of the temple. One's soul should be a house of prayer, but how often does one make it a den of thieves! One could wish that Christ would come to drive away all of them; but one must do one's part in the cleansing.

In other words, our spiritual life must begin by doing violence to ourselves; only through self-conquest can we conquer our three enemies, the world, the flesh and the devil. It is submitted that the first three Beatitudes are the best weapons with which to fight the three enemies. The world sets the highest value on riches and honors: we counter it with the spirit of poverty, which reminds us that a man's "life does not consist in having more possessions than he needs," and that "that which is high to man is an abomination before God" (Luke 16:15). The flesh is inclined to indulge in sensual pleasures: we counter it with the spirit of mortification, which helps us to chastise our body and bring it into subjection. In this connection, it is well to recall the words of St. Paul: "Just as you once made over your natural powers as slaves to impurity and wickedness, till all was wickedness, you must now make over your natural powers as slaves to right-doing, till all is sanctified" (Rom. 6:19). The devil insinuates into us thoughts of pride and rebellion against God: we fight him with the weapon of humility and meekness. We should possess an implicit confidence in the goodness and wisdom of Our Father, so that we can say with Job, "Although he should kill me, I will trust in him" (13:15). We must not be ruffled and lose our temper in the face of any events, however adverse they may be, for everything happens by the permission of God for our good. Here again St. Paul comes to our aid with his wise counsel: "For you have not yet resisted unto blood in the struggle with sin. And you have forgotten the exhortation that is addressed to you as sons, saying 'My son, neglect not the discipline of the Lord, neither be thou wearied whilst thou art rebuked by him. For whom the Lord loveth, he chastiseth; and he scourgeth every son whom he receiveth.' Persevere under discipline. God dealeth with you as with his sons; for what son is there, whom the father doth not correct? But if you be without chastisement, whereof all are partakers, then are you bastards and not sons"

(Heb. 12:7–8). Christ Himself has told us, "Take My yoke upon you and learn of me, because I am meek and humble of heart; and you shall find rest to your souls" (Matt. 11:29).

5. CHRIST AND THE BEATITUDES OF THE ACTIVE LIFE

Having followed Christ thus far to the best of our very limited ability, we may pass on to the Beatitudes of the active life. How Christ hungered and thirsted for justice can be seen from the wholehearted zeal with which He carried out His mission on earth. "My meat is to do the will of him who sent me, to accomplish the task he gave me" (John 4:34). "I am come to cast fire on the earth. And what will I, but that it be kindled? And I have a baptism wherewith I am to be baptized. And how am I straitened until it be accomplished?" (Luke 12:49–50). This is the spirit in which to go about our own work for the glory of God. Each of us has a work to do, however humble it may be. It is not the magnitude of the work, but the greatness of love with which we do it, that counts in the eyes of God. Father Francis B. Thornton has said, "Wherever holiness takes root, there springs a burning bush of love." Even if your job in life is no more than to be a housewife, you may at least turn your fireside into a burning bush of love. Holiness does not consist in doing great things, but in doing everything for the love of God. In the words of Brother Lawrence of the Resurrection, who was a discalced Carmelite lay brother serving in the kitchen, "I turn my little omelette in the pan for love of God; when it is finished, if I have nothing to do, I prostrate myself on the ground and adore my God, who gave me the grace to make it, after which I arise more content than a king. When I cannot do anything, it is enough for me to have lifted a straw from the earth for the love of God."[3]

Justice requires us to acquit ourselves of our duties to God; but one of the principal duties we owe to God is to be merciful to our neighbor. In this sense, mercy is an integral part of justice. This is clear from the parable of the unforgiving servant, to whom the master said: "Thou wicked servant, I forgave thee

---

[3] Brother Lawrence, *The Practice of the Presence of God*, ed. Francis J. Thornton (Garden City, NY: Image Books, 1957)

all thy debt, because thou besoughtest me; shouldst not thou then have had compassion also on thy fellow servant, even as I had compassion on thee? (Matt. 18:32). In fact, "God so loved the world as to give his only begotten Son: that whosoever believeth in him may not perish, but have life everlasting" (John 3:16). It is not possible to love God without loving what He loves. As St. John says, "If we love one another, God abideth in us: and his love is perfected in us." For "God is love: and he that abideth in love abideth in God, and God in him" (1 John 4:12, 16). Christ Himself went about doing good, both corporal and spiritual. Any Christian, therefore, who is interested only in his own salvation is not likely to be saved.

How closely the love of God and the love of our neighbor are related to each other can well be illustrated by two quotations from the works of Blessed Henry Suso. He loved God as much as anyone. It was he who wrote the superb poem entitled "What Thou Art to Me":

> As the Bridegroom to his chosen,
>> As the King unto his realm,
> As the keep unto the castle,
>> As the pilot of the helm;
> So, Lord, art Thou to me.
>
> As the fountain to the garden,
>> As the candle in the dark,
> As the treasure in the coffer,
>> As the manna in the ark,
> So, Lord, art Thou to me.
>
> As the ruby in the setting,
>> As the honey in the comb,
> As the light within the lantern,
>> As the mother in the home;
> So, Lord, art Thou to me.
>
> As the sunshine in the darkness,
>> As the image to the glass,
> As the fruit unto the fig-tree,
>> As the dew to the grass;
> So, Lord, art Thou to me.[4]

---

[4] S. M. C., O. P., *Henry Suso, Saint and Poet* (London: Blackfriars Publications, 1947), 49.

Certainly, no one has given a better expression to the tender
affection he feels for Our Lord. Yet Our Lord once taught him
a salutary lesson in fraternal charity. Here is what he wrote:

> I once refused to hear the confession of an afflicted soul
> that had been directed to me. "Tell him to go to another,"
> I said to the porter, "for I cannot hear him now." But I
> had scarcely said those words when the sweetness of the
> divine grace which I had been enjoying vanished alto-
> gether and my heart became as hard as a stone. Amazed,
> I asked God the cause, and he interiorly responded:
> "Just as you abandon this afflicted soul and send him
> away without any consolation, so I also have abandoned
> thee in that same instant and have taken from thee the
> sweetness of My grace and the joy of My consolation." I
> immediately began to weep and beat my breast and I ran
> to the porter's office to call the person, who was leaving.
> After hearing his confession and bringing him consola-
> tion, I returned to my cell to meditate. Then God, who is
> goodness itself, deigned to give back to me the joy which
> I had lost by my lack of condescension and abnegation.[5]

Nothing can be more intriguing than to consider the inter-
actions between fraternal charity and contemplation. Fraternal
charity leads to contemplation, which in turn replenishes and
intensifies fraternal charity. Of course, men have different apti-
tudes: some are more in their element in active life, and others more in contemplative life. But, as St. Thomas says, "those
who are more adapted to the active life can prepare themselves
for the contemplative by the practice of the active life; while
nonetheless, those who are more adapted to the contemplative
life can take upon themselves the works of the active life, so
as to become more apt for contemplation" (*S. T.*, IIa, IIae, Q.
182., Art. 4).

One who lives in a cloister can be very active in fraternal
charity. No apostolate can be more effective than the apostolate of prayer. It is all the more precious for its hiddenness.
On the other hand, one who lives in the world can enjoy

---

[5] Arintero, *The Mystical Evolution in the Development and Vitality of the
Church*, 2:134, note 22.

contemplation also in a hidden way, by seeing Christ in his neighbor, by walking in the presence of God, by looking at everything as a symbol of the living Truth, by making his soul a garden of delight where his Divine Lover may feed among the lilies, by turning his body into a temple of the Holy Ghost. For what is contemplation but a "science of love" — in the words of St. John of the Cross, "an infused, loving knowledge of God"? This infused, loving knowledge is open to everybody, whether he lives in the cloister or in the world. In fact, the more one is engaged in exterior activities, the more need there is for him to cultivate the spirit of recollection. Just because he does not enjoy the silence and solitude of the cloister, he should build an interior cloister in his heart to enjoy the Divine friendship; so that although he is on earth, his conversation is in heaven.

6. CHRIST & THE BEATITUDES OF CONTEMPLATION

In order to build such an interior cloister, our heart must be thoroughly cleansed. "Blessed are the clean of heart, for they shall see God." This Beatitude requires that in our love of God there should be no mixed motives, that we should be so thoroughly inebriated with God as to forget ourselves, that not only the conscious part of our soul but also its unconscious part should be permeated with the Spirit of Love. We can never attain this state by our own efforts. All that we can do is to open our soul nakedly to the influence of the Divine Sun, and let Him shine into every nook and corner of it so as to kill all the germs of self-love and pride lurking in places unknown to ourselves. There are periods in our spiritual life when the gift of understanding has opened our eyes to our hidden sins and defects to such an extent that we are tempted to despair. In trying to cure ourselves of one defect, we often fall into a greater defect. Sometimes in trying to pull out the weeds, one uproots the wheat along with them. Violence, which was a virtue in the beginners on the way, would work disastrously here. One cannot too often remind himself of Our Lord's words: "Such things are impossible to man's powers but not to God's; to God, all things are possible" (Mark 10:27). In this stage, you

have to enter upon a second childhood. In the words of St.
Thérèse of Lisieux, "Let God play the part of Papa; he knows
what is best for baby." Here all human prudence and worldly
wisdom, which you may have acquired during the preceding
stage of active life, must be left behind. You must be converted
into a little child — childlike without being childish. Our Lord
repeatedly stressed the importance of being a little child. Once
"he rejoiced in the Holy Spirit and said, O Father, who art Lord
of heaven and earth, I give thee praise, that thou hast hidden
all this from the wise and the prudent, and revealed it to little
children. Be it so, Lord, since this finds favour in thy sight"
(Luke 10:21). On another occasion, people were bringing little
children to Him, that He might touch them. When the disciples saw this, they rebuked them. "But Jesus called the children
to him and said, Let them be, do not keep them back from
me; the kingdom of heaven belongs to such as these. I tell
you truthfully, the man who does not accept the kingdom of
God like a little child, will never enter into it" (Luke 18:15–17).

The doctrine of spiritual childhood is of special importance
to the present age. Since the Renaissance in Europe, mankind
has developed its natural talents to such an extent that it can
fly in the air and split the atom. Psychology has probed deep
into the complexities and subterranean urges of the human
soul. It is about time to return to simplicity and to remember
our dependence upon God. Spiritually, man will never become
mature unless he is converted into a child again. It is providential that God should have raised up a saint like the Little Flower of Lisieux to re-emphasize the message of spiritual
childhood in an age when it is most needed.

Commenting upon the Teresian doctrine, Fr. Garrigou-
Lagrange offers an illuminating distinction between spiritual
childhood and natural childhood:

> In the natural order, in proportion as the child grows, the
> more self-sufficient he should become, for some day he
> will no longer have his parents. In the order of grace, on
> the contrary, the more the child of God grows, the more
> he understands that he will never be self-sufficient and
> that he depends intimately on God. As he matures, he

should live more by the special inspiration of the Holy Ghost, who, by His seven gifts, supplies for the imperfection of his virtues to such an extent that he is finally more passive under the divine action than given up to his personal activity. In the end he will enter into the bosom of the Father where he will find his beatitude.[6]

Not only does the Holy Ghost supply for the imperfection of our virtues; He also helps us in our prayer: "when we do not know what prayer to offer, to pray as we ought, the Spirit himself intercedes for us, with groans beyond all utterance: and God, who can read our hearts, knows well what the Spirit's intent is; for indeed it is according to the mind of God that he makes intercession for the saints" (Rom. 8:26–27). If we do not give place to these groans beyond utterance of the Spirit, but persist in articulating and formulating our prayers with as much meticulous care as a lawyer would employ in pleading his case before the court, we shall not arrive at contemplation.

We now come to the last two Beatitudes: Peace and Joy, which should be treated together, as they represent two phases of the same state. The most wonderful promises of Christ concern peace and joy. "Peace I leave with you, my peace I give unto you; not as the world giveth do I give unto you" (John 14:27). "Abide in my love. If you keep my commandments, you shall abide in my love: as I also have kept my Father's commandments and do abide in his love. These things I have spoken to you, that my joy may be in you, and your joy may be filled" (15:9–11). Note that the peace and the joy promised are His peace and His joy. No human relation, whether it be between father and son or man and wife, bears any comparison in point of intimacy to His relation with us. To use the image of a tree, the Father is the root, the Son is the trunk, the Holy Spirit is the sap; and we are the branches. The Father "hath sent the Spirit of his Son into your hearts, crying: Abba, Father" (Gal. 4:6). In mystical parlance, this is the awakening of Christ in the soul, and lo! a new man is born into the world. One of the sure signs that the new man is born is

---

[6] Garrigou-Lagrange, *Three Ages*, 2:437.

an enhanced filial devotion to the Blessed Virgin; because the same Spirit that cries within us, "Abba, Father," cries "Mama, Mother." When this happens, we possess the liberty, peace and joy of the children of God, for the very Love that unites the Son to the Father is active in our souls.

The mystical writers like to speak of this state as one of spiritual marriage. St. John of the Cross has written beautifully about it in *The Spiritual Canticle*:

> The Bride has entered
> Into the pleasant garden of her desire,
> And at her pleasure rests,
> Her neck reclining on the gentle arms of the Beloved.[7]

In such a state, the soul's only occupation is love, and even the body becomes a willing servant of God. "For the body now works according to God; the inward and outward senses are directed towards Him as to all their operations; and all the four passions of the soul she likewise keeps bound to God, because she neither has enjoyment save from God, neither has hope in aught save in God, nor fears any save only God, neither does she grieve save according to God; and likewise all her desires and cares are directed to God wholly."[8]

Such souls may be said to be truly deified. They repose in the peace of Christ and rejoice with His joy. When alone with God, they pray for others. When duty calls them to serve others, they would willingly leave the repose of Mary for the works of Martha. "But," as Father Arintero says, "they are not at all perturbed as was Martha herself, for in the midst of a prodigious external activity, internally they remain tranquil and recollected, conversing in their hearts with God as if they were all alone. There is no danger that they will soil their feet with the dust of earth or be contaminated by a worldly atmosphere. Rather, they sanctify the ground which they tread and they purify and perfume the air with the virtue which they exhale."[9]

---

[7] *Works*, 2:306.
[8] *Works*, 2:343.
[9] Arintero, *The Mystical Evolution in the Development and Vitality of the Church*, 2:174.

This is the beginning of heaven on earth. For heaven is where God is; and Christ has promised us that if we love Him and keep His commandments, the Father will love us, and the Holy Trinity will make Their abode in us (John 14:23). What a promise this is! But Christ has never failed anyone, and can never fail us. For "in him all the promises of God become certain" (2 Cor. 1:20). Countless saints have been brought to the goal by Him. We are yet far from the goal; but it is a goal worth striving after and worth any sacrifice that may be demanded from us.

7. THE CYCLES OF THE SPIRITUAL LIFE

The spiritual life does not consist merely in writing or reading about it. An author can produce a romance without being one of its heroes. In this supreme romance between God and the soul, I am still a beginner eager to improve himself. The fact is that the spiritual life moves in cycles. A beginner may cover the whole cycle *in his own mode*. That is to say, he may try to have some idea of all the three stages of love, mainly through faith and knowledge. Then another cycle should begin for him, in which he will make up his mind to practice his knowledge seriously, at least through hope and fortitude. Actually, he does not go very far; all the same, he must have the whole Way in view and ardently desire to reach the goal. Then a third cycle will begin for him, in which the Divine Lover will quicken him with His Spirit of Love and infuse into him the gifts of understanding and wisdom, so that he will be able to cover the whole road actually, not merely in intention or in desire.

On this point, my friend Dr. Paul Sih has discovered a very interesting analogy. This is what he has written to me:

> Recently I painted some woodwork at home and the thought came to my mind that painting quite naturally forms an analogy to the development of the spiritual life. A worthwhile and satisfactory painting job usually calls for three coats of paint, first sealing, then priming and finally finishing. The first coat which is usually done with shellac is to cover the scars and fill up the cracks and crevices of the surface. The second coat is to prime the

surface with color which is smooth and lovely but which gives no brightness. It is only the third coat that brings out the beautiful undertones and gives a long-lasting, bright finish. Although the effects of these three coats are quite different; the first is for orientation; the second, fortification; the third, perfection, the need for covering the whole ground in each coating is the same and no single inch may be neglected. Of course, the finishing touch is most difficult and calls for more time and skill.

I wonder whether these three coats of paint may not be likened respectively to the purgative way, the illuminative way, and the unitive way of climbing up the mountain in our spiritual journey. I shall be very much delighted if you will give your comment on this analogy, or should I say discovery.

This analogy appeals to me as extremely appropriate. I am specially impressed by the fact that each of the three coats must cover *the whole ground,* though each in its own mode and manner. Sealing covers it lightly, priming covers it solidly, and finishing adds splendor to the color. That means that even the beginner must know where he is going and learn, however faintly, about the Way he is to take in order to reach the goal. Although actually he can only take a few steps, he has to cover the whole Way in intention. The proficient covers the whole way by the active practice of moral and theological virtues, and does it with steadfast purpose and earnest desire. Actually he goes farther than the beginner, but with all his strenuous efforts he comes to find that he is still far from the goal. The finishing must be done by the Divine Painter Himself, with the passive cooperation of the soul. He lifts the soul to a higher plane, but at the same time makes the soul start the journey all over again, right from the first step, and leads it on up to the last. This time, it covers the whole Way, not only in intention or in desire, but in actual truth. But it is to be remembered that what is actuality in this life is in reality only a potentiality *vis* à *vis* the life of bliss in heaven. In the meantime you can make as many cycles as God wants you to. It is just like attending Mass. Every Mass begins with acts of contrition and ends with Communion and thanksgiving. It covers the whole Way; but you can repeat it every morning. The same is true of the liturgical year, which forms in itself a complete cycle. Advent, Christmastide, and Epiphany form one period, corresponding to the budding of love. The season of Septuagesima, Lent, and Passiontide correspond to the flowering of love. Finally, Paschaltide, Pentecost, and the Time after Pentecost correspond to the age of ripening; and this completes the cycle. But this does not mean that one year is enough to perfect your love. As Dom Guéranger has pointed out:

> The cycle of the liturgy, with its rays of light and grace for the soul, is not a phenomenon that occurs only once in the heavens of holy Church; it returns each year. Such is the merciful design of God, "who hath so loved the world as to give it His only-begotten Son"—of God, "who came not to judge the world, but that the world may be saved by Him." And holy Church is but carrying out that design by putting within our reach the most powerful of all means for leading man to his God, and uniting him to his sovereign Good; she thus testifies to the earnestness of her maternal solicitude. The Christian who has not been led to the term we have been describing by the first half of the cycle will still meet, in this second, with important aids for the expansion of his faith and the growth of his love. The Holy Ghost, who reigns in a special manner over this portion of the year, will not fail to influence his mind and heart; *and, when a fresh cycle commences, the work thus begun by grace has a new chance of receiving that completeness which has been retarded by the weakness of human nature.*[10]

This is true, *mutatis mutandis,* of the Threefold Way of Love. If we have not done well in the past—and who has?—then let us begin anew, and we can begin right where we are, or, what seems to me to be the better way, begin at the beginning (though each may do this at his own level). The Way of Love is a spiritual way, and therefore it must not be followed mechanically, but *in spirit and truth.*

---

[10] Dom Prosper Guéranger, *The Liturgical Year,* trans. Laurence Shepherd. vol. II (New York: Benziger Brothers, 1910), preface, 10–11.

The way I have sketched in this book is only the ordinary way of souls: but even within this ordinary way, there are infinite individual variations. It can be said that God has as many methods of teaching as there are individuals in His creation. I have seen beginners who practice the virtues so heroically as to put older Christians to shame. In fact, one of the great benefits incidental to apostolic work is that it keeps one in touch with new converts whose fresh fervor and joyful faith are so infectious that one's own spiritual vigor is being constantly renewed through them. I suspect that the Holy Spirit is particularly active in new converts. Sometimes they are given penetrating insights by which older Christians can well profit. For instance, the following passage is from the hand of a new convert, Mrs. Richard Chun of Honolulu:

> To trust God is like giving Him a blank check bearing our signature, and asking Him to fill in the amount He thinks we owe Him for all His loving services. This comparison was brought home to me when my husband showed me a check which was made out to him and signed by a wealthy patient who had recovered from pneumonia. The patient had left it to my husband to fill in the amount of the check; he was willing to pay any amount. Of course, he knows that my husband is very reasonable. Still, he could be taking a chance. My first reaction was: "What trust!" Then I began to wonder how many of us have as much trust in God as that patient has in my husband. I, for one, will find it difficult to give the Lord such a check. I can almost hear myself whispering, "Please, Lord, up to this amount only."[11]

Such a beginner is certainly capable of teaching her god-father!

8. THE RHYTHM OF THE SPIRITUAL LIFE

"Whoever does not advance, falls back." Perhaps no principle has been so often repeated as this. It has its foundation in the parable of the sower (Mark 4:1–9). Our Lord's own interpretation of the parable is as follows:

---

[11] From *Ave Maria*, Vol. 74, No. 4, p. 113.

What the sower sows is the word. Those by the way side are those who have the word sown in them, but no sooner have they heard it than Satan comes, and takes away this word. In the same way, those who take in the seed in rocky ground are those who entertain the word with joy as soon as they hear it, and yet have no root in themselves; they last for a time, but afterwards, when tribulation or persecution arises over the word, their faith is soon shaken. And there are others who take in the seed in the midst of thorns; they are those who hear the word, but allow cares of this world and the deceitfulness of riches and their other appetites to smother the word, so that it remains fruitless. And those who take in the seed in good soil are those who hear the word and welcome it and yield a harvest, one grain thirtyfold, one sixtyfold, one a hundredfold (Mark 4:14–20).

Of these four categories of persons, the first can be left out, because they do not even begin their spiritual life. The second class consists of those beginners who enjoy the freshness of their new faith and feast greedily upon the sentimental excitements incidental to any new way of life. But they have no stamina. As soon as their first fervor subsides, they fall away. They fail at the very first test, because they have a superficial conception of religion and do not practise it seriously. They should know that true religion does not consist in having elated feelings and beautiful thoughts, but in doing the will of God as revealed through the words of Christ. They should remember what Christ Himself had told us: "Whoever, then, hears these commandments of mine and carries them out, is like a wise man who built his house upon rock; and the rain fell and the floods came and the winds blew and beat upon that house, but it did not fall; it was founded upon rock. But whoever hears these commandments of mine and does not carry them out is like a fool, who built his house upon sand; and the rain fell and the floods came and the winds blew and beat upon that house, and it fell; and great was the fall of it" (Matt. 7:24–27).

By those who receive the word in the midst of thorns are meant, it would seem, persons who are more advanced than the beginners. The serious desire to practise their faith is not lacking, but other desires coexist with it. So long as these latter desires are subordinated to the former, and do not grow inordinate, these souls can continue to advance. But just because such individuals are very active, they are in danger of mistaking the means for the end, and going astray. At the outset they may have undertaken certain things for the glory of God, but when their undertakings have prospered they become so attached to them that they forget the glory of God for their own glory. A concealed egoism gnaws like a canker at the roots of their being. They keep constantly reminding themselves: "It is *I* who have built up this family, this school, this publishing house, this church." "It is *I* who have written this book, who have converted so many people." "It is *I* who have attained, with strenuous efforts, to such a high state of holiness; and this is why God loves me." They may still speak often of the grace of God, but in their hearts they attribute their successes to themselves. Even if they still regard themselves as instruments of God, they feel themselves to be indispensable instruments. In order to show them what they really are, God sometimes permits them to fall into temptation and become worse than the beginners. No one of us is immune from this danger. Let us therefore realize that no one is indispensable, that God can "raise up children to Abraham out of these very stones" (Matt. 3:9). But in no event must we despair, for it is never too late to begin anew. Only let us take to heart the words of the Psalmist:

> Unless the Lord build the house
> They labor in vain that build it.
> Unless the Lord keep the city,
> He watcheth in vain that keepeth it (Ps. 126:1)

But even in the case of "those who take in the seed in good soil," there are certain rhythms which belong to the normal course of spiritual growth. In climbing a mountain, it is not a thing to be worried about if you take a little rest at certain halting places, enjoy the panorama for a moment and refresh your spirits with a certain amount of recreation, in preparation for mounting higher. Our Lord Himself sat by Jacob's well, when he was wearied from the journey (John 4:6). In our progress there is a rhythm of tension and relaxation. Grace is strong, but nature is weak. Grace is ever steady, but nature is subject to ebb and flow. If, therefore, we do not feel ourselves any holier today than yesterday, or even this month than last month, we should be watchful but need not lose our peace of mind over it. We can never be sure about the actual degree of our own progress; it may be that precisely in moments when we feel ourselves most imperfect, we are really better in the eyes of Our Lord than when we felt grand. In any case, we should remember that Our Lord is not a ruthless driver but an understanding friend. In the Canticle of Canticles, the bride fell asleep three times, and three times did the Bridegroom adjure the daughters of Jerusalem "that you stir not up, nor make the beloved to awake, till she please" (2:7; 3:5; 8:4). It is His love that presses us on.

EXPLANATIONS AND ACKNOWLEDGMENTS

It has taken me fifteen years, off and on, to write this book. It was on the night of December 7, 1937, that I first translated the Psalm of the Good Shepherd, which forms, as it were, the leitmotif of the present work. Ever since then I have not ceased to meditate on the Way of Love.

My first acquaintance with the "three ways of the spiritual life" was through Tanquerey's *The Spiritual Life: A Treatise on Ascetical and Mystical Theology,* which my confessor in Hong Kong gave me to read in 1939. That experience confirmed my interest in the growth of the spiritual life, and introduced me to the works of great spiritual writers such as St. John of the Cross, St. Teresa of Ávila, St. Francis of Sales, and many others.

While I was translating the Psalms and the New Testament, I had constantly in mind the progress and degrees of love. During my stay in Rome, I made myself the pupil of some of the outstanding authorities on theology, and whenever I was not occupied with my diplomatic duties I used to call on them, and they were most generous in giving me their time and attention. I drew my instruction and inspiration from various sources—Jesuits, Dominicans, Carmelites, Benedictines, Maryknollers, and other priests. Learned professors from the Angelicum, Gregorian University, the University of Propaganda, Collegio Beda, and the Carmelite Seminary not only welcomed my visits but deigned to call on me and sup with me from time to time. Some of them were so generous as to spend hours with me, patiently thrashing out many a difficult point in ascetical and mystical theology. To take one point, for instance: the precept of love is somewhat differently formulated by St. Mark and St. Luke. The former has: *"And thou shalt love the Lord thy God with thy whole heart, and with thy whole soul, and with thy whole mind, and with thy whole strength"* (Mark 12:30). The latter has: *"Thou shalt love the Lord thy God with thy whole heart, and with thy whole soul, and with thy whole strength, and with thy whole mind"* (Luke 10:27). As you will see, St. Mark puts "thy whole mind" before "thy whole strength," while St. Luke puts it the other way round. Which is the right order? My Dominican friend preferred St. Luke's, while my Benedictine friend preferred St. Mark's. Where great authorities differ, one has to use one's own judgment. To my mind, probably both of them were right, only they were looking from different standpoints. If we are dealing with the progress of love in this life, St. Mark's version seems to fit the experiences of the saints better. If we regard the Beatific Vision as the terminus of our journey, then St. Luke's version is more suitable. But if we look still farther and consider the resurrection of our bodies as the consummation of the Divine romance, then again St. Mark's version, which ends with "thy whole strength," is to be preferred. As the scope of this book is confined to the growth of love in this life, I have not hesitated to adopt the order of St. Mark.

Those who do not know Catholicism are apt to think that in our Church everything is laid down *ex cathedra* in black and white, so that Catholics need not think for themselves. The fact is that, within the framework of dogma, there is ample room for differences of opinion and for creative work and original thinking. The Church of Christ is a house of many mansions, but there is no mansion for provincialism. Although I have profited by my association with first-rate theologians of different schools, I recognize ultimately only one Father, one Master, and one Teacher, — the Holy Trinity.

In the Fall of 1949, I began to teach Chinese philosophy at the University of Hawaii, and that gave me an opportunity for going more deeply into the three main currents of Chinese thought, Taoism, Confucianism, and Buddhism. They again reminded me of the three ways of Christian asceticism and mysticism. Taoism, with its doctrine of detachment, Confucianism, with its emphasis on the practice of virtues, and Buddhism, with its universal compassion and its leaning toward contemplation, seem to form a continuous ascent to Truth in the sphere of natural religion, corresponding roughly to the threefold way of love.

In the Spring of 1950, the School of Religion affiliated to the University of Hawaii invited me to offer a course on Christian Mysticism, which I did with the approval of the Bishop. I taught Christian Mysticism for two terms and Thomistic Philosophy for one term. It was a happy experience for me. The students were of different races, religions and sects. There were Confucianists, Buddhists, Catholics, and Christians of different denominations; but they were united in their common interest in the things of the spirit. Some of them I count among my dearest friends. The lectures which I gave then have been incorporated into the present book.

Since I came to Seton Hall University, I have been busy teaching jurisprudence and other courses on law. But my present confessor urged me to bring this book to completion. More than half of this book has been written under his wise and patient direction.

In the production of this book, I have received so many helps from different sources, that I do not know where to begin in acknowledging my indebtedness. My friends have prayed for me, they have encouraged me, corrected me, given me valuable suggestions, sent me books to read, helped me in typing out the manuscripts and in editing them. I had intended to mention the names of all to whom I feel deeply indebted; but as I wrote them down they filled three pages, and the job was only half done! Finally I consulted a holy and wise priest as to what to do about it. He looked at the list and smilingly asked me, "Is this an exhaustive list?" "No," I said, "far from it!" "Then," he said, "the best way would be to leave out all the names, and let your friends enjoy their sweet anonymity. If the book will redound to the honor of God and benefit the souls of readers, as I think it will, then you can pray to God to shower a thousand-fold blessing upon each and every one of the kindly spirits who have in one way or another helped you to produce it."

Just today I have received a letter from an esteemed friend in Honolulu, from whom I had not heard for ages. The letter contains a passage which I want to quote: "God is truly kind and merciful to have blessed a fool like me with so many good friends. Friends in Christ can never be forgotten. As I say my rosary and finger my beads, I think of my friends far and near. I tell our Blessed Mother to bind our friendship with our prayers just as the chain binds the beads together to form a rosary." This is exactly how I feel toward my friends. May God bless them and all my readers!

JOHN C. H. WU
3 Reynolds Place,
Newark 6, N. J.
January 30, 1953

INDEX[1]

1 The name of Christ is not listed because He is, after all, the subject of the entire book.

ABOUT THE AUTHOR

 JOHN CHING-HSIUNG WU (1899–1986) was a Chinese intellectual, jurist, and writer born in Ningbo, China. His vast political and academic career included service as head judge of the Shanghai Provisional Court, an adviser to the Chinese Delegation to the United Nations, and as Minister Plenipotentiary of China to the Holy See. He received a fellowship from the Carnegie Endowment for International Peace, and he did research and taught law at many universities, including Harvard, the University of Paris, the University of Berlin, Northwestern University, Seton Hall University, and The College of Chinese Culture. His books, written in Chinese, French and English include works in the fields of philosophy and law, and a spiritual autobiography, *Beyond East and West*. John Wu earned a Bachelor of Laws from Soochow University eventually serving as Dean of its Law School. He earned a JD from The University of Michigan Law School and began over a decade long correspondence with Justice Oliver Wendell Holmes, Jr. He received honorary doctorate degrees in law from Boston College, The University of Portland, and St. John's University. He was married and had thirteen children.

www.ingramcontent.com/pod-product-compliance
Lightning Source LLC
Chambersburg PA
CBHW021718120626
46545CB00004B/1616